Bending Granite

Advance Praise for *Bending Granite*

Among the many mysteries of life, one of the greatest to me is how thought becomes action. Facing defects and unrealized hopes, the options for paralysis are abundant: fretting, endless planning, meeting after meeting, depression. But as *Bending Granite* makes clear in its stories of engagement and change, action—guided by science and learning—can cure that paralysis. A wise idea, attributed to several gurus, is this: "Everything is impossible, until it's not." This book shows how possibilities get created. —Donald M. Berwick, MD, President Emeritus and Senior Fellow, Institute for Healthcare Improvement

***Bending Granite* is a brilliant compilation of stories and insightful lessons learned by some of the pioneers of quality improvement in Madison, Wisconsin.** The content is a masterful balance of theory and actionable reality. It is fun to read, almost like having a personal conversation with the authors. Most importantly, it is as relevant today as it was at the outset of the quality movement. We need this book now more than ever! —Anne Conzemius, Founder and CEO, SMART Learning Systems

***Bending Granite* bridges the gap between theory and application.** If you want to be inspired and informed about how leaders implement real change, this is the book for you. Through powerful storytelling we are reminded to consider the whole system—social and human—beyond just the technical tools. A must read for leaders and change agents, an excellent resource for the entire team.... and an enjoyable read. —Stephen K. Hacker, past-Chair of the American Society for Quality (ASQ) and co-author of *Leading Self First Before Leading Others*

***Bending Granite* illustrates through true stories how the power of real people working together can transform a community.** —Michelle Mason, President and CEO, American Society of Association Executives (ASAE) and its Center for Associational Leadership

There are two kinds of teaching. One is that I tell you what I know. The other is that I tell you a story. Stories are much more powerful. That is why *Bending Granite* is so powerful. —John McKnight, Co-Founder, Asset Based Community Development (ABCD) Institute and Senior Fellow, Kettering Foundation

***Bending Granite* goes beyond the traditional top-down approach to change.** These stories inspire people to attempt what they perceive to be impossible or improbable. —Greg H. Watson, Ph.D., Chairman, Business Excellence Solutions Ltd. and honorary member and past-President, American Society for Quality (ASQ)

Bending Granite

30+ true stories of leading change

Tom Mosgaller, Maury Cotter,
Kathleen A. Paris, Tim Hallock,
Michael Williamson

Bending Granite
30+ true stories of leading change
Compiled by Tom Mosgaller, Maury Cotter, Kathleen A. Paris,
Tim Hallock, Michael Williamson

Editing by Gregory F. Augustine Pierce, Maury Cotter, and Kathleen A. Paris
Text design and typesetting by Andrea Reider
Cartoon on page 245 by Dana Fradon, originally appeared in *The New Yorker* magazine
Chart on page 255 by Associates in Process Improvement, www.apiweb.org

The stories and quotations in this book are true, although details may have been influenced by the authors' memories of the events described. Some of the names and details in this book have been intentionallv changed to protect the privacy or feelings of people involved.

Published by ACTA Publications, Chicago, Illinois, (800) 397-2282, www.actapublications.com

Library of Congress Catalog number: 2022933236
Hardcover ISBN : 978-0-87946-712-8
Paperback ISBN : 978-0-87946-716-6
Printed in the United States of America by Total Printing Systems
Year 30 29 28 27 26 25 24 23 22
Printing 10 9 8 7 6 5 4 3 2 First
Text printed on 30% post-consumer recycled paper

Contents

CONTENTS

CONTENTS

CONTENTS

CONTENTS

Dedication

Bending Granite is dedicated to the thousands of people who lived these stories. Change leaders from every level stepped up, collaborated, and used data to improve the quality of their products and services, and more importantly, the overall quality of life for employees, customers, and our community. They challenged norms by applying improvement approaches in all sectors, from health to education to government to manufacturing and even to families—collaborating across sectors and taking on seemingly unbendable challenges.

We also dedicate this book to the mentors and teachers, nationally and internationally, who helped guide our groundbreaking, cross-sector improvement and change efforts: W. Edwards Deming, Joseph Juran, Myron Tribus, Bill Hunter, to name a few. We were also blessed to have internationally recognized professionals within our Madison community, including Brian and Laurie Joiner, Peter Scholtes, and the Joiner Associates team, who were prominently mentioned in many of the stories here and generously volunteered their expertise in their hometown.

All these change leaders contributed to improving our community and world. More importantly, they helped bend ways of thinking and approaching challenges to create a culture of bold improvement that continues today.

Preface

Greater and More Beautiful

Bending granite defies the laws of physics but not the limits of our imagination. Granite is rock—hard, solid, tough, resistant to change. Like granite, many of our most durable institutions today—government agencies, schools, businesses, healthcare facilities, community organizations—are designed not to bend easily but rather to do the same things over and over in predictable and orderly ways. They can become impervious to change, however, inflexible in the face of opportunities, better at creating floors, walls, and ceilings of policies, protocols, and standards than adapting to rapidly changing times and abandoning things that no longer work.

These are stories by difference makers who were passionate about their organizations and persistently and patiently nudged them forward day by day, one improvement at a time. No big bang, no instant pudding, no quick fixes here. Only through the steady drip, drip, drip on their individual pieces of granite were they able to shape but not break the organizations they loved. Theirs are stories of continuous improvement.

~

Whether you are a student, a frontline worker, a community organizer, a not-for-profit executive or board member, a middle manager, a small business owner, or the CEO of an international conglomerate, we imagine you picked up this book because you are driven to help your organization or community improve the quality of your operations, services, products, and relationships with your customers and stakeholders.

Many of you are leading change as part of your job or volunteer responsibilities, tackling seemingly unbendable challenges in education, health, environment, politics, race relations, or economics. Some of you may be shaping and navigating your career options in an ever-changing landscape. And all of you have challenges that are urgent and personal. Bottom line, we believe you want to make a difference. But we also know that doing so can sometimes feel like "bending granite."

The contributors to this book cross many categories. They come from industry, government, education, healthcare, private and public companies, the armed services, families, farms, and more. They have all been agents of change. And they have the bruises and scars to prove it, as you will see from their stories. But they each also wear an invisible badge of fulfillment that comes from having achieved some amazing results. Their stories are filled with real people, doing real work, and trying to do it better.

~

One thing that holds all the contributors together is that we are now or have been based in Madison, Wisconsin. The quality improvement movement was taking off across the nation at the time most of these stories occurred, and we all began adopting these approaches in collaboration across different sectors of society. Even Dr. W. Edwards Deming, one of the founders of the quality improvement movement, initially said this couldn't be done in the public sector. But then the Madison police department was able to "bend granite" to emphasize peacekeeping versus traditional law enforcement. Hospitals began using data to cut infection rates and shorten wait times. The state's biggest university, a research powerhouse, crossed disciplines to discover new knowledge and created better ways of meeting the needs of its students. Meanwhile, a plethora of Madison companies and not-for-profits were setting out to improve the quality of their services and products. All this, and more, was happening at the same time in Madison, prompting change agents from across public and private sectors to create a convening organization, the Madison Quality Improvement Network (MAQIN), that connected and encouraged us to share and leverage our impact.

That was a beginning. Fast forward to today, Madison is consistently ranked as one of the best places to live in the nation. The stories in this book offer an inside view of change in over thirty organizations, and some of the stories span thirty years or more. The terminology and tools have evolved over time, but the fundamental elements continue to help affect change. All the authors paid attention to purpose, processes, and people. Therefore, this book is organized around these fundamental elements of Purpose and Strategy; Customer Focus; Systems Thinking; Process Design and Improvement; Managing by Facts; People, Culture, Community; and Leadership.

Today's gnarly, complex problems require systemic and innovative approaches. Our world needs people like you with bold vision and energetic strategies who can lead change from where you are right now. (Notice that the change agents in these stories are often not the CEOs, although they need to be on board and supportive.) Consider that each of you has both a circle of control—those things you can directly change—and an even wider circle of influence. Your power to lead includes all the things that you impact directly and indirectly—by the behaviors you model, the partnerships you seek, the stakeholders you communicate with, the conversations and ideas you share. You may not have direct control over all these elements and players, but you are still more than capable of helping to shape what happens next.

As you read the stories, consider the three questions at the end of each. They are designed to help you think through and discuss with others how you can create positive change needed in your unit, your organization, your world.

Pericles, the "mayor" of Athens, Greece, more than 2000 years ago, asked young people there to make this pledge: "Thus, in all ways, we will transmit our city to the future greater and more beautiful than it was transmitted to us."

We hope you will make things greater and more beautiful than they already are, even if you have to bend granite to do so.

Tom Mosgaller, Maury Cotter, Kathleen A. Paris,
Tim Hallock, Michael Williamson,
Dave Boyer, Guy Van Rensselaer
Please engage with us at BendingGranite.org

Chapter One

Purpose and Strategy

Introduction

The Power of Purpose

Two people are working hard laying bricks for the current renovation of Notre Dame Cathedral, constantly measuring and leveling each brick. One worker is asked, "What are you doing? His irritated answer: "I am obviously laying bricks." The other is asked the same question, "What are you doing?" She replies with pride: "I am rebuilding a magnificent cathedral."

This is derived from an old parable, but relevant today. The second worker understands her purpose and aim. You can imagine how that affects her motivation and desire to put forward her best effort to rebuilding that cathedral in Paris... and the reactions of others to what she is attempting to do.

W. Edwards Deming, one of the founders of what has become known as "quality improvement" offered his enduring Fourteen Points for improving organizations. It was no accident that in his first point, he urged leaders to "Create constancy of purpose for improving products and services."

~

How many times have you been in a store when someone working in the aisles or checkout counter says, "I don't know why we do this, but...." People cannot give good service, solve problems, or even lay down bricks well without understanding the larger purpose of what they are doing. Deming said that without constancy of purpose, any company or enterprise or institution will be stuck in what he called "short-term thinking."

But in today's world, which has been changed forever in reaction to the world-wide pandemic, massive racial reckoning, and seemingly intractable income and wealth inequality, we have come to the realization that so much of what worked for us in the past will not transfer into the future. Organizations will have to pivot. New aims must be identified; and new processes adopted. Leadership will be required to do this, and they must find a way bring their people along with the changes and to keep them focused on the ultimate aim. A constant focus on purpose, while evolving strategically, is necessary in a changing world.

A window shade company recognized a need to provide more for its customers than just covering for their windows. The company moved from thinking of itself as being in the "window shade business" to being in the "light control business." A not-for-profit recently stopped referring to itself as a "book publisher" and now tells its employees and customers that it is a "producer of gifts in book form." These kinds of updated statements of purpose have opened up new product and service opportunities to both companies. It could do the same for your organization or institution.

Clarity of purpose will illuminate those things that most need to be improved in your workplace or volunteer environment. A medical equipment maker regularly holds meetings where employees meet and get to know patients who have that company's products implanted in their bodies. Frank conversations revolve around the real-life experiences of the customers. Imagine what a motivator this is for employees to go back and develop methods for making devices that are as safe and effective as possible!

It is almost impossible to know which processes to improve in the absence of purpose. Without a clear definition of purpose (read mission) and strategies to fulfill that mission, employees in for-profit and not-for-profit organizations interpret their purpose as best they can (they are laying bricks), and others—including customers, clients, other stakeholders, and the general public—react accordingly. The result is that energy and talent are often wasted rather than focused on organizational success. Here are three real stories by lifelong leaders of change David Couper, Jim St. Vincent, and Dave Gustafson that focus on creating constancy of purpose for improving products and services.

Bending Granite

by David C. Couper

Surely the most dramatic finding in this project is
that it is possible to "bend granite...."

National Institute of Justice (1993)

The picnic tables were weighed down with chicken and ham sandwiches, big bowls of potato salad, fruit salad, seven-layer salad, potato chips. One roaster held spaghetti with meatballs the size of baseballs. Another pan featured pulled pork beside a mountainous platter of snowy buns. Cakes, brownies, cookies filled another table. Lemonade and iced tea were on tap and served from oversized glass pitchers. It was a beautiful day on Madison's South Side.

The event was the retirement party organized by local citizens for a Madison Police Department community police officer. The salt-and-pepper-haired officer was surrounded by kids, parents, grandparents, friends, neighbors—everyone shaking his hand, giving him high-fives, fist-bumps, elbow-touches, and big hugs. He had been the community officer in this neighborhood for many years. No one here wanted to see him go, but he was looking forward to a relaxed life of a retiree.

As the man of honor sat down with his plate of food, a disturbance brewed across the street. A group of young men had been arguing. The argument turned into shouting and then pushing and shoving. The officer quickly put his plate on the ground and moved to get up to intervene. As he moved, one of the neighbors put her hand gently on his shoulder, and said, "You just sit down and enjoy your lunch, Bill. I will take care of this."

And she did. She walked over to those young men and with unmistakable authority, stopped the fight, and the party went on peacefully for a long time. This is what community policing looks like—cooperation and a shared commitment to a safe society.

This is what community policing looks like—cooperation and a shared commitment to a safe society.

With community policing, the power is in the relationships between citizens and officers. Officers do not just arrive when someone dials 911. They are in the neighborhood every day, visible in places where people live and work. People know them personally, and they know the people.

Community policing empowers people both to solve their own problems and to work together with police to solve problems collaboratively. In this model, police officers are less enforcers and more keepers of the peace—as in *keeping* everyone safer. This was the vision of policing that I had when I became the chief of police in Madison. And the community policing principles such as decentralized decision-making, listening to our "customers," seeking root causes, and using data for decision-making were the embodiment of quality management. But even the founder of what came to be known as "the quality improvement" movement,

W. Edwards Deming, doubted that this kind of approach would work in government. Yet the years the city of Madison began implementing Deming's ideas into its police and other city services were golden. And that is not just in my biased opinion. I love this definition:

Quality is a comprehensive approach to the organization and the design of work processes. It is a way to think about stuff. It is a way to treat each other. It is a way to constantly improve everything we lay our hands on. (Cheaney and Cotter, 1991)

I served as Madison's chief of police from 1972 to 1993. I call them the "golden years." Those days were a time when unique, challenging ideas about systems, teams of people, and work caught fire and raised the hearts, spirit, and productivity of city workers. Many of us who were able to integrate these new ideas about systems, teams, and work saw the positive results. The universal principles of leading change by focusing on systematic improvement that had such positive impacts then are the very ones needed now in every sector of our country. Here is our story.

I was not interested in juggling another change that this new mayor was proposing.

In 1983, the newly elected mayor of Madison, Joe Sensenbrenner, was moved by what he was reading and learning about W. Edwards Deming and improving systems. I had been chief of police in Madison for ten years by then. At the time, I had my hands full trying to heal the wounds from the Vietnam "War at Home," from fighting the police union, and from integrating a nearly all-white, all-male police department. I was not interested in juggling another change this new mayor was proposing. Instead, I sent a deputy to the mayor's first discussion about Deming's ideas.

~

It wasn't that I didn't believe in achieving excellence. I did. What I didn't have was a plan to operationalize it. In my first year in Madison, I had offered this vision that fundamentally reshaped the purposes of policing:

1. Decentralize police services and develop neighborhood and team policing; be closer to the people we serve.
2. Build a people-oriented organization sensitive to, and understanding of, human behavior, which means hiring educated police officers and working with community members to prevent, diminish, and even eliminate crime and disorder.
3. Develop a high capacity for conflict management and crisis intervention to reduce the acrimonious relationship between police and students (in what is one of the biggest "college towns" in the world) by developing new strategies and tactics to replace tear gas and nightsticks.

I also presented the long-term goal of making "the quantum leap necessary to field a behavioral and human services expert which shall be known as a professional police officer" (see Couper and Lobitz, 2014). A quality orientation separates the warrior cops from the guardians of the peace—the men and women in policing who see their function as crime fighters or rule-enforcers compared to those who see their job as working closely *with* community members to achieve safe and orderly neighborhoods. I wanted our officers to see themselves more as keepers of the peace than law enforcers.

I read deeply into leadership literature. Tom Gordon's *Leadership Effectiveness Training* and Robert Greenleaf's concept of servant leadership reinforced my nascent understanding of what Deming was proposing and strongly influenced how I would lead and train leaders in the Madison police department. I came to see the immense opportunity to improve our work as a police agency by thinking in systems, working together, getting closer to the community, and making data-based decisions. It also meant that I needed to change—to listen to those who delivered the service (cops) as well as those who received it (residents and businesses and service providers). Deming's teaching enabled me to put into organizational practice my own deeply held values around participation, problem-solving, leadership, and continuous improvement.

A behavioral and human services expert which shall be known as a professional police officer.

~

To better understand how community policing was going, every year I would spend a month working side-by-side with front line officers on all the shifts to keep me close to the work. I actually witnessed policing from the street up, and at the same time was able to send an unmistakable message about customer focus and learning as critical to effective leadership. We ultimately moved from being a learning organization to one committed to teaching and sharing with others what we were learning. The twelve quality principles that were essential to our transformation are described in my book, *The New Quality Leadership Workbook for Police* (Couper and Lobitz, 2015).

1. Believe in, foster, and support teamwork.
2. Be committed to the problem-solving process; use it and let data, not emotions, drive decisions.
3. Seek employees' input before you make key decisions.
4. Believe that the best way to improve the quality of work or service is to ask and listen to employees who are doing the work.
5. Strive to develop mutual respect and trust among employees.
6. Have a customer orientation and focus toward both employees and residents and businesses.
7. Manage the behavior of 95 percent of employees and not the 5 percent who cause problems. Deal with the 5 percent promptly and fairly.
8. Improve systems and examine processes before placing blame on people.
9. Avoid top-down power-oriented decision-making whenever possible.
10. Encourage creativity through risk-taking and be tolerant of honest mistakes.
11. Develop an open atmosphere that encourages providing and accepting feedback.
12. Use teamwork to develop agreed-upon goals with employees, and a plan to achieve them.

We began to experience the power of "we" in our cross-functional team meetings.

~

As these new and radical ideas took root, we began to experience the power of "we" in our cross-functional team meetings. We began to use trained facilitators at all our important, decision-making meetings. We told our leaders to "lead by wandering around," and for the first time we asked our officers about their work and deeply listened to their answers. I decided to engage by scheduling a score or more of employee meetings, asking them: "What needs fixing?" and "How can I improve?" (It was, as they say, a "significant emotional experience." On the days I held these meetings, I came home from work with tears in my eyes. But we all got better.)

Through a newly established, community-wide organization called the Madison Area Quality Improvement Network (MAQIN), I began to see that what I was experiencing and learning not only applied to government but also local businesses, job creation, industry, better healthcare, and improved educational practices. We began to talk with, share, and learn from one another.

I personally sent out a "customer feedback" form to persons identified in every 50th case number.

Probably nothing more profound, yet so unrooting to police culture, was the idea that members of our community were our "customers." As I began to teach these ideas outside of Madison, no idea received greater pushback and resistance than identifying community members as "customers." Audiences were astounded to learn that I personally sent out a "customer feedback" form to persons identified in every 50th case number—and that included persons who had been arrested and jailed!

~

You cannot do your job if you do not have the support of the community, and police officers should represent the community they serve. When I first became the chief of police in Madison, we had 300 employees and only one of them was black. The MPD was composed of white, male, mostly high-school graduates.

I wanted well-educated officers. Even though we did not have a formal four-year degree requirement, we eventually were able to attract more applicants with baccalaureate degrees, including many from minority backgrounds. I found that the most effective recruiting results were obtained by likening police work to joining a domestic Peace Corps and describing it as an essential job in our community in need of people with solid backgrounds in social work, conflict resolution, and helping professions.

We also provided postsecondary incentives by offering higher pay for those working on or who had completed baccalaureate and graduate degrees. Through aggressive recruiting and the compelling vision, we communicated that we were a place for college graduates. We were able to raise the educational level, integrate the department on both gender and race, and receive praise from our community for doing so. To help ensure increasing diversity in the department, I called for more diversity in the MPD Academy, the program for training new officers. If a search for new officers yielded no minority members or women, I sent the hiring team back to the drawing board to try again. Despite initial opposition from my fellow police officers, we recruited nationally from the best, most diverse, and educated pool of potential officers, receiving over 1000 applications for a recruitment class. In time, half of the Academy classes were women and people of color.

I also instituted an Officer's Advisory Council (OAC) which played a major role in the leadership and administration of the police department. The OAC decided policies on issues such as uniforms, weaponry, vehicle purchase, and other issues impacting the daily work of the department. I added the head of the union to my management team. My idea of an elected employee advisory council and placing the union head on my management team remained in place for a number of years after my retirement. Many systems in hiring and training have continued.

Data for decision-making was one of the principles of this transformation effort.

~

Data for decision-making was one of the principles of this transformation effort. How effective were we as a police department in implementing Deming's ideas? I needed to know the answer to this question, so I requested an independent evaluation by the National Institute of Justice to measure the outcomes. Results of their three-year study showed that MPD had significantly changed for the better. They found that our new style of "quality leadership" was apparent throughout the department. We had created a new, flatter organizational design—both structural and managerial—to support community-and problem-oriented policing; in effect, we were able to "get closer" to those whom we served.

They concluded that our attempt to bring comprehensive and effective change to our operations was successful:

Surely the most dramatic finding in this project is that it is possible to "bend granite...." It is possible to change a traditional, control-oriented police organization into one in which employees become members of work teams and participants in decision-making processes.... This research suggests that associated with these internal changes are external benefits for citizens, including indications of reductions in crime and reduced levels of concern about crime.

What did I learn from these efforts? First, it's a lot easier to talk about making improvements than to do it. Second, doing it can be harder than you can imagine. Today, I would add a third: Sustaining change is even more difficult than making it.

Transformations—especially those that are so massive in scope as Deming taught—must have a totally supportive leader who is truly committed and seen to "walk the talk."

~

To lead significant change in an organization like a police department takes a healthy mixture of passion, patience, and persistence. What I learned most was that organizational transformations—especially those that are so massive in scope as Deming taught—must have a totally supportive leader who is truly committed and seen to "walk the talk."

Today, in the 2020s, the United States leads all other democratic nations in the use of deadly force against its "customers." Looking at the issues post-George Floyd and others surrounding the lack of connection, trust, and accountability between law enforcement and the communities we serve, I have to say that many of the lessons we learned in the past about achieving excellence still have much relevance. Important methods still exist that can help police renew trust and support from the people we serve. Militarization is not the way forward, nor is training police recruits as if they had joined the Marines.

Militarization is not the way forward, nor is training police recruits as if they had joined the Marines.

~

After I retired from law enforcement, I did not forget what I had learned leading improvement efforts. As a church leader, I have brought many of the things I learned from Deming with me: the importance of customer feedback in deeply listening to others; continuing to practice those twelve principles of leadership; and the importance of facilitating meetings so that everyone has a voice. What I learned not only helped me become a better police leader, but I think it also helped me to be a better person.

References

Cheaney, L. and Cotter, M. (1991). *Real people, real work.* Statistical Process Controls, Inc.

Couper, D.C. and Lobitz, S. (2014). *The new quality leadership workbook for police: Improvement and leadership methods for police* Amazon.com.

Couper, D.C. (July 1973). "The First Seven Months and the Next Seven Years." Presentation to Madison Downtown Rotary Club.

Wycoff, M.A. and Kogan, W.G. (1993). *Community policing in Madison: Quality from the inside, out: An evaluation of implementation and impact executive summary.* National Institute of Justice.

Rev. David C. Couper, now an ordained minister in the Episcopal Church, was Madison's chief of police from 1972 to 1993. Under his leadership, the department was transformed as he brought educated women and minorities into a virtually all-white, all-male police department. The third edition of his book, *Arrested Development* (2021), articulates his concern about the increasing militarization of our nation's police forces and their slow progress in changing to meet the new challenges they are facing.

Questions for Reflection and Discussion

1. Pick one of the author's dozen practices from the list in this story that you have tried or at least seen being tried in your workplace. Tell what happened.
2. Do you think the principles or practices of leading change outlined in this story can be used to address current systemic problems in the workplace or society? Why or why not? Give examples either way.
3. Besides policing, what other institutions or organizations need serious transformation? Name and describe one of them that you are involved with or work for.

From Fast Follower to Industry Leader

by Jim St. Vincent

We didn't accept the premise of Peter Drucker that "Culture eats strategy for breakfast." We believed cultural alignment was key to our strategy, but we also believed strategy should drive culture. Change begins from the top in what you say, and particularly what you do, we thought. Cultural change is intentional, strategic, aligned among leadership, and takes sustained effort over years of reinforcement.

The body language said it all. His jaw was set, and he stood straight and tense in the doorway of my office after a key meeting with teams of employees involved in our systematic improvement efforts. "We have to talk," he said.

"What's going on?" I asked.

"I have worked my whole career to get to this point where I can make the decisions. Are you telling me that now I have to turn it all over to the employees?"

"Yes. That is exactly right."

This conversation I had with a top executive took place over twenty-five years ago. In a nutshell it tells the story of American Family Insurance shifting and reshaping its traditional culture to match its current strategy of innovation.

"Culture eats strategy for breakfast."
Peter Drucker

In meetings at American Family Insurance during the 1980s, the common question was "What is State Farm doing?" We continually strove to keep up with the competition. We considered ourselves a "fast follower" in the industry—a good, safe place to be, it seemed at the time.

I was working in the Corporate Research and Development Division at American Family when my boss asked me to research quality management by attending a local quality conference. In the coming months, I attended a seminar led by leaders of this movement, including W. Edwards Deming and Joseph Juran, in back-to-back weeks. A whirlwind of information was coming at me, but the philosophy resonated. In particular, the focus on customers seemed key since American Family Insurance is a mutual company owned by our policyholders. That means we have no stockholders whose interest might conflict with our customers' needs.

"It does not suffice to meet the competition.
You need to make an end run and do better."
W. Edwards Deming

~

Another hook from the seminars was the idea of getting ahead of our competition. Deming said, "It does not suffice to meet the competition. You need to make an end run and do better." American Family was a regional carrier, dwarfed by the likes of State Farm and other huge insurance companies. If we were first, we might fail, we all worried. By following our strategy, however, we were doomed to follow. This "aha" moment inspired a quality journey that has evolved for over thirty years and transformed American Family's place in the national insurance industry.

In 1987, our senior leadership team and I attended a local Hunter Conference on Quality sponsored by the Madison Area Quality Improvement Network (MAQIN). Over the next year, we discussed articles, white papers, and books on achieving excellence. We provided professional coaches for all leaders who were open to a new way of leading. We made mistakes, we learned, and we adjusted (which in the improvement world is referred to as "Plan-Do-Check-Act").

In 1989, we again attended another Hunter Conference, plus we participated in a separate three-day orientation to quality methods at an offsite meeting. As an outcome from these sessions, the senior leadership team at American Family selected three projects that would report back to us quarterly with learnings and results. We purposely kept those early projects small, taking small risks with employees who were willing to try new things. These projects included things like cash handling, phone responses to customer calls, and improving our claim-handling process. The projects focused on both external and internal customers.

I fully expected the quantifiable results of those small projects to make a difference in the general commitment to quality methods and philosophy. But I underestimated the positivity of the response. While we achieved the desired quantifiable results in the test projects, the real impact was the change in the attitudes of employees participating in the projects. You could clearly see their ownership of the processes for which they were now responsible. These were employees from the front line, serving external and internal customers on a daily basis, who had never even met our senior leaders much less been in meetings to present their process, findings, and answer questions about achieving excellence. Their engagement in the methods, the learning, and the results of our systematic improvement efforts were obvious to everyone. Imagine a new front-line employee of American Family Insurance exchanging ideas with the CEO in a meeting—magical!

Imagine a new front-line employee of American Family Insurance exchanging ideas with the CEO—magical!

~

In 1990, we made a proposal to our senior leadership team that we formally incorporate systems-improvement concepts into our strategic plan, create formal customer-focused pilot projects reporting to the senior leadership team, and create a small Improvement Resources department with coaches to lead implementation. Our definition of what we were trying to do was widely distributed: "Total quality management is a management strategy that provides American Family a structured method to focus on customers, use data, and work together. It is also a philosophy recognizing that all work is a process and that improvement is everyone's job." Quality meant that improving our processes to meet or exceed our customers' needs and expectations regarding the value they received from us was now a stated and accepted element of the culture of our company. Our corporate mission statement at that time stated, "We are committed to improvement of our business so that we represent a best value to consumers and a strong, growing and friendly organization to our customers, agents, and employees."

A few key components of the proposal:

- Development of new management methods for American Family to improve profit, productivity, and morale by focusing on customer satisfaction.
- Orchestration of quality-improvement efforts at the top while insuring on-going involvement by employees at all levels.
- Expectations of hard and time-consuming work by all.
- Funding and time made available for on-going learning at all levels about achieving excellence through constant improvement.

Key tenets of all our action plans:

- Focus on Customers.
- Improve Processes.
- Take a Team Approach, including Customers.
- Make Decisions Based on Data.
- Reduce Process Variation.
- Eliminate Complexity.
- Prevent Errors.
- Maintain Improvements.
- Improve Continuously.

The proposal was approved. Those early efforts led to expansion of our coaching resources, including internal volunteer coaches, plus a full-time staff of twenty. In 2000, we merged the American Family Improvement Resources department into a newly formed Organization Effectiveness department. To execute improvements, they worked with teams to understand the immediate (and subsequent) impact of any change on our company's strategy, structure, processes, people, and culture. That department continues today.

American Family Insurance has grown by leaps and bounds, both organically and through mergers and acquisitions. It is now a national insurance player. Remember my earlier comment about our being a fast follower? You would never hear that today. Instead, American Family is a leader in the industry in the pursuit of continuous improvement. In the spring of 2020, during the COVID-19 pandemic, American Family was the first insurance company to announce refunds to its customers for auto insurance because driving miles had nosedived. We passed our savings back to our customers when they needed it most. We've since had two more rounds of temporary rate reductions because of the pandemic. And the rest of the industry followed, some willingly, others with customer pressure when they saw what early leaders in the industry were doing.

Our company's customer focus, improvement efforts, and teamwork continue. We adopted Lean Six-Sigma—a team approach to reducing waste and improving performance—and established a group of coaches focused on applying Lean to creating continuous improvement and disruptive innovation. The core tenets today in the company include what we call "test and learn," which mirrors the traditional systems-improvement "Plan-Do-Check-Act" method. We have a group solely focused on innovation efforts, and a venture capital group (one of the first in the industry) that invests in startup companies both within and beyond the insurance industry that we and our customers might benefit from. We take the learnings from these entrepreneurs and at times invest further in their innovations for company-wide application. American Family has gone from fast follower to industry leader.

We decided on and built the culture we needed and wanted.

While many organizations—in both the private and the public sectors—embraced systematic improvement and quality management early-on, many did not sustain the momentum. What was different at American Family? It was the unwavering support of top leadership and their clear understanding that the company's culture and strategy must be aligned. (Otherwise, the first would eat the second for breakfast.) When we decided strategically that we would no longer be the follower, but that we would become a leader—a disrupter, if you will—we knew we also needed to develop a corporate culture that would support innovation, continuous improvement, and customer-focus. In other words, we decided on and built the culture we needed and wanted.

Organizational culture is defined in various ways, but for the most part, there is agreement that culture consists of shared beliefs and values that inform the behaviors that result from them. It's the way all work gets done. Jack Salzswedel, CEO of American Family during most of this time period, led the top-down effort to transform both strategy and culture. He said to his executive team, "Culture begins with every single one of us, and leadership plays a key role in what that culture is by what you say and what you do." He was consistent in this message in every talk, blog, conversation, and decision.

Culture-shaping meant we had to look at everything we do. For example, American Family deliberately looks to hire the best and the brightest from both inside and outside of the insurance industry, as well as systematically growing our own leaders. We know we need an intentional mix of diverse people to make the changes that need to be made. We encourage risk-taking and the testing of key assumptions. (If we test our assumptions along the way, we learn quicker and take smaller risks.) At each milestone of a project, the big question is, "What have you learned and how will you use that knowledge?"

This type of culture shift also required a major shift in Human Resources (HR) approaches. The majority of our traditional HR policies have been eliminated or modernized. Bereavement leave is an example. The old policies requiring a certain relationship and exact days off have been replaced with flexibility to work out time away—with the supervisor within the company guidelines of empathy—that meet employees individual needs while covering their work. Our new policy simply states: If you require time off due to the death of a friend or relative, see your manager.

Our dress code is very practical: Dress for the Day. We embrace the 95/5 per cent rule. We believe that 95 per cent of our employees and agents have common sense and want to do what's best for our customers, each other, and the company. So, we don't make rules for everyone that are needed only by the 5%.

Two years ago, we also began the American Family Institute to affect social change that helps our communities, which fits perfectly with our commitment of service to our customers where they live, work, and play. The Institute includes a social investment group that looks to impact communities through four key focus areas:

- Resilient communities—reducing climate change and preparing our communities for climate changes.
- Creating economic opportunities for all—breaking the cycle and removing barriers to those previously incarcerated.
- Learning and academic achievement—innovation in kindergarten through 12th grade education to eliminate race, ethnicity, and gender as predictors of educational outcomes.
- Healthy youth development—reducing the impact of adverse childhood experiences.

American Family Insurance is by no means a finished product, and I am now happily retired, but I am proud of how the company I worked for infused the principles and approaches of quality improvement into every aspect of how it does business, how it treats its employees and customers, and how it serves our community. I'll eat *that* for breakfast any morning.

Reference

Guley, G and Reznik, T. (2019). *Culture eats strategy for breakfast and transformation for lunch.* Jabian Consulting. https://journal.jabian.com/culture-eats-strategy-for-breakfast-and-transformation-for-lunch/

James (Jim) St. Vincent worked for American Family Insurance from 1984 through his retirement in 2021. He began as an auditor and was promoted ten times in five different divisions of that company. From 2013 to 2021, Jim served as Vice President of Human Resources, which included accountability for talent acquisition, talent management, compensation, benefits, employee relations, organization effectiveness, and HR business enterprise coordination across all operating companies. He continues his leadership as a volunteer in several community organizations in the Madison, Wisconsin, area.

Questions for Reflection and Discussion

1. What makes you proud of the organization or institution you work or volunteer for? Be specific. What is one thing you could do to help improve it? Be specific.
2. What strikes you about Peter Drucker's famous statement "Culture eats strategy for breakfast"? What does it say to you about what is going on in the world right now? Give at least one example. How can culture be put to use in the effort to make the world "Greater and more beautiful than it was"? (The pledge all Athenian civic leaders made at the time of Pericles.)

3. Pick one or more of the following tenets of American Family's improvement action plans and say what strikes you and why.
    - Focus on Customers.
    - Improve Processes.
    - Take a Team Approach, including Customers.
    - Make Decisions Based on Data.
    - Reduce Process Variation.
    - Eliminate Complexity.
    - Prevent Errors.
    - Maintain Improvements.
    - Improve Continuously.

From "Paths to Recovery" to "NIATx"

by Dave Gustafson

"Simple can be harder than complex: You have to work hard to get your thinking clean to make it simple. But it's worth it in the end because once you get there, you can move mountains."

Steve Jobs

I learned to respect women and the wonderful things they can do. And I learned to listen and not talk a lot. Those things framed my life. My dad died when I was eleven, and my mom and grandmother raised me. Mom put all three of us kids through college on her secretary's salary. I never felt poor. And she taught all of us that we could do anything.

When I was a student at the U of Michigan in the 1960s, a non-profit organization called the Community Systems Foundation (CSF) provided Industrial Engineering services to hospitals based on principles later called "Quality Improvement" or "QI." CSF designed and implemented practical, data-driven, decision-making methodologies. We addressed any problem, not in isolation but as nested within multiple systems. And we engaged the stakeholders—the community members—in the process. As W. Edwards Deming said, "Put everybody... to work accomplishing the transformation." Over fifty years later, CSF is worldwide, and its clients include hospitals, libraries, municipalities, government agencies, NGOs (including the United Nations), and more.

When I came to the University of Wisconsin after graduation, Madison was already a quality improvement hotbed. Several faculty members were studying how to improve organizational functioning. Andre Delbecq and Andy Van de Ven (creators of the Nominal Group Process), Al Filley, Gerry Nadler, along with community folks such as June Spencer and Tom Mosgaller, studied and taught quality-based principles all over the country.

We started what we called "Learning Collaboratives," where multiple hospitals would jointly attack the same problem at the same time, sharing learning along the way.

Early in my QI-in-healthcare days, colleagues and I who met regularly as "a birthday club" created the Institute for Healthcare Improvement. IHI was led by Don Berwick and Maureen Bisognano but involved all of us. We did many things at IHI, but one of them was to start what we called "Learning Collaboratives," where multiple hospitals would jointly attack the same problem and share learning along the way.

My colleague Todd Molfender and I were asked by the Robert Wood Johnson Foundation (RWJF) to lead one of their national programs focused on improving processes in addiction treatment agencies around the United States. RWJF was big on catchy names, and after a few months of debate (literally), our projects were given one: "Paths to Recovery."

Now, I did not know anything about addiction, so with the support of the others on the team, I got myself admitted for heroin addiction to two treatment agencies in Madison and New York City.

~

Now, I did not know anything about addiction at the time, so with the support of the others on the team I got myself admitted for heroin addiction at two treatment agencies—one in Madison and the other in New York City. The idea was for me to try to experience what it was like to be addicted. I stayed overnight at a detox facility and at an inpatient facility. Everyone there knew I was fake, but I learned much about addiction and how it is treated. Have you ever seen someone sitting huddled up in a corner shaking with DTs? Frightening! We now call those kinds of observational experiences "Walk-Throughs." After going through all sorts of paperwork, they told me (the patient) that I needed to be admitted to residential care but there was no room for me and that I should call back once a week to see if they had room. I did that, each time being greeted by a recording that said simply, "Leave a message." That was it; no identifier—just "Leave a message." Seven weeks later, I got in! Can you imagine what could have happened in those seven weeks if I were really addicted to heroin? In 2010, 38,329 people died of opioid overdose. The Centers for Disease Control and Prevention recently estimated that more than 103,000 people died of overdoses in 2021, a 28% increase from 2020. That was the highest number of overdose deaths ever recorded in the United States of America in a single a year—more deaths than if a Boeing 757 crashed each day of the year!

At the same time, Ann Hundt, then a graduate student, and I scoured the literature on organizational change, because I thought QI might just be organizational change under a new name. I still think it is. We found only a very few high-quality research studies. They were conducted by folks like Bob Cooper, Madesto Madique, Andre Delbecq, and Andy Van de Ven. The latter two had studied NASA success, applying their principles to community service agencies around the USA—principles such as deeply understanding customer needs and reaching outside the organization for improvement ideas. I tried to steal as much as I could from these brilliant folks. Ann and I looked for commonalities among these great studies. We came up with six fundamental (albeit not always obvious) principles that always seemed to turn up in successful organizations and were missing in unsuccessful ones:

- Deeply, deeply, deeply understand your customer.
- Show how your improvement project can help the CEO achieve one of his/her/their organizational goals.
- Put an irresistibly influential person in charge of the improvement team.
- Get ideas for improvement by looking at the work of others successfully doing the same thing, but in other industries.
- Run a series of small but very fast pilot tests, each building on what you learned from the previous one, until you get it right. (Until then, you're only trying stuff; now you are ready to make a change.)
- Don't collect a lot of data and don't use existing data. Pick one or two things to measure and measure them well and anew.

I love the simplicity of these principles and felt that many QI approaches out there were way too complex. These six principles formed the foundation for the simple process we then used in our RWJF work.

~

As the project took off, Paths to Recovery was able to exert influence nationally. We addressed Congress and took part in leadership activities in D.C., such as national conferences and international meetings.

With RWJF and funding from the federal Substance Abuse and Mental Health Services Administration (SAMHSA), we sponsored competitions to get treatment agencies to join us in our Paths to Recovery project with just three goals: to reduce the time needed to get into treatment, to keep people in treatment when they did get in, and to increase the number of patients who could be treated at one time. CEOs had to do a "walk-through" and get "admitted" to treatment in their own agency to be eligible for the competitions. You would be surprised by how many CEOs found embarrassing gaps in service (such as no one answering the phone at their agency when people used the number in the yellow pages to call for help.) We looked for simple improvements that could be implemented easily.

We looked for simple changes that could be implemented easily.

The competition-winning agencies did amazing things with those three goals. Over time, many more treatment agencies joined in and we decided to change the organization's name and started calling it "NIATx" (originally the acronym stood for the Network for the Improvement of Addiction Treatment; "Tx" being the acronym for "treatment" in health-care settings; but now it's known simply as NIATx, which reflects its growth and expansion into fields other than addiction treatment). The name is perhaps not as descriptive as "Paths to Recovery," but "NIATx" has stuck to this day!

I remember riding with my colleague Dean Lea in a car in New York State near Lake Champlain after visiting an agency whose appointment book was filled up for weeks ahead. When we looked back, we could see that half of the appointments had been canceled or were no-shows. Dean said, "Why bother to have appointments if so many people don't show up?" Today, hundreds of treatment agencies have walk-in times because of NIATX's finding that no appointments are needed when it comes to addiction. Get people into treatment whenever they show up. Simple changes.

We continued to hold conferences, and the SAMHSA continued to push the NIATx process. Tom Mosgaller—then the leader of the American Society for Quality—also helped promote our work. Talk about passion! What Tom did for systematic improvement efforts throughout Madison is the stuff of legends.

~

By the time our grant funding ran out in 2017, we had about 3700 treatment agencies across the U.S. that were claiming that they had been "NIATx-ed." We conducted a randomized trial to evaluate NIATx's and Learning Collaboratives' impact in 200 treatment agencies across the U.S. with additional grant funding. What elements made the difference?

We found that the key to success was teaching our consultants to work between agencies to get them to learn from one another and encourage one another to stay on course. Not expensive consulting contracts—just an advisor, once a month, touching base with each partnering agency—sharing ideas, asking questions, and encouraging each to learn from each other. Simple changes.

From these 200 agencies, we documented lots of great ideas and put them into a database for others to use. And, of course, because that's what people like us do, we wrote a book in 2011 titled *The NIATx Model: Process Improvement in Behavioral Health.*

We found that the key to success was teaching our consultants to work between agencies to get them to learn from one another and encourage one another to stay on course.

~

In parallel to helping to start a national movement for system improvement for addiction treatment, I was always interested in using computers to improve individuals and organizations. It felt to me that there should be ways to automate large parts of healthcare, so we developed a computer-based system to help cancer and HIV patients (among others) cope more effectively with their diseases. We are now building smartphone systems to help families of those struggling with alcohol and other drug abuse. In my mind, families are critical to success, and if they learn to use a few simple tools, they can help protect themselves and their loved ones. A lot of the things we are doing with those patients and families are built around those same six fundamental principles Ann Hundt and I developed for NIATx.

Todd Molfender and I got another federal grant to figure out how to implement the computer systems (aimed at people with alcohol or drug addiction) throughout the state of Iowa. We were convinced that family involvement holds the key to treatment success and that smart speakers and smart displays (rather than laptops and desktop computers) are the way to automate and engage families around addiction treatment.

Hillary Clinton was right: *It does take a village!* Call it what you want—QI, organizational change, couples therapy, industrial engineering, methods improvement, supply chain management, NIATx—it takes a lot of disciplines and perspectives to make a change that is a true improvement. So, being true to our shared human nature, we will all continue to rediscover the wheel and call it by different names; but in the final analysis, our shared goal is to make the world a little better place. As we listen to each other and care about the people we serve, we will make the simple changes that need to be made.

Looking back on it, I have never done one thing by myself except go to the bathroom (smile). I get a lot of excessive credit for the work of great groups of people. Thanks to all of you, only a few of whom I have mentioned here, the quality improvement movement is not dead; it has just changed its name and will reappear in even better forms. Just watch.

References

Business Week (May 25, 1998). *Apple: Is its comeback for real?*

The W. Edwards Deming Institute (April 17, 2017). *The transformation is everybody's job.* https://deming.org.

David (Dave) Gustafson, Ph.D., directs the University of Wisconsin–Madison's Center for Health Enhancement Systems Studies, including the national program office for the Network for Improvement of Addiction Treatment, and the Center of Excellence on Active Aging Research (a.k.a. the Agency for Healthcare Research and Quality). Dave is a member of the National Academy of Engineering, a Fellow of the Association for Health Services Research, and a leader in the American Medical Informatics Association, the WK Kellogg Foundation, and the Institute for Healthcare Improvement, which he co-founded and was board vice-chair.

Questions for Reflection and Discussion.

1. As Shakespeare once said, "What's in a name?" Give an example of the name of an organization or institution that had a great name or acronym that helped it do its job, and maybe one whose name did not help quite so much. (Note: This is meant to be a fun question!)
2. Do you agree with Steve Jobs that "Simple can be harder than complex, but it's worth it in the end"? Tell a story from your own experience or that of another that illustrates this principle.
3. Do families and what goes on in homes help or hinder small changes in the improvement of the quality of life for those with addictions or mental health challenges? Explain your answer with real examples. What societal changes might help make the situation better for them?

Chapter Two

Customer Focus

Introduction

For Whom Do We Exist?

The cartoon shows a full waiting room at the Department of Motor Vehicles. A man leans over to the skeleton next to him and asks, "Been waiting long?" Of course, this joke only works because DMVs everywhere are notoriously slow and complicated. But not in Madison, Wisconsin. Since the mid-nineties, you can get your driver's license updated, including eye test and photo, in four minutes.

Customer focus is at the core of leading systematic change. Fulfilling what customers need or want is the foundation for any organization, any product, any service; it is the reason your for-profit or not-for-profit institution exists. If you are trying to improve something, you must start with understanding who it is for, what they want or need, and how to interact with them.

We intuitively get that concept when we are thinking about the new car that we want to buy, the meal we just ordered, or the running shoes we are having delivered (for free) the next day. Corporations had a rude awakening in the 1960s when Americans started buying German and Japanese cars and U.S. car manufacturers were literally at a breaking point. The Japanese and Germans had learned to build a car that was reliable. And they had noticed that women were beginning to drive, so they designed cars that weren't all built for six-foot men. American car manufacturers finally started listening to customers as a matter of survival. This was the breakthrough industry that launched systematic improvement efforts in the U.S.

But back to the DMV. People everywhere have to get a driver's license, and there is no competition for where they can go. So, why bother listening? Why pay attention to customers' wants and needs?

Why did the Madison DMV care about making it easy to get a driver's license?

Various systematic improvement approaches were embraced as a prime value throughout Madison and implemented quickly and successfully across organizations of all types. Corporations such as American Family, Placon, and Home Savings and Loan were quick to adopt the quality approach to their businesses. And so did the city, the university, state agencies, the school district, the police department, hospitals, and...the DMV.

But wait. It's easy to see how this concept can help make an insurance company more efficient and profitable. But how do you set out to "please" someone you just arrested? Why worry about how long people have to wait to get their trees trimmed? How can the concept of "customer" service fit in the public sector? The answer was complex, but not so surprising.

~

Wants v. Needs

A Japanese camera company once simply asked their customers (and potential customers) what they wanted, that is, how they would like to see their cameras improved. Customers asked to have the buttons moved so they could reach them more easily, to have the strap hang differently, other simple things that maybe the company could have thought of on its own...but hadn't. The camera company, however, looked further. They examined the photos that had been discarded in the trash and saw a lot of bad pictures with fuzzy images, low light, etc. They realized that, in addition to customer "wants," what was "needed" was a way to take better photos. They then invented auto focus and auto flash. These revolutionary features were developed thanks to a relentless drive to learn what their users really needed.

Students have wants and needs too. You don't ask fourth graders what math concepts they want to learn. Teachers and principals and school boards know what fourth graders need to know and design curricula and lesson plans accordingly. But it might also help all of us learn better if the kids are asked about their wants and needs. We might find out that they can't read the board, or don't get anything for breakfast, or are being bullied.

Someone who is arrested might not get what they "want" so much, but you can find out what they need such as clear information or medication, and they can be treated fairly and with respect.

People paying for a new car or driver's license may not enjoy the fee, but they can have an easy process for paying and a timely delivery of the license... and perhaps some communication about the good being done with the funds received. Improving public services so they are easy for people to use can increase compliance and ultimately save taxpayer dollars in decreased costs for staff and administration. The freed-up resources can be used for other, possibly more impactful, efforts. Efficient and respectful services tend to generate public goodwill and cooperation.

~

Customers and Stakeholders

Who is your customer, anyway?

Sometimes it's obvious. You buy a tube of toothpaste, you're the customer. Some organizations, however, especially in the public sector, have many levels of "customers" as well as other "stakeholders." While customers use or consume the services directly, stakeholders are all the people or groups affected in some way by the organization's products, services, or decisions. (That is, they hold a "stake" in it.) The customer is always a key stakeholder.

When the Department of Natural Resources, for example, issues a boat license, all the people who use the lakes now and in the future are their stakeholders—not just the immediate new boat-owner-license customer. When a meat plant is inspected, consumers are stakeholders, and so are the employees. Universities' stakeholders include students, faculty, staff, parents, grant funding agencies, donors, employers who hire students, and everyone now and in the future who benefits from academic research. And here's another thing: some of these stakeholder groups have conflicting wants/needs.

And so, when you begin to make any systematic improvement, first think about the customers and stakeholders: For whom are we doing this? Who else is impacted? And what do they all want and need? Here are three stories about those questions by Tom Mosgaller, Cathy Caro-Bruce, and Connie Thompson.

Walk in Their Shoes

by Tom Mosgaller

You can observe a lot by watching.

Yogi Berra

"Did you say he threatened to kill himself?"

"Yes, he just told me he had had enough and wanted me to open the gun safe so he could get his rifle. I told him I wouldn't do it, but he is very agitated and says he will find a way into the safe. I am worried for my family."

That was the beginning of the call I made to the intake specialist at our local mental health facility. Our 23-year-old nephew, Brian, was living in a bedroom above our garage after his parents had thrown him out. He was an avid hunter, but I had secured his gun as a requirement for his moving in with us. Brian has had numerous run-ins with the law and suffered from a number of mental health issues, including depression and attention deficit disorder. He had spent part of the winter at a men's shelter and would do most anything to avoid going back there. The good news was that he trusted me, and he knew if he cooperated and followed my rules he would have a roof over his head, food in his belly, and an uncle who would have his back.

After the intake specialist ran through the suicide protocol for me, she recommended I bring him in immediately. We both were concerned he might harm my wife and family.

Fortunately, this was only a fictional scenario my colleague and I had developed for experiencing how clients were treated at one of our city's oldest mental health providers. We call it a "walk-through," and doing one is the first thing we required of every member of any team in any organization looking at improving the quality of their service. We need them to appreciate firsthand and at that specific time what it is like to be their client. This method was sometimes resisted but always insisted upon by us, and it was always eye-opening to our clients.

We need them to appreciate firsthand and at that specific time what it is like to be their client.

~

Here is a story of a walk-through that I did in the process of designing a simple problem-solving process at the University of Wisconsin-Madison College of Engineering to help them improve addiction treatment and mental health services across the country. It was called NIATx (formerly the acronym stood for the Network for the Improvement of Addiction Treatment; "Tx" being the acronym for "treatment" in healthcare settings, but now it's known simply as NIATx, reflecting its growth and expansion into fields other than addiction treatment).

The director of a mental health facility had heard about NIATx and called us. They knew they had problems but wanted fresh eyes to look at their intake process. The initial walk-through phone call I had made to the intake specialist set the entire change process in motion.

When my colleague and I got to the facility after my call, we put on our game faces as client and uncle, got out of the car, and approached the building. The front entrance was under renovation, and jackhammers were busting up the concrete walkway. A crew was pouring cement for new steps. We began to navigate our way when a mason pointed at a yellow plastic crime scene tape going around the side of the building. I made a mental note that no one had given us a heads up that they were under construction. Also, I wondered if that crime scene tape could trigger an anxiety attack for my "nephew" Brian. I also wondered how many people came to the facility but decided to leave rather than asking the construction crew for directions.

I wondered if that crime scene tape could trigger an anxiety attack for my "nephew" Brian.

Once Brian and I got into the reception area, we had to figure out how we let someone know we were there. Brian pointed to a glass window across the room with a round hole in it. The lighting behind the window was so dark it was hard to see if anyone was even sitting behind it. We walked cautiously across the dimly lit reception area, which was full of other clients—some sitting, some pacing around, and a few at a table in the corner bent over and apparently taking a nap. The only directions were an old sign with black lettering on a blue piece of paper right below the window that said, "If you have been here more than 30 minutes, inform the receptionist." That sight raised a red flag in my brain that we were going to be there for a while, and we hadn't even checked in yet!

I put my face up to the glass hole, stated my name, and introduced Brian. I explained that the intake specialist had told us to come in immediately to see a counselor. The receptionist said she had not received any notification we were coming and told us to take a seat.

I tried to plead my case and asked her to talk to the intake specialist to get verification of the urgency in Brian's threats. She looked at me, and I could tell from her gaze that she had seen it all, heard every story, and had no patience with pleading. She did say they would get to us "as soon as possible."

"What does, as soon as possible mean?" I asked. But she was getting irritated, and I could feel the hair on my neck going up and sensed all the eyes in the reception area were focused on us. To her credit she said she would try and find out if we were to get immediate care and pointed to a couch across the room.

Nothing like a little drama in the lobby of a mental health facility to break up the boredom of a long wait for everyone else!

Brian's fake anxiety was rising. Whenever he felt out of control, he would start wringing his hands, tapping his feet, and rocking back and forth. I tried to calm him down while keeping one eye on the window with the hole in it. After thirty-five minutes, I went back up to the hole, peaked in, and asked how much longer it would be. I tried to whisper to her that Brian was getting agitated. She said, "Do you see all these other people? They have stories too. We are down two staff, and we are working as fast as we can. Now sit down!" And she went back to her computer screen.

As Brian's agitation increased, I knew there would be a point where he would just get up and bolt for the door. When I sat down, I told him it would be only a few more minutes. (Of course, I really had no idea how long it was going to be.)

"Do you see all these other people? They have stories too."

Brian elbowed me in the ribs, "Are you seeing what I'm seeing?" Strolling around the lobby was a young man moving from one person to another. He finally came over to us and quietly asked, "Are you interested in buying some stuff?" At first, I didn't know what he meant by "stuff." Then it hit me, why not! If you're a drug dealer where would be a better place to sell drugs than at your local behavioral health facility? The reception area was full of anxious and depressed clients. There was plenty of background noise from the entrance remodeling to drown out sound, and the only staff person was sitting on the other side of a glass barrier focused on her computer screen. I told him we weren't interested right now. He winked and gave me his card with only a name and number on it. Before he moved on, he said, "Maybe next time."

Fifty minutes after we had first gone up to the window the lady behind the glass with the hole in it said she had talked to the intake specialist and moved our mental health assessment with a counselor up and it looked like we would probably be seen in the next half hour. I looked at my nephew. I could tell it was too late. He shook his head to let me know he couldn't stay there any longer. I understood, and we walked back out through the construction noise and got in our car.

~

We could now come off script, take off our game faces and actually talk about all the things we had seen in those fifty minutes. Yogi Berra would have been proud of us. We had observed a lot by watching.

As we sat in the parking lot debriefing the walk-through, I told my colleague that the experience we had just gone through reminded me of the monthly radio test of the national emergency-broadcasting weather warning system with those screechy noises in the background. My scripted nephew and I had walked through the intake process, and we saw a lot of opportunities for improvement. I dreaded to think of what would have happened if Brian's situation had been real.

Yogi Berra would have been proud of us.

We still had the most important step of our walk-through process to do. The next day we met with the executive director of the facility we had just visited, while our experience was fresh. We described our experience step by step from the phone conversation with the intake specialist to our arrival at the facility to the encounters of looking through the round hole in the glass with the receptionist to the experience with the drug dealer to our final exit without getting service—or even a pleasant goodbye—during what they all thought was a real, life-and death emergency. He just sat there in shock. To his credit, he didn't try to make excuses for what we experienced or defend the system.

We told him we did walk-throughs of different facilities every month as a way of keeping us grounded in what it feels like to be in the shoes of a client. We reminded him we were not there to judge or blame but to help him improve care for his clients.

Before we left, he stood up and asked, "Where would we start?" I said "We would start by working with a team from the facility flow-charting the intake process as it really is. That would include the intake specialist, the lady behind the glass with the hole in it, their supervisor, and a counselor. You would serve as the leader of the team."

To his credit, he didn't try to make excuses for what we experienced or defend the system.

~

The next week the executive director called to ask if we would work with him and his team on improving the intake process. This director had the courage to do his own walk-through (properly disguised, which was not difficult because of the poor lighting and construction noise), see for himself what could be improved, and face the possibility of doing better. The director immediately organized several staff teams:

- One team worked on making sure that when the construction on the front of the building was completed and the crime scene tape came down that the new the public face of the agency was more welcoming. This included better exterior lighting, brighter colors and plants, and a big sign above the new entry that made it easier to identify the facility as a welcoming caring place for clients and their families and listed the first steps they needed to take for service.
- Another team took on transforming the waiting room from a drab, dark, and cramped room with old worn carpet to a welcoming environment with a fresh coat of paint, appealing pictures of hope and renewal, and a new carpet. Most importantly, the desk

behind the glass with the hole disappeared. It was replaced with a non-intimidating intake desk and an intake specialist with a new attitude that reflected a "Welcome, glad you are here today! How can we be helpful?" message. The handwritten 8 x 11 sign—*If you are not seen in 30 minutes, tell us*—was gone, along with the insulting message it sent to clients. An improvement in attitude was emerging.

- All of these small physical improvements led to the team pilot -testing and adopting a customer care approach that included a twenty-four-hour-reminder-call system to help clients and their families remember their appointments. The "We care about you" attitude was demonstrated with a follow-up call within three days of each visit to check on how clients were doing. Had they gotten their medication? Did they get the follow up scheduled with their counselor? These changes dramatically reduced no-shows and the previous revolving door of clients.

Today, five years later, this facility continues to do monthly walk-throughs, and use the NIATx model for continuous improvement. It has become a recognized leader for quality in the behavioral health field.

Walking in someone's shoes may not actually put you in their shoes, but it gets you a whole lot closer to their story than blaming them from behind a glass with a hole in it.

Tom Mosgaller is past president of the American Society for Quality (ASQ) and the Madison Area Quality Improvement Network (MAQIN). Tom's work experience includes being Director of the Office of Organizational Development and Quality for the City of Madison, VP of HR and Organizational Development for the Marshall Erdman

Company, and Director of Change Management for the University of Wisconsin-Madison College of Engineering. In addition, Tom has served on numerous community boards including as chair of the Badger Rock Middle School, and member the national Public Health Foundation (PHF).

Questions for Reflection and Discussion

1. Tell the story of one of your own moments of frustration as a customer of a company or agency. How did you react at the time? Did you ever see improvement? Describe it.
2. What are the ethical and practical considerations you see in doing a "walk-through" with a busy (and often harassed and underfunded) organization? Would you be willing to do one? Why or why not?
3. Think about the customers, users, or clients of your organization. What are their experiences? What kind of walk-through exercise might help you find out?

Voices of Inside Experts

by Cathy Caro-Bruce

I walked by her desk daily, mostly averting my eyes from the piles and piles of paper. The stacks that surrounded her, often reaching unthinkable heights, were all credit hours that had to be entered into our clunky system for recording professional learning experiences for teachers.

The papers kept coming and she could never get on top of it, even staying extra hours to try to get ahead. Her mood was understandably a bit sour at the prospect of doing this task day in and day out, and I would pass by exuding both sympathy and judgment. It seemed to me that this was her job and that maybe she wasn't very good at it. Once in a great while I wondered if perhaps the job was simply impossible for anyone to do well.

After attending a workshop in 1993 that was sponsored by MAQIN (Madison Area Quality Improvement Network) on using flowcharts to thoughtfully examine systems within organizations, however, I approached our beleaguered program assistant. I asked her if she would like to meet with a group of us to take a look at all of the systems for which she was responsible and figure out how we could make these processes better. She seemed surprised but willing. Her shoulders also loosened as I told her a nugget of my new learning that 90% of problems in an organization are system problems, not people problems! Thus, began my journey of reflection and understanding about how quality tools could be effectively used in all sorts of settings in K-12 education.

For this staff member, the opportunity to describe to her supervisors and team members the inefficiencies and redundancies of our current processes and to offer her ideas for more effective ways to deliver services to teachers was life-changing or, at the very least, job and morale-changing! Many of her ideas were embraced as the department became more tech-savvy and definitely more efficient. Those piles soon disappeared from her desk.

~

At the heart of this story is valuing the voice of the people most closely connected to the work. This is not a new idea, but in the world of education, there is often a belief that only *outside* experts know best how to design systems for leading schools, delivering instruction, and implementing educational change. While we can certainly learn from those outside voices, I have also learned that honoring and respecting the voices, experiences, and expertise of those within the organization is far more powerful and sustaining. Putting the voices of teachers and principals front and center—that's what the stories in this book represent. Here are a few of mine.

At the heart of this story is valuing the voice of the people most closely connected to the work.

After our initial success in cleaning off our assistant's desk, we renamed our team at the Madison Metropolitan School District from "Curriculum and Staff Development" to "Staff and Organization Development." The name change was subtle, but it reflected our understanding that we could only help individuals within the school district make helpful improvements if we thoughtfully examined and improved the systems that were in place. We enthusiastically found ourselves embracing quality principles throughout all of our work.

As we became more knowledgeable, our team began to offer workshops for principals, teachers, and other district staff on Running Effective Meetings, Building Teams, the Change Process, Leadership, Data Collection and Analysis, Decision-Making, and Facilitation. Principals in particular were appreciative because real-world applications on systems-improvement methods had not been part of their graduate course experiences.

Teachers enthusiastically embraced these learning opportunities because they could use their voices on leadership, grade level, and curriculum teams to make real change in their schools. And, as we were offering workshops for the classroom, we were also living the principles in our work with our administrative teams in the central office and in the administrations of schools throughout the district.

In one middle school, for example, there was a large and quantifiable achievement gap between that school and most of the other middle schools in the district. We brought a group of teachers together and did a root cause analysis of why this gap existed. After identifying one of the key drivers of the gap—that high academic expectations were not consistent schoolwide—we used the "Five Whys" strategy of systematic improvement to uncover what was really going on in the school.

The Leadership Team determined that one of the main causes of the educational gaps at this particular school was that the schedule was designed so that students had either study halls or "specials" (art, music, physical education) first period, which seemed to bring more of a "social v. academic" focus to the start of the day. Those involved in this workgroup came to believe that in order to change the culture of the school, every student there needed to start the day with academics. The team redesigned the schedule so that students were more academically focused in their first periods. This signaled a shift for students, staff, and parents and was a change the school could control. The teachers were ready to embrace the changes because they were involved in the design of the new structure and had tremendous ownership in making this new schedule work.

~

The biology department at a high school in our district was struggling with who was going to teach the "Basic Biology" course each year. Determining which teacher would take on this position was a yearly challenge. Picture the composition of the class—students who had not been successful in middle school were being referred to this low-level class. Imagine the daily challenges for the teacher who had to put up with the disruptions, paper airplanes, lack of motivated students, and no role models of students who cared about biology.

Meetings throughout the summer with all the biology teachers at the school led to an objective look at the current structure. They developed a set of shared beliefs about learning and biology. One example: "We believe that all students, regardless of age, sex, cultural or ethnic background, disability, or interest and motivation in science, have the ability to learn and be successful in an integrated Biology I classroom."

Early on, the team examined actual student achievement data, using a Root Cause Analysis. As a result of this work, strategic priorities and action steps for the coming year were identified, including the complete untracking of ninth grade biology courses. That meant that the low-level class went away. Students were no longer assigned to biology classes based on their grade point averages or past achievement.

As the year progressed, improvements were made to this plan, and a rotation system was implemented for those teaching ninth graders. Students' grades improved once they were being taught in heterogeneous classrooms. The biology teachers were incredibly proud that their voices had resulted in these significant changes and received a district award for their work.

Students' grades improved once they were being taught in heterogeneous classrooms.

~

We were on a roll. The Staff and Organization Development Team was receiving positive feedback from schools across the district. We found ourselves working with teams to construct flowcharts to find ways to make improvements. Along the way, we saw teams building more trust with one another and exhibiting a willingness to take risks to open their doors and work more collaboratively on issues of mutual interest. Flowcharts for Referrals to Special Education, Class Placement of Students, Steps for Designing Field Trips, Parent Communication, Math Assessments, Decision-Making, and Implementation and Evaluation of Curriculum were showing up in teams at many K-12 schools in the district.

Language around continuous improvement in schools began to shift. No longer were administrators and consultants from outside the individual schools telling teachers and principals where they needed to focus their time and resources. The school staff was collecting data—often using new strategies, sharing data, analyzing data, and designing actions to address organizational gaps that they themselves had identified. Schools even began to hold and enthusiastically participate in all-day professional learning experiences called "Data Retreats."

Language around continuous improvement in schools began to shift.

What was most interesting and revealing to me during this time of new learning and growth for teachers and principals was the reaction of curriculum specialists and other administrators throughout the district who perceived their positions as defined by their area of expertise—their specific body of knowledge that they wanted to impart to the rest of the staff. Many questions from the curriculum specialists were thrown at the school teams and to our Staff and Organization Development Team as teachers and principals were doing their own data collection and analysis. The most common question we encountered was: "What if they come up with the wrong conclusion?" This pushback led to a journey of many meetings with reflective conversations on what were the ultimate desired outcomes for our schools and students. What questions should we be asking if we disagree about the conclusions of the data conversations? What was the role of the curriculum specialists in supporting schools around data if teachers and principals themselves were analyzing data and designing action steps? Many of these questions were not resolved easily or collaboratively, and different departments continued to work to some degree in isolation.

~

One elementary school had a significant change in staff, and the principal was looking to bring the new teachers into the culture of the school by having teachers tell the stories of the improvement of the school over time. We combined what we called an "Affinity Process" (a brainstorming and sorting exercise) with the development of a historical timeline by asking the staff to put the names of significant people, curricular initiatives, challenges, milestones, crises, celebrations, and community initiatives on the timeline with individual self-stick notes. They could then see these notes populate the timeline, sorted by decades and years, on a chart that went across a wall of the room.

Teachers then told stories about the themes they saw. It was an opportunity for the new staff not only to learn about the people and history of the school but also about what was really important to that school and why. One teacher stood up, her voice shaking, and shared about the year a teacher had died and how a bench was dedicated to her, and she said, "If any of your kids do anything to disrespect that bench, I will be really upset." How important it was for everyone to hear those words. That bench remains in the park next to that school to this day.

At another school that also created a timeline, staff found out that one of the teachers had brought "Ready, Set, Go" conferences to the school (meetings with teachers and families early in the year to exchange information and queue students up for success). These meetings had then been adopted districtwide. No one knew this particular teacher had done that!

And at another school that had gone through a tough crisis, they used the timeline to talk about everyone's feelings and how they were trying to move on and heal from that hard and challenging year. The affinity/timeline process allowed teacher voices to be honored and valued in ways that were very special and reinforced the culture that the school was trying to rebuild.

~

By attending workshops with some of the quality experts in Madison, the Staff and Organization Development Team learned different strategic planning strategies, which influenced the existing School Improvement Planning (SIP) process in our school district. Teams at schools comprised of teachers, support staff, administration, parents, and community members completed a visioning process for their school—where they would like to see the school in five years. They developed a mission statement identifying core values driving the goals and action plans they were adopting.

Quality-improvement tools helped identify the highest leverage strategies to meet the goals. Teams evaluated options using what we called the "4 x 4 lens of Cost/Impact and Urgent/Important." They learned how to use a variety of data collection strategies and to write statements that reflected their conclusions. They learned about doing Force Field Analysis and Gap Analysis when those conversations required more structure.

When teams broke into smaller sub-teams, they were given what we called "Charge Statements" to identify the expectations and boundaries for their work. Teams used visual dialogues and mapping to portray change initiatives. These visuals assisted them in communicating to the whole staff the directions in which their teams were moving.

One of the most powerful learning tools was our ability to model the practices that we were learning. We didn't just teach about running effective meetings. At all of our meetings we always had clarity around desired outcomes, defined roles and responsibilities, decisions that had been made, and dedicated time at the end to provide feedback and talk about how we could improve on the meeting. Teachers and principals experienced these practices and took them back to their schools. It wasn't just that teachers were learning new ways of working, but their sense of efficacy and the ability to take on new leadership roles in their schools led to more enthusiasm and job satisfaction.

One of the most powerful learning tools was our ability to model the practices that we were learning.

~

What we also designed over thirty years ago was a professional development experience called Classroom Action Research that continues to this day. Groups of teachers, principals and other staff met monthly to discuss research questions that they had about their practice, their classroom, or their school. They focused on topics of importance in the district such as Homelessness, Outdoor Learning Labs, Mindfulness, Reading Comprehension, Culture and Climate, Special Education, English Language Learners, Early Algebraic Thinking, Restorative Practices, Literacy, and the use of iPads, to name a few.

Members came to the group with their own research questions. They collected and analyzed data about their questions, determined what to do as a result of this learning, and then wrote and published their work. At monthly meetings, participants would share their findings and other group members would ask critical questions to push the individual's thinking in deeper directions. Often the question might change as people learned more from the data and took new actions in their schools. The Plan-Do-Study-Act cycle was at the heart of the process and led to exponential learning for everyone.

The Plan-Do-Study-Act cycle was at the heart of the process.

Classroom Action Research resulted in outcomes that were unimaginable when this initiative started. Teachers from our district taught classes at University of Wisconsin campuses, presented at state and national conferences, wrote for journals, and participated in other research sponsored by universities and foundations.

Teacher and principal voices continued to be the clear driver of professional learning and improvement in the Madison schools. We saw the benefits in so many ways. Their experiences, their wisdom, their smarts, their ownership of the work, and their accountability for the work were all essential in moving schools forward. Having the resources and opportunities to learn about continuous improvement practices and strategies contributed greatly to the development of many structures that were at the foundation of being a responsive system and a learning organization. It was an exciting time!

Maybe those huge piles of paper sitting on top of our program assistant's desk so many decades ago were merely a visual nudge to get us started on the journey to various improvement efforts in the Madison Metropolitan School District. But what I really believe is that putting teacher and principal voices front and center in improving our schools changed our lives forever and for the better.

Cathy Caro-Bruce is a retired educator who worked as a Staff and Organization Development Specialist in the Madison Metropolitan School District for over thirty years, and then as an Educational Consultant with the Wisconsin Department of Public Instruction for eight more years. She worked with school staffs and district teams in the areas of planning, team development, creative problem-solving, systems thinking, and building consensus. She started a Teacher Center in the District, and for fifteen years coordinated the Classroom Action Research program.

Questions for Reflection and Discussion

1. In your experience, what is the proper role of administrators and outside consultants in leading effective improvement efforts in schools? What is the role of the principals and teachers? School boards? Parents? Students? Politicians? The general public? Explain your answers with examples from your own experience or that of others.
2. What does it mean to "own" a change? How does it affect how you accept and carry out that change? What might be some possible outcomes of not listening to the voices of those in your institution who are most directly impacted by any changes?

3. Make a list of situations from that need immediate attention in your organization. Which do you feel most passionate about? What actions did the author take to engage both internal and external customers that would be helpful for addressing and improving your top issues?

The Shirtless Dancer Guy

by Connie Thompson

In 1997, I decided to start a new job in a new industry and go back to school—all at the same time. I was looking for a more fulfilling career, my next adventure. I had previously worked many years in retail and was burned out, unhappy, and really needing something completely different.

I took a huge leap of faith and a big pay cut when I was hired by the City of Madison to work in a new position called Customer Service Coordinator in a new department of the City of Madison, Wisconsin: the Monona Terrace Community and Convention Center. Why would I want to take a pay cut and work in an industry in which I had absolutely no knowledge or experience? What, you might ask, made me think that I would be successful or that it would work out? In fact, it was that I was desperately in need of a career that would be both rewarding and enjoyable. This was a time in my life when I had to make a big change. So, I took a chance. This is a story of how it paid off.

I remember the first few months being a whirlwind of activity. I went from getting my orientation to city policies to being told that I needed to hire and train approximately thirty employees within the next four weeks when we would be holding our grand opening. Yikes, I thought, how is this going to work out? In my prior career I had been a store manager and then a district operations expert. Yet even though my new job had nothing to do with retail, the planning, organizing, hiring, and training of staff was very similar. Because we were a new department with very few individuals who had actually worked in the hospitality industry, we had to be very agile, great communicators, and intensely collaborative. In essence, we were building the internal systems for the new organization as we went along.

Now, I do not recommend doing things in your institution that way. We all would have preferred to have two or three months to develop our policies, procedures, and training. To start, I had only five full-time employees in my department and no standard operating procedures. Not a very organized or effective method for success, but it was the new challenge I was looking for... and more.

We had Monona Terrace Board members driving our riding vacuums and emptying trash.

~

We somehow managed to get the building opened for business and lived through the enormously popular grand opening of the Monona Terrace Community and Convention Center. I swear that every Madison resident showed up to tour the building that first weekend. This was both a blessing and a curse. While we wanted city residents to be excited about our grand opening, we were very under-staffed and undertrained. In fact, we were flying by the seat of our pants. We had Monona Terrace Board members driving our riding vacuums and emptying trash. The Associate Director was literally personally helping set up the rooms for events. All Monona Terrace managers and employees were pitching in—it was an all-hands-on-deck situation. While this was chaotic due to the huge crowds, it was also thrilling and an amazing example of teamwork. In my mind we not only survived; we thrived in a difficult situation. Against all odds, we hit a home run.

This success was significant because prior to construction there had been a long delay in getting the building approved and funded. The last attempt included a contentious referendum that narrowly passed; 51% wanted us built and 49% did not. Here was a lesson in the importance of clarity of purpose. The name of the center was expanded to show the purpose as an asset for the people of the community. Tom Mosgaller said, "Without the community emphasis, I don't know if we should even have the Monona Terrace Community and Convention Center." We spent the next several years proving that city residents had made a good choice in voting (albeit narrowly) to build this beautiful and unique Frank Lloyd Wright-designed convention center.

The first full year that we were open was 1998, and everyone wanted to hold an event at Monona Terrace. We hosted 1051 events that year, at least two times more than was advisable. We served 361,000 event attendees and visitors to the building. This meant turning rooms over two to three times a day. It was madness, and we certainly did not have the systems or people in place to do this at a high level or for a prolonged period of time. Another issue that we encountered was capacity within the building. In some cases, the events that had been sold were too big for the spaces rented and required major adjustments to their room set-ups. We were also experiencing operational defects due to staffing, training, and systems issues. On the bright side, the entire Monona Terrace team worked together to get through these issues without the customers even knowing that there were any operational issues. Our overall customer satisfaction rating was 98% satisfied. Percentage of repeat business was a very respectable 61%.

It was madness, we did not have the systems or people in place to do this.

~

So, we were definitely doing many things well, but we all knew we had work to do and many things to improve. Our event services staff and some managers, had taken to calling their morning building and room set walk-offs, "Morning Madness." They were seeing that our set-up quality requirements were not being met. There was sloppiness in the details, which included table linens and stage drapes not properly configured, detail vacuuming not done well, trash cans not being wiped down, carpet stains in the rooms. The list was long.

Someone from the upper management team, I believe it was the Executive Director Joan LeMahieu, wisely put a call in to Tom Mosgaller, the city's Director of Quality and Productivity, to come help us fix these issues. A process-improvement team was immediately set up to map the existing processes, identify the root causes of problems, gather data, develop potential solutions, implement the best options, and then maintain the gains. In addition, Tom trained us in techniques such as how to use Plan-Do-Check-Act (PDCA) and other tools to fix problems. These effectively ended "Morning Madness," but it took a good year to put all of the systems, policies and procedures, and training into place.

This is where the real growth occurred. Our leaders became better at leading. Our staff became better at identifying and communicating issues and poor outcomes. We all became better team members and better at working together to solve problems. Our internal and external service levels improved and moved toward being exceptional. Our organizational culture became a best-practice-worthy example, and we collaborated so well that employee satisfaction was off the chart. Customer survey data was also unbelievably high. We added a measure to our customer survey—willingness to return—and it has been 99% since 2000. While many things were going well and headed in the right direction, we still knew we had more work to do, so we embraced additional improvement training and eventually we were able to drive it down to the frontline level and make it part of our organizational culture.

It was during the early years that we realized the importance of all managers and lead workers being well trained in both systems and people management. By then, Tom Mosgaller had developed a top-notch Supervisory Academy for the city. It was a huge time commitment several months long, but well worth the time. We had four people from Monona Terrace attend, and I was fortunate to be one of them. It was in this training that I was exposed to the Quality Improvement movement's systems and methods.

One of the requirements at the end of the program was a final improvement project. The project I chose to improve was our staffing model. We had originally tried to staff the operations department with a few full-time permanent employees and a lot of part-time employees. This is the model used in our industry, especially in big arenas, but it was not very effective for us due to low local unemployment rates and economic growth rates that gave people seeking jobs many opportunities. In short, we could not keep part-time staff on board. It seemed like the second that we got them trained and performing at a high level, they either found another job that gave them more hours or was full-time with benefits. Turnover definitely contributed to our quality levels being inconsistent at times.

They either found a job that gave them more hours or was full time with benefits.

I took on the task of studying convention center staffing models and ultimately identifying the best approaches for us. During this benchmarking process, I identified the need to implement a third shift. Two shifts of staff could not keep up with the workload, and the second shift ended up with a lot of overtime because they could not leave the building until all their work was completed. This was not an effective use of our payroll budget.

Another discovery was that it would be better to differentiate staff to develop different expertise. The original staffing model had all part-time staff being assigned based on need, not interest or experience. This also led to inconsistent quality levels, turnover, and low levels of productivity. In response, I suggested operations workers be specialized as either set-up workers or building cleaners, but they would still be used to cover shifts or if needed for a large event turnover.

Lastly, I identified the need for two Assistant Operations Managers. The Operations Manager just did not have time to complete their required duties and responsibilities. This had led to scheduling issues and running out of supplies and failing to hire enough part-time staff in a timely manner. My suggestions were accepted by the Associate Director and the Operations Manager and were implemented within six months. Having more full-time staff, an additional shift, and another level of management really helped the operations department stabilize, organize, and be in the best position to continue the early quality work that we had achieved.

Sometime shortly after graduating from the Supervisory Academy, I was visiting Guy Van Rensselaer, another consultant with the city, about helping me with some additional improvement projects at the center. As I was leaving to go back to Monona Terrace, Tom Mosgaller motioned for me to come in and talk with him in his office. I had no idea what Tom wanted to speak to me about. The conversation went like this:

"Hey Connie," said Tom, "I have noticed that you really like this quality thing and saw the project that you did for the Supervisory Academy—it was good work. If you are interested in learning more in this field, there's a program at Edgewood College that you should check out. The guy in charge of the program is Dan Schroeder. Give him a call."

I said, "Okay, thanks. I will; sounds interesting."

Tom's great advice was well-timed. I went on to graduate from the Industrial/Organizational Psychology program and then got an MBA with an emphasis on Pedagogy and Organizational Development. I have put that knowledge to good use in the operations department at Monona Terrace.

I saw great opportunities to tighten up our standard operating procedures, improve our processes, up our quality game (especially our training program). I remember my excitement; it was like being given the keys to the candy shop. I had new knowledge, skills, and abilities that could revolutionize our department's quality levels.

It was like being given the keys to the candy shop.

However, much to my surprise, my excitement was not universal. Initially, I felt like the shirtless dancer guy in the video called "How to Start a Movement." Yes, I was that awkward lone dancer out there dancing to the beat of my own drum, without concern about what others thought of me. I had tools that would fix our organizational problems, make our lives easier, and deliver better outcomes for our customers. What was taking so long for my team to get the value of this quality movement? So, like the shirtless dancer guy, I persisted. I kept dancing and trying to sell my team on the virtues of improving processes and systems, and finally I was able to get my first follower on board. And we danced together for a short while and then, little by little, more people in my department saw the value and joined us. Pretty soon we were all dancing together and had started a true movement for continually improving our department.

Over the next several years, I worked with my operations staff, the lead workers, and managers to identify potential areas to improve. We put together teams to work on improvement projects such as back/shoulder injury reduction, comprehensive operations worker training, clean facility quality control, back-of-house organization, and guest service attendant training. All these we evaluated using objective data.

We also brought in Guy Van Rensselaer to train staff on using LEAN waste-removal procedures. We added questions to our customer survey that they told us was important to them: courteous staff, staff available when they needed them, staff adaptable to changes, rooms set up to their specifications, rooms and building clean.

By identifying the seven types of waste and then eliminating or greatly reducing them, we have seen impactful results. We also improved our customer response time from fifteen to six minutes and achieved 98% satisfaction with our adaptability to make last-minutes changes. Room set-up quality errors were reduced from an average of five per shift to none, and customer satisfaction with room set-up was improved to 98%. Event paperwork errors were reduced from 30% to less than 2%. By eliminating cleaning errors, we achieved 100% customer satisfaction of building cleanliness. In general, we achieved overall customer-service satisfaction of 99%.

Customer service is everyone's job.

The greatest improvement of all, however, was in staff courtesy. We had provided customer service training on a yearly and sometimes bi-annual basis, but our results did not achieve consistently high ratings until we trained each individual department on exceptional customer service *specific to their job duties.* Often staff think that if they are back-of-house employees or in positions that do not directly interact with customers, they don't need to be trained in customer service or interact with customers.

Innovation comes from people who take joy in their work.

Once we understood the problem that not all employees understood their role in customer service, we were able to change the training and expectations to this: Customer service is everyone's job. Over the years, this has become a source of pride and we share and celebrate all customer comments, letters, and surveys with every single staff person. We raised our scores in courtesy from 95% to 99% satisfaction.

~

In 2020, I became Executive Director of Monona Terrace Community and Convention Center. From the beginning, we have been guided by several important insights from the late, great W. Edwards Deming:

- Quality is everyone's responsibility.
- Quality comes not from inspection, but from improvement of the process.
- The greatest waste is failure to use the abilities of people, to learn about their frustrations and the contributions that they are eager to make.
- Innovation comes from people who take joy in their work.

But how do you know when you have really succeeded in establishing a strong culture committed to continuously improving everything we do? Here are some of the things that I saw within my team that made me know they got it. I saw team members leading at every level—as one big team with everyone contributing to improving our processes. For example, operations workers who were not lead workers or supervisors take personal responsibility to train and coach new staff on how to set rooms properly and show them when they do not meet our specifications and standards. I saw staff implementing innovative ways to do their work on their own. For example, they started using the patterns on the carpet to set the tables so that the rows were perfectly aligned and the distance between tables was exact. Previously we had used long tape measures to set the rows, which was time consuming and less accurate.

One day when I was walking through a room being set up by a group of operations workers, I heard one of them say to a coworker who was leaving to get some equipment, "Hey, when you go get new equipment, take back equipment that needs to be put away too; don't waste the trip. The employees themselves had determined that it was inefficient to send staff to get new equipment and then later take back all the unused equipment. So, they made a rule that if you were going to get new equipment you had to take equipment you no longer needed and put it away.

I saw my people asking a lot of questions, trying to understand processes, systems, and break downs, mapping out processes, measuring outcomes, forming cross-functional teams to develop new solutions. For example, one insidious quality issue that pops up from time to time is the hand off from one step in a process to the next step. As you might guess, sometimes changes happen in one area that impact the next area and that can lead to big issues if the communication of those changes is not timely or well-coordinated. Sometimes, a change in one area can make it impossible for the next area to complete their work. Our workers are constantly anticipating and solving that problem before it even occurs.

So, don't be afraid to be the shirtless dancer guy, that lone nut who isn't afraid to try something new and isn't afraid to fail or look ridiculous. Even better, if you see a lone nut dancing by themselves, don't be afraid to join them. They might be inventing something great. Have the guts to stand up and join in. You may just be starting a movement if you do.

Connie Thompson is the Executive Director of Monona Terrace Community and Convention Center, where she has served in various roles for the past nearly twenty-five years. She served most recently as the Associate Director of Operations and Quality at Monona Terrace. Thompson is also a certified venue manager through the International Association of Venue Managers and was an adjunct professor of Organizational Behavior and Leadership at Edgewood College, where she taught for over ten years.

Questions for Reflection and Discussion

1. Have you ever felt like you were the "shirtless dancer"? Tell the story. Or if not, explain why it is not your thing. Would you join the shirtless dancer if you saw him? Why or why not?
2. Is it true that "customer service is everyone's job"? Explain your answer, with examples.
3. What do you think of these four insights by W. Edwards Deming:
   - Quality is everyone's responsibility.
   - Quality comes not from inspection, but from improvement of the process.
   - The greatest waste is failure to use the abilities of people, failure to learn about their frustrations and the contributions that they are eager to make.
   - Innovation comes from people who take joy in their work.

Chapter Three

Systems Thinking

Introduction

A Virtuous Cycle

A system is a set of things—people, cells, molecules,
or whatever—interconnected in such a way that they produce
their own pattern of behavior over time.

Donella H. Meadows

If you cut a cow in half, you will not have two cows. This is the lesson of systems. In a complex system, everything is connected to everything else, even if we don't see it. It is the millions and billions of connections that make a system in nature or in a human organization what it is—a system.

In 2019, an infectious virus was discovered in a small town on the other side of the globe. Within six months, we couldn't buy toilet paper, stock in Zoom was skyrocketing, airlines were going bankrupt, sweatpants were the new fashion, people were making sourdough bread, rush hours disappeared, and new car lots were empty. It turns out, the whole world is an interconnected system.

Peter Senge wrote extensively on organizations as systems in his classic, *The Fifth Discipline*. Systems behave in unpredictably predictable ways. For example, some changes made in a system will create virtuous cycles, where positive actions build on each other and the situation continually improves. For example, strong leadership development programs and coaching can lead to better leaders, who lead to productive and satisfied employees, better services/products, happier customers, which ultimately results in a successful organization. It is a "virtuous cycle."

~

Some changes made in a system, however, can result in a "vicious cycle" of increasing dysfunction. For instance, buying based on lowest bid can lead to poor quality parts, which cause the product to fail, and unhappy customers who quit buying, and funds that go down so you can no longer afford quality parts. Some solutions can make things worse, like creating a policy where no one can flex their vacation because it resulted in a problem once, often long ago and far away. Some changes made to systems will show up in unexpected ways a long time after the action was initiated. A law was passed to allow flexibility in approving herbal medicines, and now their proclaimed benefits can't be completely trusted.

All systems have built-in limits to growth and expansion. For example, earth's environment can only bear so much carbon dioxide before its sub-systems break down. Just look outside your window.

We may know this intellectually because we can see systems in nature. Often, however, the understanding that we are nested in larger systems is forgotten in the course of organizational planning and decision-making. Research by McKinsey tells us that globally almost half of the decisions made today in organizations fail to net the intended results (43%), so "improvement" becomes not much better than tossing a coin. (See De Smet, Koller, and Lovallo, 2019). We often only see our part of the system, and the rest is like wiring in the walls—unseen but essential.

~

Donella Meadows' famous article "Dancing with Systems" offers keys for working within systems:

> Systems thinking leads to another conclusion–however waiting, shining, obvious as soon as we stop being blinded by the illusion of control. It says that there is plenty to do, but of a different sort of "doing." The future can't be predicted, but it can be envisioned and brought lovingly into being. Systems can't be controlled, but they can be designed and redesigned. We can't surge forward with certainty into a world of no surprises, but we can expect surprises and learn from them and even profit from them.

Meadows advises us to expose our mental models, talk about our assumptions. She urges us to let information flow freely. Go for the good of the whole, she advises, even if it seems to disadvantage sub-parts. Stay humble and be a learner, she says. In short, she reminds us that we can't really *control* systems, but we can *dance* with them.

In his famous Red Bead experiment, Deming illustrated how little control individual employees have over the systems in which they work. Participants (workers) were asked to take a paddle and scoop from a bowl of red and white beads. Their job was to get only white beads, not red ones. Red beads were "errors." He instructed, encouraged, and rewarded those with the most white beads, and berated those with too many red beads. He kept pushing, and they kept trying, but they had no control over how many red beads landed in their scoop. They had no control over the system. Deming said that workers work *in* the system, while leaders work *on* the system.

It is the job of leadership, Deming said, to make sure the systems in their organization are coherent, efficient, and effective. These systems improvements, however, can only be done successfully with full engagement of those who work in them. Front-line workers hold keys to improvement. Here are four stories on systems thinking by Turina Bakken, Guy Van Rensselaer, Luis Yudice, and Janice Smith.

References

De Smet, A., Koller, T., and Lovallo, D. (Sept. 4, 2019). *Bias busters: Getting both sides of the story.* McKinsey and Company.

Meadows, D. (2008). *Thinking in systems: A primer.* Sustainability Institute.

Meadows, D. (no date). *Dancing with systems.* The Donella Meadows Project: Academy for Systems Change.

Adjusting to Meet the Moment

by Turina Bakken

...if you don't know what to do,
you do more of what you know how to do.

Bolman and Deal, 2017

She was nervous. The young woman with brown eyes and curly dark hair sat rigidly in her chair right in front of me and tried to look calm. It was the first day of a Marketing Principles class at Madison College.

I guessed she was from somewhere in Europe. Having lived in and traveled extensively across Europe and having been a student there myself, the telltale signs of graph paper, a protractor, and a plastic box for colored pencils were evident. Those academic tools were commonplace in Europe. In addition, unlike many of the American students, she sat in the middle of the first row in the classroom.

As the instructor, I was sitting on the edge of a desk in the front of the room, leading first day introductions and hoping to put everyone at ease. When I called on her to introduce herself, she quietly said, "My name is Ema. I am from Kosovo."

Anywhere I travel, I always learn three phrases in every county—please, thank you, and how to order beer. So, hoping to welcome her I said the only phrase I knew from her home country, "*Tri piva molin.*" After a look of surprise, a broad smile lit up her face. I smiled too. The phrase, which translates to "Three beers, please" didn't fit, but it was all I could think of, and to attempt to put her at ease. I adjusted to meet the moment, and we had made a human connection—a connection that remains all these years later. Two years after that initial connection, Ema and I would share the Madison College commencement stage, where she bravely delivered the commencement address as a college graduate in front of thousands of people.

W. Edwards Deming, one of the main founders of the Quality Improvement (QI) movement, often said, "Drive fear out of the workplace." I have lived by that principle, doing my best to drive fear out of the classroom so that all students feel welcomed and a sense of belonging. Only then can true learning occur. This and so many other quality practices have informed my work, learning and leadership over the span of my career.

"Why is this a thing?" Of course you should use data for decision-making!

~

In my first professional role after undergrad, I coordinated the continuous improvement program at UW-Madison's Management Institute (now Executive Education). As I prepared to promote a quality workshop on data for decision-making, I asked myself, "Why is this a *thing*?" Of course you should use data for decision-making! But I had no idea at the time how many decisions are made based on unchallenged assumptions, how much time is spent solving the same problem over and over again, or how many meetings went awry without a clear purpose or framework to get better results.

~

I could have stayed comfortably in that role at UW-Madison, but I was looking for a new challenge, so I accepted the position of Communications Director for a small, non-profit called the Madison Area Quality Improvement Network—MAQIN. At MAQIN, I was fortunate to interact with and learn from Madison's stars in the field of quality improvement—including Dave Boyer, Brian Joiner, Barb Hummel, Peter Scholtes, and many of the other contributors to this book. I met Meg Wheatley, Dan Oestreich, Michael Brassard, Alfie Kohn, Daniel Kim, Peter Senge, and many other inspirational thinkers and change leaders. I learned much from these professionals in workshops, conversations, over dinner, or on rides to the airport. I soaked it all in, not realizing at the time the cumulative, profound effect they were all having on me and would have on the rest of my career.

As MAQIN changed form and staffing models, however, I accepted a position at Madison College as a faculty member in the Marketing Program. I wasn't an expert on curriculum design and, in fact, had never taught in a formal classroom setting, but I knew how to organize and run a good meeting and thus knew the importance of having a clear purpose and outcomes for every class. I managed time, recapped important points, kept it light while maintaining accountability, and—most importantly of all–engaged students in their own learning. As with Ema, I tried to instill a sense of community in the classroom.

My students were rich in diversity: in age, race/ethnicity, socioeconomic status, number of first-generation college students, and more. In that diversity, students had life experience that positioned them to add value to class learning in some important and often unique ways.

I had come to appreciate the power of inquiry instead of thinking that change agents have to know everything. Questions were about curiosity, a door to new possibilities. To my students I said many times, "It is better to have *some* of the questions than *all* of the answers." When the pressure of having a correct answer is lifted, it is a sense of relief for students to *be* in the question, to *live* in the possibilities.

I encouraged students to be open to different possibilities, to use critical thinking and analysis, to remember to "trust their gut." I always remembered a session on data from one of the first Hunter Conferences sponsored by MAQIN. The speaker reminded everyone that our own intuition is such a valuable data point and that we always need to combine our own experience and intuition with the data in decision-making. In teaching about Marketing Research, for example, I pointed out that data will shine the light on the problem, but it will never tell you what to do. "That's why we need you—to translate the data into meaningful action or improvement."

Everything about my teaching approach was based on what I had learned about focusing on quality. I used principles of Servant Leadership from Kouzes and Posner, Idealized Design from Ackoff, and Systems Thinking from Senge and Kim. Chris Argyris's "Ladder of Inference" (see Senge, et al., 1994) had permanently changed the way I communicated and solved conflict.

As I moved from faculty to academic leadership, including Associate Dean, Dean, Associate Vice President, and then Provost, the tools and practices of change management and continuous improvement became even more influential and important to my work. In fact, I used Systems Thinking as the conceptual framework for my Ph.D. dissertation, something not often used in academic research but an approach that garnered me the Dissertation of the Year award in my academic program.

~

In March 2020, as COVID-19 cases escalated throughout the U.S. and the world, the floor literally fell out from under us at Madison College—as it did in organizations everywhere. Our collective experience and insights on quality in leadership, learning, communication, decision-making, design thinking, scenario planning, systems thinking, culture, teamwork, people—everything—was needed in the spring of 2020 to transform our college of 34,000 students and 2,500 employees in a way that was organized, safe, and in everyone's best interests.

In a matter of days, the college went nearly 100% remote, with thousands of on-line course sections. Face-to-face instruction was paused, travel and athletics postponed, meetings cancelled, staff sent home—uncertainty, anxiety and fear rising by the hour. A thousand questions were before us and there simply was no roadmap, no example to lean on for a guide. All our knowledge about how to successfully deliver education and services had to be adjusted to meet the moment. COVID may have been the greatest crisis to face Madison College since its inception in 1912. The pandemic crisis disruption presented a blank slate, and as we quickly realized, might also become a great gift if we met the moment.

Integrated systems that ordinarily would have taken months or years to develop were built collaboratively in a matter of days or hours.

What transpired in the weeks and months after that was an opportunity to infuse new ways of thinking and doing that would serve students in ways we could have never imagined. Integrated systems that ordinarily would have taken months or years to develop were built collaboratively in a matter of days or hours. We were given a chance to re-invest in and celebrate our culture as a foundation for the future. While stress and anxiety were high, so was innovation and transformative change. A solid grounding in organizational change theory, practice, and tools provided a base for Madison College to stand on while we survived, learned, and moved forward together.

Just a sampling of the questions we faced: How would we prepare and support almost 1,300 faculty members to teach remotely? How must we to attend to equity in remote instruction? How could our technology infrastructure expand and adapt to deliver programs and services remotely and ensure that students, faculty, and staff have access to the technology needed to do their best work? How would we maintain integrity in our renowned hands-on programs like nursing, apprenticeship, advanced manufacturing, and criminal justice? How might we maintain academic continuity and student services? How will we take care of our employees' needs? What about the facilities, public safety, crisis communication, the budget—and seemingly everything else?

As the college's provost and academic leader, my first task was to calm the initial chaos and recognize the complexity before us. To do that, I used all the learning from my MAQIN days. From Russell Ackoff, we approached the current reality with an Idealized Design frame of mind (Ackoff, Magidson and Addison, 2006). Ackoff would say, "Pretend that your organization was destroyed overnight, how would you redesign it?" The power in that approach was to remove preconceived notions and assumptions about how things were supposed to work, in order to "see" truly innovative possibility. We based our immediate planning on scenario thinking and designed multiple scenarios to meet the multiple realities that might emerge. Guided by our president and with my cabinet colleagues, and with critical input from the rest of our college community, we began the difficult but inspirational work of reconfiguring every part of our institution, with the health and safety of our students and employees and fidelity to our mission as our umbrella.

Systems Thinking from Peter Senge and Daniel Kim helped us recognize that many new systems would have to be created and then made to interact successfully for the college to operate mostly virtually. As they noted, the sum of the parts does not equal the whole, it's the synergy between the parts (Senge, et al., 1994). Silos had to be broken down instantly, and we collaboratively rebuilt service and academic systems and processes not only to work in this new reality of COVID, but to offer our employees and students other support they needed in this disruptive time.

The sum of the parts does not equal the whole.

We made it visual—we sketched out how new systems would look and how they would interact using less than perfect, but meaningful, interrelationship diagrams and process maps. We used whatever data we could get, including qualitative data from our employees and students and benchmarking data from across the country to test our assumptions. We honored and leaned on intuition and experience as valid data points. All the Brassard and Scholtes process improvement tools helped us at some point.

As leaders, we used Bolman and Deal's Four Frames (2017) to evaluate what we were doing. How does each solution look through the various structural, human resources, political, and symbolic frames? Were we paying adequate attention to each of the frames? What were we missing? Bolman and Deal have famously noted that if you don't know what to do, you do more of what you know how to do. That can be detrimental if you do the same things you always did and expect different results. We had to admit what we didn't know, what we had never seen before, and then ask good questions and rely on one another and find a way forward.

Meg Wheatley's work helped us stay focused on the human side of change, to ensure that our relationships with one another—relationships based in our values and shared governance principles of respect, equity and inclusion, fairness, and transparency—remained at the heart of all our actions. One of the very first decisions, announced in March 2020, was that the college would continue to pay all employees through June 30—including faculty, staff, student employees, and part-time. (As of this writing, we have continued our way through the pandemic disruption without layoffs or furloughs.)

Communication—transparent, honest, constant communication—was critical. Our crisis communication team managed the website and external communications. We focused on bulletins, video messages, and all-employee forums that provided open communication and questions on topics that mattered. We continue those communications to this day. We also found innovative ways to honor our most treasured traditions—graduation, college community days, employee recognition, student and employee orientations and much more.

As provost, I leaned on the SCARF model from the Neuroscience Leadership Institute (see Rock and Ringleb, 2013). The essence of my messages considered status (acknowledging expertise wherever we could find it); certainty (trying to create some sense of what is and what will happen to reduce fear during massive uncertainty); autonomy (trying to offer some sense of control and choice); relatedness (building on our common connection and belonging); and fairness (increasing a sense of values, of justice, and the idea that "We are all in this together"). It was those tenets of communication that guided my messages to my team, faculty, staff, students, and the public. We realized that, quite simply, as their worlds became separated, people needed to be a part of *something*. The college helped hold people's lives together in many ways.

In addition to communications with our college community and external stakeholders, I had to build a leadership structure—a structure that avoided redundancy, added clarity, and reflected trust in those who were in key positions to do what they had to do. We sketched out a cascading communication and leadership plan on day one that guided our work. (I kept a map of the new structure for Academic Affairs on my whiteboard for months, even though a year later I had nearly completely redesigned it based on what we had learned from the crisis.)

"Let's do it now, because we know it is the right thing to do."

Every day, I created a list of at least ten people to connect with informally just to check in personally, to ask the simple but powerful question, "How are you?" They responded with gratitude, observations, suggestions, ideas, or questions. It was enormously helpful to me as an executive leader to know where the pain points were and what things were working for our faculty and staff. With the shutdown, I had lost my ability to walk around, to have those critical (and fun) hallway conversations, to keep a pulse on the place. Those daily check-ins gave me the affirmation that I needed to know I was doing the right things right (see Ackoff), and where I needed to do more or move forward differently. And it mattered to people that they were being asked, being "seen" in the isolated world of the pandemic.

More than ever, political (with a small "p") history dissipated. We had to trust, to trust that we were doing what we could and what we must for our students and our employees. A phrase I heard daily, or sometimes hourly, was "Let's do it." Not, "Let's do it after several months of meetings and bureaucracy," but rather, "Let's do it now, because we know it is the right thing to do."

Inspiration, ingenuity, and resilience reigned at Madison College. Too many stories to tell, honestly. Many, many faculty and staff members came forward with ideas and solutions during this time and simply said, "I can help; I'll do this." For instance, Bill, a faculty member in our paramedic program, had been experimenting on his own with cutting-edge virtual reality and simulations in his teaching. We shifted his role to support all faculty during COVID, and he is now one of our lead faculty members on this issue as we expand sophisticated simulation and virtual reality into programming across the college.

In all the disruption during that Spring semester of 2020, student course withdrawals actually *dropped* from pre-pandemic levels. While the crisis caused great stress in our enrollment metrics, by and large our existing students stuck with us and came back the next term to continue their academic journey.

Course success, as a leading indicator to degree completion, dipped only slightly in online courses, but showed improvements after two terms—evidence of our investments in faculty, academic technology and equity in remote instruction. COVID performance bonuses were awarded that next year to all part and full-time employees, to say thank you and recognize each unique contribution.

If you asked me what any leader of change needs to keep in mind, I would first say, let go of certainty and admit you don't know all the answers. Inquiry and collective voice are your best strategies to inform a future you could never have imagined.

Second, remember that it's not about you—it's about them—the people you serve. People first, always. Simple as that.

Let go of certainty and admit you don't know all the answers.

Finally, always keep in mind and check that Ladder of Inference you have in your head. Your own unconscious beliefs and assumptions can keep you from seeing clearly and can stand in the way of your imagining new possibilities.

Higher education has been forever changed. We didn't see the COVID disruption coming—and when it hit, it hit hard. For Madison College, this disruption has resulted in a flowering of creativity, innovation, and a new sense of care around teaching and learning, with a focus on equity, access, and success.

From the positive impact on Ema-from-Kosovo to helping lead a major organization through COVID-19 to a new and promising future, I have stood on the shoulders of the thinkers, leaders, writers, and change agents that I have been blessed to learn from. And that, in closing, has helped reshape Madison College and put us in a position to impact our students and communities of the future in the most meaningful ways possible.

References

Ackoff, R. L., Magidson, J., and Addison, H.J. (2006). *Idealized design: Creating an organization's future.* Wharton School Publications.

Bolman, L.G. and Deal, T.E. (2017). *Reframing organizations: Artistry, choice, and leadership* (6th edition). Jossey-Bass.

Rock, D. and Ringleb, A. H. (2013). *Handbook for Neuroleadership,* Neuro Leadership Institute. CreateSpace.

Neuroscience Leadership Institute. https://neuroleadership.com.

Senge , P.; Roberts, C., Ross, R.; Smith, B.; and Kleiner, A. (1994). *The fifth discipline fieldbook. Doubleday.*

Turina R. Bakken, Ph.D., is the Provost at Madison College in Madison, Wisconsin. In her nearly twenty- five years at the college, she has held a variety of senior leadership positions and served for a decade as a full-time faculty member. She was awarded the Distinguished Teacher of the Year award in 2006 and received the College's Outstanding Employee award in 2010. In 2016, she received the Dr. Idahlynne Karre Exemplary Leadership Award from the global leadership training organization, The Chair Academy. Her experience also includes management and board positions in the fields of marketing, quality management, product development, and sports broadcasting. Bakken holds a doctorate in Educational Leadership and Policy Administration (ELPA) from the University of Wisconsin-Madison.

Questions for Reflection and Discussion

1. Which of these pieces of the author's advice for leading change seem most helpful to you? Why? Explain your answer with examples:
   - Let go of certainty and admit you don't know all the answers.
   - Inquiry and collective voice are your best strategies to inform a future you could never have imagined.
   - It's not about you—it's about them—the people you serve. People first, always.
   - Your own unconscious beliefs and assumptions can keep you from seeing clearly and can stand in the way of your imagining new possibilities.
2. Do you have any stories of positive things that came out of the COVID-19 pandemic? Tell one or two of them.
3. Systems thinkers tell us that a so-called "solution" applied to a systemic problem sometimes makes a problem worse. Why do you think that is? What tools did the author and her team use for avoiding that common phenomenon? How might you use those tools?

The Urban Forest

by Guy Van Rensselaer

The bearded man was chained to the stately spreading oak tree. A huge padlock at his waist secured the chains. Nearby, a uniformed arborist stood holding a chainsaw, staring in disbelief at the chained man. The man glared back defiantly. At his feet lay a carnival of water bottles, juice boxes, baggies of snacks, homemade cookies, and love notes from supporters.

On the other side of Penn Park in Madison, picnickers heard the chained man's cry, "I'm not going to let you butcher this tree." A Forestry Unit foreperson approached him and said, "We need to trim the limbs that are a safety hazard. People get killed by limbs like these when they fall," he added, pointing upwards.

"Don't say you're just trimming this tree. You're going to butcher it. This tree has been here for 100 years and will be ruined when you people are done with it. I know how this works!" The foreperson said they would be coming back in a week to do what needed to be done and advised the man to go home.

The city of Madison, Wisconsin, has had a love affair with trees for well over a century.

When the Forestry crew arrived the following week to remove the troublesome branches, the man was again chained to the tree with snacks and notes at his feet. This time, a group of local residents were gathered, watching to see what would happen. Again, the foreperson tried to convince the man to open the lock on the chains and go home, the police were called, and the foreperson said he would be bringing in the Fire Department next with bolt cutters. Finally, the police officers explained to the man that charges could be brought against him for endangering public safety, and shortly after that he wearily unlocked the padlock and stepped out of the chains. "This isn't right," the man shouted as he walked away, eyes glistening. He didn't look back.

The guy just loved trees. The city of Madison, Wisconsin, has had a love affair with trees for well over a century, starting in 1894 with the Madison Park and Pleasure Drive Association. As the city grew and developed streets, it became the practice to plant trees on the terraces (the area between the street and the sidewalk). In addition, homeowners and other property owners were encouraged to plant trees to enhance the beauty and health of the city. Snapshots of Madison from the early 1950s revealed massive elms arching over streets, verdant parks lush with many species of hardwoods, and beautiful well-maintained trees on almost every private lot.

Catastrophe came in the late 1950s in the form of Dutch Elm disease. The city employed multiple means to save its elms, all unsuccessful. The die-off was so complete that the Forestry Unit did little else but remove dead and dying elms for the next fourteen years. By the time the disease had run its course, thousands of stately trees had died. The longstanding policy of the city—to replace every dead tree it took down—compounded the annual workload. Annual pruning was suspended and, as a result, thousands of trees were planted every year with little or no maintenance during their critical first ten years. Ultimately, all the elm trees were replaced. As the city grew, the tree population grew proportionately.

~

Due to the lack of initial annual pruning, the city had many thousands of juvenile trees in dire need of proper trimming. There were approximately 90,000 terrace trees and 250,000 park trees. The Forestry Unit was charged with the maintenance of all of them.

During windstorms, thousands of limbs would fall and create hazardous conditions for pedestrians, bicyclists, and motorists. Even in the heavily forested cemetery, the arborists had to spend an excessive amount of time repairing the damaged trees. (Those visiting their dearly departed had to be protected from their own demise at the hands of damaged trees!)

The Forestry Unit had difficulty keeping up with the workload even in the best of times. The actual maintenance cycle had grown to over 12 years. Without proper maintenance, the trees became unruly and took considerably more time and effort to correct. Juvenile trees had developed faulty architecture, which inevitably led to extensive damage during major storms. Often, regular maintenance would be suspended to deal with storm damage. This only exacerbated the problem.

Terrace trees were the top priority for the safety of commuters and pedestrians—which meant that the maintenance of park trees was put on the back burner, even though they required the same care as the terrace trees.

As each tree aged without proper maintenance, it became more unruly and took considerably more time and effort to correct.

Because private property trees and shrubs were the responsibility of property owners, the brush from their maintenance was collected and processed by the Streets and Sanitation Division. Private property trees also suffered after every storm, and property owners felt the city brush pick up was too slow and not frequent enough. They complained that the brush on the terrace not only looked bad but also killed their grass. This dissatisfaction was amplified anytime there was storm damage. Streets and San was stretched to the limit to maintain the cycle in the best of times, let alone after storms.

For the Forestry Unit, the problem was how to catch up and adhere to a proper maintenance cycle for the "urban forest" that is Madison, Wisconsin. For the Streets and Sanitation Division, the question was how to speed up brush removal, especially after storms.

In the 1990s, systemic-improvement teams were established in both Forestry and Streets and San. The teams consisted of a "vertical slice" of each agency, which meant that they had representatives from all levels of the hierarchy in each. These vertical teams reported to Guidance Teams from each agency, which were composed of agency supervisors and managers.

Employees were encouraged to submit potential solutions to the problems identified by the project teams and, wherever possible, employees were involved in the evaluation of the potential strategies.

Using the Seven-Step Problem Solving methodology, we realized that the existing data was made up predominantly of so-called "lagging" indicators, such as quantity of work, hours applied, equipment utilization, productivity, etc. These measures were all well and good, but they offered little or no guidance for solving the problems.

~

As is often the case, where helpful data is absent, everyone has assumptions that are unverified but become institutional "knowledge." In this case, for example, Streets and San believed that the best (quickest) way to remove brush from residential terraces was to use garbage trucks. To test this assumption, a series of experiments was conducted comparing collection times for different types of disposal: garbage packers, stake body trucks, clams, and on-site processing. The results surprised everyone. Garbage trucks turned out to be the *least* productive means for getting rid of brush.

As a result, both improvement teams began to review their other assumptions and verify them with new data. The Forestry team conducted a complete census of terrace trees—not only their numbers, but tree condition, varieties, and girth (which could be used to estimate age). From this information, leading indicators of forest health were identified, such as age of trees, rainfall, and high-heat days (especially important for juvenile trees). Then experiments were designed and managed and education was provided to city leadership and the general population.

We learned through these improvement processes the simple truth that we needed to do a better job of educating people about trees.

We learned through these improvement processes the simple truth that we needed to do a better job of educating people about trees. We initiated one-on-one meetings with citizens, gave presentations for neighborhood associations, wrote articles, and created flyers and brochures which city council members distributed.

To eliminate surprises, we regularly knocked on the doors of homes where terrace trees needed to be removed due to damage or disease, explaining what would happen and why. When new trees were planted on the terrace, we provided written instructions for care and the amount of watering needed in those first few critical years.

Similarly, the Streets and Sanitation Division reached out to property owners with information as to when, how, and where to place brush for effective and faster collection. Residents were also taught how to dispose of brush if they missed scheduled collections.

Significant effort was focused on what we called "Holding the Gains" achieved by the projects. Leading indicators were identified and routinely collected and promulgated by employees. Periodic reviews became the norm. Many residents welcomed up-to-date information about the state of the trees in their neighborhood, as well as the city.

~

Some things we learned—First, it is necessary not only to involve the employees in data collection but also to educate them thoroughly on why the data is important and how it will be used. By initially not sharing this information, we inadvertently increased fear in the workforce.

Second, an educated population can be a blessing or a curse. Many residents take the time to learn everything they can about "their" trees but not about "all" trees. But what is good and accurate for the individual specimen tree may be irrelevant or opposite of what is needed for the forest as a whole. So continued education and outreach remains essential.

Maintaining a healthy urban forest requires the cooperation of the entire system of city services, as well as of its citizens and businesses.

Third, maintaining a healthy urban forest such as that of Madison requires the cooperation of the entire system of city services, as well as of its citizens and businesses. For instance, government purchasing services may default to selecting less expensive trees, whether or not the quality of the stock is adequate. Or longstanding city policies may force impractical moves such as planting trees where they cannot flourish. Human Resources may balk at paying for additional skills needed for contemporary forestry. New building projects commonly scrape away the good soil and leave a thin layer of soil so grass and trees can get started; this practice makes it difficult to establish and maintain healthy trees. The urban forest that is Madison, Wisconsin, is a complex system and requires a system to maintain it.

Ultimately, the success of continuous improvement efforts is dependent on broad-scale and in-depth change management activities. Not only do processes, systems, products, and services need excellence, but citizens, customers, product and service providers, beliefs, attitudes, and visions need to aspire to excellence as well. It is generally not effective to change just one part of a system and expect improved results.

Did the city of Madison have to change to save its trees? Of course it did. But changing its processes and services was the easy part. Changing fundamental beliefs about what an urban forest is and should be was far more difficult. The city had to remind itself that citizens see the individual tree before they can comprehend the forest. Communication and education for all stakeholders illuminated the urban forest as an interdependent system rather than a collection of trees.

Guy Van Rensselaer was the Organizational Development Specialist for the City of Madison. He led hundreds of Quality Improvement projects throughout city government, as well as the not-for-profit sector. Since 1992, he has been providing various quality methods workshops for the Certified Public Managers program at the University of Wisconsin-Madison. In addition, he has provided quality and leadership workshops for many cities and counties throughout Wisconsin. With luck, he says, he'll soon finish writing his book about change in early twentieth-century rural America.

Questions for Discussion and Reflection

1. Describe a time when you couldn't see the forest for the trees. How did you get yourself out of that?
2. How does real "education" of residents, voters, businesses, and public officials happen? Give one or two examples from your own experience or that of someone else you admire.
3. Think of a major decision that you are involved in making right now. Identify a few options for that decision. Now, think about how each of those options will impact customers or consumers. How will each impact other parts of your organization?? When viewed systemically, which option(s) seem the most promising or feasible?

The Sergeant's Role in Leading Change

by Luis Yudice

I was a sergeant when Total Quality Management (TQM) was introduced to the Madison Police Department (MPD) in the late 1970s. I was appropriately cautious. Given the nature of policing, the concept of loosening the reins of the organization and giving greater voice to the employees seemed just too good to be true. What was the catch?

Having previously served in the Marine Corps (as our Chief David Couper had), the traditional paramilitary style of management suited me just fine. Orders came from above, each rank passed them on to the next level and ultimately, we sergeants were responsible for ensuring they were carried out by the "troops." The thought that ideas and plans for serving our city could germinate from the bottom level of the organization was not in our consciousness.

The thought that ideas and plans for serving our city could germinate from the bottom level of the organization was not in our consciousness.

The story of how continuous improvement in policing unfolded in Madison in the 1980s and 1990s is a tale of an adventurous undertaking that led to transformative change. It also created turmoil, led to the questioning of long-held principles about policing, and ultimately positioned the MPD as a national leader in progressive policing.

These changes included a total restructuring of the organization, as well as the reassessment of how we managed, supervised, and controlled personnel and the flow of ideas. The development of new tools and strategies unleashed the human potential of our talented commissioned and civilian personnel. But all this required the flattening of the chain of command, investment in training for every member of the department, and buy-in from command staff—as well as a long-term commitment on everyone's part to the new management model.

When Mayor Joe Sensenbrenner introduced quality improvement concepts to city government, Madison was a city in transition, already marked by greater urbanization with hints of potential big-city problems. Violent crime was increasing; school safety concerns led to early experimentation with the placement of officers in schools and the arrival of crack cocaine, gangs, and violence soon wreaked havoc in many of our neighborhoods. Madison was caught off guard and unprepared, and so were those of us in law enforcement. Addressing these complex and violent situations demanded creative minds, flexible thinking, and a data-driven process capable of identifying root causes to help focus the department's stretched resources to where they were most needed.

~

Madison at the time badly needed a different approach to the "top down" model of traditional policing, which was proving too rigid and not suitable to adapting to the fast-changing developments in our city. It required police officers to become problem solvers, outside-the-box thinkers, and employees empowered to initiate solutions. Above all, it needed an organizational model that allowed for the free flow of ideas, unencumbered by bureaucratic levels of control.

It needed an organizational model that allowed for the free flow of ideas.

Techniques and processes from systematic improvement enabled the department to effectively respond to these challenges. By creating coalitions involving government, churches, the private sector and community groups, the city was able to revitalize some of its most violent neighborhoods and address the underlying causes of crime and disorder. It required mayoral leadership, teamwork at all levels, and a commitment from our officers to abandon the old order for new and creative strategies.

Utilizing these concepts, the department worked alongside other city departments such as housing, health, building inspection, and community development to gather critical information indicative of the health and well-being of those communities. This information was compared to police calls for service and other factors that ultimately guided our selection of the neighborhoods most in need of city services and police intervention.

~

The creation of what we called "Neighborhood Officer" teams occurred partly as a result of this process. Guided by data, thirteen "at-risk" neighborhoods were selected for the placement of a single officer in each area who worked closely with residents to reduce crime in their communities. These officers needed technical skills to both identify neighborhood conditions that enabled crime and disorder to occur and root out those responsible for crime and violence. They also needed social skills to create trust and credibility with those they served.

This program was extremely successful and became emblematic of community policing in Madison. Driven by highly motivated officers who were given great latitude to meet the needs of their neighborhoods, neighborhood officers formed strong partnerships with local residents who came to think of these officers as their "own." For example, Vera Court, a poor and densely populated rental community, was one of the targeted neighborhoods. Its recovery was the result of an alliance created by private and public efforts. At the heart of that community was a resident known simply as "Big Momma," who ruled as if everyone was her family. Her partner and close ally was Officer Bill Lahr, who saw Big Momma in much the same way. The two were an unstoppable force of good. They reinforced community norms, created a safe environment for residents, and gave voice to people who would otherwise have been neglected and isolated.

Neighborhood officers formed strong partnerships with local residents who came to think of these officers as their "own."

But the key to success did not rest solely with these community police officers. Critical support from patrol officers, departmental supervisors, and top management was needed to reinforce the strategies that had been created for each neighborhood. The program needed "buy-in" from these groups in order to implement creative and non-traditional approaches to long standing social problems. For example, rather than responding with arrests and citations, officers now sought alternatives such as recreational opportunities for youth, jobs, and resources for families. The new paradigm allowed and encouraged officers to flourish in many areas. They engaged with community centers, participated in youth mentoring programs, and became advocates for their communities.

For most officers, the search for quality policing brought welcome changes. It offered police officers an opportunity to have their voices heard and to redefine themselves as individuals who could contribute to positive change in an environment that rewarded initiative and creativity. Process improvement tools such as Pareto charts, Scatter Diagrams, and Flow Charts, soon became well known and were incorporated into the improvement projects needed to advance to the rank of sergeant.

For others, however, change was more difficult. Learning to let go and trust that the majority of employees would do their jobs well did not come easy. One of W. Edwards Deming's principles of Quality Improvement is that as much as 94% of variation in performance is caused by the system, with as little as 6% caused by people. This is difficult for those managers and supervisors who believed that a well-run department needed lots of rules, regulations, and policies to maintain order and discipline. Change was tough on some on-the-ground officers, as well—particularly for those who preferred the old way. They showed up for work, did what was expected, and that was the end of it.

But these changes were perhaps most difficult on our first-line supervisors—that is, we sergeants who had the most direct contact with the patrol officers who made up the bulk of the department. Under the traditional model, sergeants were the first line in the chain of command. We supervised, directed, and reviewed our officers' work product, investigated misconduct, and responded to citizen complaints. Sergeants were responsible for conducting the department's annual performance evaluations. (In another context I am familiar with, the Marine Corps has the equivalent of police sergeants called "Gunnys"—a Gunnery Sergeant, which is the seventh enlisted rank in the USMC, just above Staff Sergeant and below Master and First Sergeant. Gunnys hold institutional memory, have more technical competence, and are respected in the USMC. In my opinion, it is the Gunnys who form the backbone of the Corps.)

The systemic-improvement efforts in the MDP sometimes upended the sergeants' authority. Officers no longer needed to check with us before going into the captain's office to discuss an idea or to complain about workplace rules. If given approval, they could implement new strategies, enlist the assistance of other city departments, or create a team with fellow officers to address problems in their beats. To a certain extent, sergeants ceased to exist. We were no longer essential. The "flattening" of the organization ensured we were no more than a place holder on the staffing charts.

The sergeants' role was sometimes reduced to that of a spectator. We were expected to coach our officers, provide them support, and give them feedback. But in general, we were asked to get out of the way of the bright and motivated officers who were leading the changes in policing that we knew were desperately needed. Most of us relished our new roles and did it well, but others were bewildered and confused. Critical responsibilities such as the investigation of complaints against police officers were removed from us and given to Internal Affairs. Performance evaluations were discontinued altogether.

Most relished their new roles and did it well, but others were bewildered and confused.

These changes tended to undermine the role and authority of the sergeants, who had the most intimate knowledge of our officers' strengths and weaknesses and, most importantly, of how they interacted with the community. Few in the organization worked as closely with the people on the ground as we did. No one else was as capable of understanding how stress, and frustration with the judicial system could potentially lead to policy violations or abuse of authority.

The sergeant's role has always been a difficult one. As neither line officers nor managers (and members of the same bargaining unit as officers in our platoons), we are expected to supervise and reinforce strict adherence to the law, department polices, and critical concepts regarding constitutional rights. Our jobs are made even more difficult by the fact that we work alongside our officers and face the same difficult work conditions that are far removed from departmental mission statements and the rarified levels of the management team.

~

The current quest for racial reckoning and social justice has again aroused our society and has questioned the legitimacy of the criminal justice system, particularly that of the police. Most police departments, including Madison's, have experienced incidents of significant officer misconduct that had been allowed to continue until they came to light due to an incident or complaint. We all wondered how could this occur and why wasn't it stopped sooner?

Law enforcement agencies are under tremendous pressure to reform and are facing monumental challenges to recruit and retain qualified officers. They can no longer afford to ignore or look the other way. For this reason, the role of the sergeant is a critical one that must be elevated, redefined, and supported more than ever. Why not utilize them more efficiently? Who else is in a better position to model progressive policing, to support officers, identify training needs, systems issues, or problematic officer behavior?

What's the ideal model? For starters, the patrol sergeant position should be elevated to the management level and be removed from the rank-file union membership. This will provide breathing room and separation from the officers and give recognition to the fact that they have a strategic role in the organization. Some departments are already experimenting with this idea by creating a field- lieutenant position that serves a similar function. However, field lieutenants have other duties, and supervision still rests primarily with the sergeants who spend virtually all of their time on patrol with their officers.

The "sergeant" position should be elevated to the management level and be removed from the rank-file union membership.

Careful selection of sergeant/lieutenant candidates should be followed by extensive training on supervision and management skills, coupled with inclusion as full-fledged members of the department's management team to provide a clear and direct line of communication between the officers, supervisors, and command staff. The training should provide technical and managerial skills, as well as exposure to community forums to inculcate departmental values and progressive policing principles.

Police sergeants have a unique and unobstructed view of the challenges faced by field officers and a deep understanding of the barriers that may prevent lofty departmental goals from being achieved. Their perspectives are critical to the root cause analysis that must be conducted before implementing new policies and practices. They deserve to be heard.

The systemic improvement movement in the Madison Police Department was a success in innumerable ways, and it led to the recruitment of many bright and committed young men and women who wanted to join our agency. It's not by accident that the MPD has been nationally recognized as a leader in policing and innovation. But perhaps we missed an opportunity to fully examine the benefits and potential negative impact that these foundational changes created for our front-line supervisors. Improvement has to be continuous, and we must adhere to this principle and accept that reassessing where we've been is part of the change process. The principles of the quality management movement provided the tools in the past we needed to reimagine the sergeant's role. They can do so again. Those same principles can help meet the needs and challenges of tomorrow's police organizations.

Luis Yudice joined the Madison Police Department in 1974. He retired as an Acting Assistant Chief of Operations after serving 31 years with the department. His assignments included: mental health coordinator, hostage negotiator, SWAT commander, captain of detectives and of several police districts in Madison. He has a BS from Edgewood College and completed a Quality Management course at the University of Wisconsin-Madison. Luis is a native of Guatemala and a US Marine Corps veteran.

Questions for Reflection and Discussion

1. Who are the "sergeants"—the front-line managers—in your organization or institution? How can you incorporate them into your operational change efforts? Be specific.
2. What do you do when you meet resistance from front-line workers in your change efforts? What can you do to reassure them and incorporate them into your plans for making improvements that will affect them?
3. How might the principles and practices described here contribute to addressing the post-George Floyd and Black Lives Matter focus on racial reckoning and economic inequality? Explain with examples.

A People Business

by Janice Smith

Our business was not cars or assembly lines. As the State Bureau on Aging of the Wisconsin Department of Health Services (DHS), we managed state and federal programs operated by county and tribal aging-service agencies. Our mission was to create opportunities for elders to maintain their independence, health, and well-being and remain a vital part of their communities. These programs included meals, medical transportation, in-home services, and opportunities for social interactions.

It was the late 1980s. My boss was telling me about a new approach to what she called "quality improvement" in city services. It was based on the work of an American engineer who helped Japan become known for making superior cars. She suggested we write a federal grant proposal to see if we could apply this framework for achieving increased quality in our programs and services for older people.

Ours was a people business, committed to recognizing, supporting, and even celebrating the individual preferences and uniqueness that come from a lifetime of experiences. We wondered, "Can a people business be improved by the same processes used by successful manufacturers?" To write the proposal, I had to read papers by statisticians, engineers, and others, including the pioneer in this movement, Dr. W. Edwards Deming. This learning process was daunting, intimidating, and overwhelming for a social worker. I was learning a new language.

We received the grant. Now what? Wisconsin already had a nationally recognized aging and community-based long-term care system. Although our leaders and advocates had always ensured our programs were customer focused, the grant enabled us to better define quality in these programs.

"Can a people business be improved by the same processes used by successful manufacturers?"

Between 1989-1992 we tested process improvement with nine Wisconsin county project teams, applying the process improvement techniques to three critical services: home-delivered meals, in-home services, and care management. We sought to answer this question: "How will we know quality when we see it? How will we do the right things right?"

We trained all our local aging and human service agencies on continuous improvement principles and methods. The energy and enthusiasm from learning something new, practical, and helpful to them (and more importantly to the people they served) was contagious. We showcased those county projects to a statewide audience so people could learn from one another. Some county agencies even used local funds to hire experienced facilitators to carry out projects after the grant ended. Success inspired success.

"Would this be a fad, or would it be our future?"

Thus began our continuous improvement adventure. We wondered, "Would this be a fad, or would it be our future?"

~

During the mid-1990s, Wisconsin was both reimagining its services for the aging network and redesigning its long-term care system. At that time, frail elders and those with disabilities faced long waiting lists for in-home care. Some couldn't wait: a nursing home became their only option—whether or not they needed or wanted that level of care. Department program leaders and advocates aimed to eliminate waiting lists for in-home care.

Part of this systems change was to create public, local Aging and Disability Resource Centers (ADRCs). ADRCs would be the place where elders and people with disabilities could obtain reliable information about care options, find help in locating services, or apply for benefits. Receiving this information meant individuals and their families could conserve their personal resources, maintain self-sufficiency, and delay or prevent the need for more expensive long-term care.

Nine ADRCs began in Wisconsin in 1998, and by 2006 the governor's budget authorized funding for statewide expansion. By 2013, 41 ADRCs were serving all 72 counties and all tribes. For a new statewide program, this was fast! Coincidently during this timeframe, quality improvement practices were becoming more prevalent within Wisconsin state government.

It was significant that the Bureau on Aging (which had implemented that earlier grant) was the state agency that designed and implemented the ADRC program. Quality improvement techniques and principles and focus on customer service were built into state legislation and rules by design. For example, one state statute required "internal quality improvement and quality assurance processes." The administrative code referenced gathering "feedback from customers" on quality and effectiveness of service. The contract between counties and the state included the requirement for an annual performance improvement project to strengthen customer satisfaction and ensure ongoing service quality.

Focus on customer service was built into state legislation and rules by design.

By 2007, the Department of Health Services had created a specific office to manage the local ADRC program—the Office for Resource Center Development (ORCD). Among its key functions was ensuring consistency, integrity and quality while supporting local ADRC success.

Starting up a new program involved helping local ADRCs to embrace the vision and make quality service a reality. It also involved moving the program from multiple pilot approaches to a statewide model so that customers would have a consistent experience.

We determined it was essential for the customers served by the program to tell us what was important to them. Therefore, our next step was to survey ADRC customers. The data produced through this qualitative research helped establish an evidence-based ADRC model that would enable us to achieve high customer satisfaction and quality outcomes across the state. "ADRC quality wrapped in a **PACKGE,**" was coined as a way to remember the six facets, or domains, of quality service derived from what customers had told us:

- **P**ersonalization.
- **A**ccessibility.
- **C**ulture of hospitality.
- **K**nowledgeable staff.
- **G**uidance.
- **E**mpowerment and control.

This customer research project created individual ADRC reports that articulated how well each ADRC was doing in meeting customer expectations and quality domain standards. ORCD staff went on a statewide "road trip," talking with each ADRC about key improvement opportunities, "These are the things that your customers are asking you to change," we were able to tell them. That was a powerful motivation. ADRCs then worked on making changes in their efforts to improve customer satisfaction, but up until then they had no sure way to determine if the changes were making a difference.

Two years later, when we had the chance to do the statewide survey again, we wanted the ADRCs to be equipped with additional powerful tools for change. So, from 2010-2012, we selected the Center for Health Enhancement Systems Studies (CHESS) based at the University of Wisconsin-Madison College of Engineering to introduce us to the NIATx model of process improvement which is based on these principles:

- Understand and involve the customer.
- Fix key problems.
- Chose a powerful change leader.
- Get ideas from outside the field.
- Use rapid-cycle testing.
- Measure one or two things really well.

The project started with training on this model, and a few pilot ADRCs benefited from NIATx coaching and from technical assistance. Staff from almost all of the ADRCs (94%) were trained on process improvement. After training, and in the course of a year, 47 ADRC projects improved processes and customer satisfaction. (See more about NIATx in the article in this book by Dave Gustafson.)

We eventually rebranded our effort, moving on from NIATx to form what we called the "Change Leader Academy." We kept phrases like "Change Leader" and got really good at letting "PDSA Cycle" (Plan-Do-Study-Act) roll off the tongue. We moved a network primarily made up of social workers (people-people) to understand how to collect data and understand why it matters.

We got really good at letting "PDSA Cycle" (Plan-Do-Study-Act) roll off the tongue.

Since then, the Change Leader Academy trains ADRC staff and state and local partners on process improvement every year. In addition, regional quality specialists and network partners have been specially trained to serve as Process Improvement Coaches. This coaching expertise, coupled with continued leadership commitment and ongoing training, has been instrumental in sustaining our quality improvement program and improving it over time.

Using the Change Leader model, ADRCs in Wisconsin mastered the process, embraced rapid cycle testing, collected data, and found ways to improve internal office processes, staff communication, and customer experience. A few examples of these quality change projects are:

- Increased walk-ins at satellite offices.
- Increased the number of deaf and hard-of-hearing customers from one per year to three per month.
- Decreased the time from the customer's initial contact to the time of their initial home visit from nine business days to three and a half.
- Reduced the time between initial customer contact and the in-person meeting with a benefit specialist.
- Increased the completion rate of memory assessments by building staff confidence through refresher trainings and by supplying new informational materials to the home visit packet.
- Increased the number of participants attending a "Living Well with Chronic Conditions" Workshop series.

~

In a large, statewide government agency, change is a constant. Within such change, the ADRC program benefited from consistency of leadership commitment to the program's purpose and methods of ensuring positive customer experiences. Continued program integrity and success also relied on the skill of executive leaders in communicating to newer governor appointees the importance of ADRCs to constituents and how the program furthers their administration's agenda.

Data from 4,300 ADRC customers in 2015 showed that 97% would recommend the ADRC to others. Reflecting back on what contributed to our success in developing a customer-focused quality-driven program, the following elements emerge:

- **Customer is at the Core.** Whatever you do and however you do it, keep asking, "How does this benefit the customer and how can we be sure?"
- **Leadership Matters.** Leaders at any level must embrace new possibilities, create a culture of excellence, respect staff contributions, maintain steadfast focus on the consumer, and seek to prevent or overcome barriers to quality service.
- **Money Helps.** Repeatedly taking advantage of federal grant opportunities made possible and/or enhanced the quality of ADRC services and the degree of customer satisfaction.
- **Training, Training, Training.** Training teaches, reminds, energizes; it must be ongoing.
- **Data-Based Decision-making.** Data is empowering. Programs are more efficient and effective when focused on the right things; data will help find what the right things are.
- **Ongoing Support for Local Partners.** Give agencies the information they need and the tools to make it happen, especially if you are "requiring" them to do something. Clarifying expectations, collaborating, and problem solving together yields results.
- **Local Ownership and Effort.** It is very satisfying for local agencies to identify their own areas for improvement and figure out how to make them better.

~

So, my boss's question was answered. Yes, principles of quality improvement are extremely usable and relevant to the design and delivery of human services. Any human service agency, small or large, seeking to improve its service or outcomes can find success by adopting process improvement and change management concepts and tools.

Any human service agency, small or large, seeking to improve its service or outcomes can find success.

Start by learning the basic principles of customer focus, systems orientation, teamwork, data-based decision-making, and process improvement via the Plan-Do-Study-Act formula. Then start small, experience success, and continuously improve. Staff will be motivated by positive results and, most importantly, customers will benefit from enhanced personal outcomes.

Janice Smith was the director of the Office for Resource Center Development within the Wisconsin Department of Health Services from 2007 until she retired in 2014. For over 35 years she managed Wisconsin's state human service programs that served elders and people with disabilities.

Questions for Reflection and Discussion

1. What is the responsibility of government in improving the quality of its own services? Give an example of where this has worked, and another example of a government service that could benefit from improvement approaches.

2. Which of the following elements strike you as the most important in the changes you hope to lead? Explain your answer:
   - Customer Is at the Core.
   - Leadership Matters.
   - Money Helps.
   - Training, Training, Training.
   - Data-Based Decision-making.
   - Ongoing Support for Local Partners.
   - Local Ownership and Effort.
3. Systems thinking reminds us that all organizations exist within a web of larger and smaller systems, all interconnected to a greater or lesser extent. Draw a Venn diagram of circles showing where your organization or unit fits relative to larger and smaller organizations or units. What can be done to create a better fit or connection with them? What connections offer opportunities not yet tapped?

Chapter Four

Process Design and Improvement

Introduction

Why the Oil Is on the Floor

Some processes are easy to see. We recognize that cooking and assembling IKEA furniture and planting a garden and even building a rocket to go to the moon are all processes. We get it that a process is a series of steps carried out to produce something we want—a product or a service. Yet processes in our own work environments may be difficult to see. Essential though they are.

If you can recognize that your entire organization is a symphony of interacting processes, you are poised to be able to create change. Many of the processes may be clearly visible as in filling orders from customers, or requesting vacation, or moving new products to market. The bad news is that some of our most important processes may be like the wiring in the walls—invisible to us yet critical. How budget decisions are actually made or how prospects become loyal customers, or how big data is used to improve profitability are examples of processes that can go unrecognized and untended. Whether big or small, evident or not, all processes degrade over time as new people come and go or the context changes.

Recognizing that a myriad of processes underlie everything an organization does or could do is a leap in thinking and positions you as a leader to focus on improving the most important processes. You will ask different questions. You will move away from "Whose job is it to do XXX?" or "Who is responsible for this mistake?" to "What is our process for doing XXX?" and "How can we improve it?"

Here are three examples of how attention to processes can be at the core of change and improvement—identifying root cause, mapping your processes, and improving your organization's capacity for making substantial improvements.

Root Causes and the Hidden Cost of Poor Quality

Jessica and Marco were cleaning up the oil on the floor of the trucking company's huge garage. They did this every day for the last hour of their shift. Once in a while, they went through a little game, asking each other five questions and giving the obvious answers, but they had no power to do anything about the situation, so they then went on to discuss the Green Bay Packers' game that week. Here was their routine:

- Why was the oil on the floor? (It was leaking from the vehicles they were servicing.)
- Why was the oil leaking from the vehicles? (There was a standard part they used that always leaked.)
- Why did that part leak? (It was of inferior quality.)
- Why were they using a part that was inferior in quality? (It was purchased because it was the lowest bid.)
- Why did their bosses decide to get the part that was the lowest bid? (It was company policy to use the lowest bidder.)

Cleaning the floor is a process. If you want to improve that process, you can either look for a more efficient way to clean the floor or you can prevent the problem from occurring by understanding the cause. Jessica and Marco's exercise is called the "5 Why's" in the systemic or continuous improvement world, and they are designed to help get to the "root cause" of a problem.

In the "old" days (that is, fifty years ago), quality and productivity used to be seen as a trade-off: if you want quality, you need to take more time (and spend more money) to get it. But Jessica and Marco's story illustrates the cost of poor quality in both time and money. It also reminds us that merely addressing symptoms of a problem (oil on the floor) is not the same as addressing the root cause of the problem.

Mapping Your Processes– The Ever-Powerful Flowchart

Anthony had waited eighty-two days to get an appointment for his son's routine check-up. Then, when the day of the appointment finally arrived, they waited nearly twenty minutes in the waiting room and another twenty for the exam to begin. This was a typical experience in the South Side Clinic. All involved—patients, clinic staff, and physicians—were frustrated. The clinic and even individual doctors tried remedies to reduce delays, but they bumped up against one barrier after another in the process.

Then one day, Dr. Gordon gathered his two fellow internists and clinic staff to flowchart the scheduling process. (They created a map of the steps currently being used to schedule a patient.) They saw several things that could be addressed. One step included checking the restrictions individual doctors applied to appointments, such as only offering physicals on certain days of the week or times of the day. Another step scheduled all patients for the same amount of time, even though they regularly had short fifteen-minute visits and much longer visits such as annual physical appointments lasting 30-45 minutes or more. Finally, they noticed the step listed as "turn room around." The wait time when patients arrive was directly tied to this step. It appeared that each physician had different methods and styles for preparing a room for the next patient.

After reviewing their process map, they decided that their practice had introduced too much complexity. To reduce delays, they would take three key actions. First, as much as possible they would eliminate all physician restrictions. Second, they would create scheduling blocks for short and long visits. And third, they would standardize the turn-around and setup procedures for all rooms and use each room as soon as it became available.

The clinic implemented and refined these changes. After working down their backlog, patients wanting care are now seen in 2-3 days, with a goal of same day appointments. The average time patients spend in the waiting and exam rooms is now around five minutes. Patients, staff, and doctors are pleased with an easier process, and their new practices have been adopted by other clinics.

Improve How You Improve and Think Big

Have you ever participated in an improvement effort that took more time and resources than it saved? Are there dozens of teams working on small things that won't address key problems or seize big opportunities? Do your improvement efforts drag out over months and years?

- If process improvement efforts are to have real impact, they must be selected carefully and carried out effectively. Here are a few concepts to consider to help ensure your improvement efforts net real gains. Identify the core processes for carrying out your mission, no more than ten. Then focus on the most essential of those.

- Use a "fast cycle" approach for process improvement, followed by PDCA for continually improving. Find an approach that concentrates improvement efforts into a few well-planned and executed meetings. You might practice on simpler processes, but then focus on your essential, core processes.
- Think big. Don't shoot for 10% improvement. What would 100% look like? Or a million!?

What are the core processes in your organization? How could you improve them by a factor of ten? A thousand? A million! Here are five stories by Dave Boyer, Tim Hallock, Kevin Little, Ben Reynolds, and Michael Williamson on how they improved processes in a range of types of organizations.

Trouble with Ant Bait

by Dave Boyer

Every process is perfectly designed to get the results it gets.

Arthur Jones

It turns out that significant parts of my university education were quite misguided. It was the 1970s, and my undergraduate Engineering and graduate Business degrees had taught me that I needed to find the most effective ways to "motivate" people, that lowering costs was my primary aim, and that I needed a "quality" department to insert "quality" into our products.

So, my early work colleagues and I learned to pay people for the volume they produced—piece rates. (We did get a lot of pieces—and high rejection rates in direct proportion to volume.) We did lower costs. (And significantly lowered the US market share for a number of our products in the bargain.) And we formed and enlarged our quality departments and inspection procedures. (And watched our reject rates stay the same or go up.)

Then along came a revolution in the U.S., first led by W. Edwards Deming and his client companies in Japan, then by groups who came together because what they called "Total Quality" made so much sense. One of the early groups was in Madison, Wisconsin, with leaders like Brian Joiner, statistician Dr. George Box, and Peter Scholtes among many others. There was a remarkable local focus on teaching and learning total quality principles, teamwork, and how to effectively use data.

That is what this story is about, but it is also about the trouble with ant bait.

My team and I used quality approaches to grow two manufacturing companies I led. Its principles are still with me every day, and I use them in my community roles to help my fellow humans make progress in significant social and environmental issues we all face.

One of the first principles, as quoted by Dr. George Box, is that "Every process is perfectly designed to get the results it gets." If Dr. Box's quote causes you to stop and think even for a moment, then it's done its job.

They were deadly to ants all right, but we had a problem. You have probably seen the S.C. Johnson "Raid" brand ant baits—little plastic houses with a cube inside of something that ants find delicious, though deadly. At my company, Placon, we produced millions of units of ant bait traps for the S.C. Johnson Company. We had built a 30,000 square-foot building just for them. Then one day, the shift supervisor brought me the bad news: "We are seeing a 5% defect rate on our ant bait cubes because of size variation. Some of them are a lot bigger and some are smaller than they should be."

They were deadly to ants all right, but we had a problem.

I asked what that meant practically. The supervisor explained, "Well, if the cubes are too big, they don't fit the plastic containers and have to be thrown out. It's money lost to us. And if they are too small, the amount of toxin may not be enough to kill the ants or else the bait traps won't last as long as we say they do and therefore people will buy our competitors' traps. That's also money lost to us." Now he had my attention.

"What do you think is causing the variation?" I asked.

"No idea," he shrugged.

Enter quality improvement. Working with consultant Brian Joiner, I convened a problem-solving team of line-workers and the shift supervisor to get at the critical issue of poison pellet size. The first thing Brian did was show every worker how to measure variability by using control charts. This empowered everyone working on the product to measure variability themselves—versus having a separate inspection process done by someone else, somewhere else, and at another time.

The team brainstormed what could possibly be causing the unacceptable variation. One idea was that it could be an issue of allowing varying amounts of moisture in the material. The team tested their hypothesis about moisture levels, but we learned that moisture was unequivocally not the problem.

The team then looked at the mechanical variables and noted that two machines operated simultaneously—an extrusion machine that produced a four-sided ribbon of clay-like material, and a knife that cut the ribbons into cubes. A team member wondered out loud if these two machines might be out of sync with each other. An obvious question that none of us had thought to answer earlier.

An obvious question that none of us had thought to answer earlier.

The line workers measured the Revolutions-Per-Minute (RPM) of each machine and found that they were, in fact, running at different speeds. If the *extruder* was running faster than the *knife,* the cubes were too big. If the *knife* was running faster than the *extruder,* the cubes were too small. When the RPMs of both machines were synced up, the cubes were just the right size. It was a Goldilocks and the Three Bears kind of moment.

The team members presented our findings to the company leadership team, and the "fix" was adopted for all three shifts. The reject rate was reduced from five per cent to less than one per cent. This was a huge cost-savings-customer-pleasing improvement, and it happened, precisely (pun intended) because we asked the people closest to the work to improve the process.

~

Since the ant bait debacle, I convened improvement teams wherever I worked. This allowed us to look at quality outcomes differently, after decades of assuming that it is primarily individual employees who drive quality results. What I mean is this. When quality problems came up, we could just add an additional inspection system. Or—we could enable employees to collect data at various points along the production line, analyze the data, determine the cause of variation, change the process, and confirm the results (the Plan-Do-Check-Act system). When we changed the design of the process in this way, we got different (and better) results.

Ensuring that such results are designed into the process has wide application today. Consider healthcare in the U.S. We know the data—we Americans have the highest healthcare costs in the world with some of the lowest healthcare outcomes among all western nations. Dr. Box might ask us to consider *how it is that those results are designed into the system?* After spending years on healthcare boards, I know many people who know the answer: It's because, by and large, for decades, we have paid providers based on their *volume* of care provided. The result of that key process design is that *providers make more money the sicker their patients are.* We have built massive systems and procedures to maximize volume health-care payments, and we have built it in a way that makes our volume payments practically unconscious.

When we changed the design of the process, we got different (and better) results.

This way of thinking is beginning to change thankfully, albeit slowly. There are now healthcare payment systems that reward the *value* of the system maintaining its patients' health. The improved health and reduced costs are undeniable. Those systems have been designed by people who have seen and documented the negative results of paying for health care on the basis of volume. There is, of course, a huge resistance to changing the process of how we pay for health care, because so many (large) incomes depend on how it's designed today. This is where quality improvement principles can help. The more people who become aware that results are driven by quality concerns, the more power there will be to improve health care and lower costs for hundreds of millions of people.

Relationship Diagrams and Systems Thinking are another set of principles and tools that are core to the quality movement. We can use these tools to map out processes and relationships to discover the best leveraged ways to impact the entire system.

At Placon, for example, we drew a Relationship Diagram of the sales process to determine which factors in our process were most likely to positively impact customer satisfaction, sales results, and profits.

It turned out that the *most* positive thing our team could do is to interview potential clients *without trying to sell them a thing*. Instead, we asked them what problems they were trying to solve, what goals they had, what worried them most. The *second most* positive thing that correlated to results was to bring a team together to create solutions from our existing products and services that would help solve our customers' current issues. Our goal was to *knock customers' socks off* with the solutions we were then able to present to them. I'm telling you this selling system worked brilliantly. The approach is the opposite of the almost universally accepted sales technique: "Here's what I have to sell. Do you want to buy some?" We had identified a real leverage point by mapping out a new selling system.

We asked our clients what problems worried them most.

~

An enduring principle for me is that you get what you measure. In the plastic-packaging company where I worked, we learned that if we simply measured the speed in packages-produced-per-hour on a machine, the hourly totals of packages increased—but it was along with defects and the potential of having to quarantine entire skids of product for inspection. Win. Lose. But when we measured variation of key process inputs—like plastic thickness, temperature, and speed, and worked to reduce that variation—then output increased along with product quality. Win. Win.

Three timeless quality principles I have learned the hard way are these:

- Recognize that every process is perfectly designed to get the results it gets.
- Find leverage points through systems thinking.
- Accept that *how* you measure is *what* you measure.

These principles corrected my early academic education and have helped me bring a much more powerful perspective to a world of design possibilities.

The movement to Total Quality was a revolution. It was a necessary revolution in many industries, and it brought significant value and quality of life to the entire country. I think the principles and tools I used during my career are timeless and are still applicable to major problems we are trying to solve in our world today – i.e., TQ ain't just for ants.

Dave Boyer is the retired CEO and Chairman of the Board of MCD, Inc., in Madison, Wisconsin. MCD provides creative packaging, graphic arts products, and print finishing. Prior to purchasing MCD, Dave was President, CEO of Placon Corp., which designs, and manufactures plastic packaging systems. He is a past Board Chair of the Madison Area Quality Improvement Network (MAQIN).

Questions for Reflection and Discussion

1. What is a "size-of-the-ant-bait" problem in your organization? What is the aim of that process? Who are the customers? What needs are being served?
2. Map that process. Include inputs, key steps, outputs, stakeholders.
3. Within your span of control or influence, what could you do to improve that process? How might you help create a process of Plan-Do-Check-Act for continuing to improve that process?

Checkers Checking Checkers

by Tim Hallock

Quality comes not from inspection,
but from improvement of the production process.

W. Edwards Deming

They took a moment to look into each other's eyes and smile. In Janet's soft, kind voice, she said, "Good morning." Jimmy's body shook with energy overflowing. Janet, a nurse's aide, had started her Monday morning shift this way for the last twenty-four years—gently waking up the residents in her care. She never called them "residents" because they were like family to her. She called them by name. Jimmy, a 47-year-old, non-verbal, intellectually disabled man with multiple syndromes that left him medically fragile, met her gaze with joy–like a child on Christmas morning. Janet lowered the side rails to help Jimmy sit on the edge of his bed. That's when she noticed something different. "What is this?" There in the middle of Jimmy's forehead, above the bridge of his nose, directly between his eyebrows, was a dark spot–the size of a dime. Thinking it was a smear, she wiped it with a damp washcloth, but it remained. She surmised it was a bruise. She would report it and have the nurse look to confirm.

Sure enough, a bruise. And although minor, they'd treat his bruise with some ice and report it in their Resident Incident and Injury Tracking (RIIT) system. RIIT would initiate a complex set of process steps to identify the likely cause of Jimmy's bruise. The facility and the Center for Medicare/Medicaid Services (CMS) took this process seriously. Regardless of its severity, all injuries need to be reported, tracked, and investigated for their cause.

Jimmy's bruise cleared up in three days. RIIT, a paper process, took almost ten days to complete. It included over twenty steps, such as getting input from all staff who had interacted with Jimmy going back three days before his minor bruise. Lead workers reviewed a stack of statements, investigated, and met with others to determine a cause and implement a corrective action plan. It is important to know that RIIT took about 25% or more of the staff's time each day. During annual CMS surveys, surveyors randomly reviewed about 10-15 of these reports—basically to see if they followed the correct RIIT process. In this case, the probable cause was identified as Jimmy bumping his head on the bed's side rail. The staff added additional padding. Mystery solved—problem fixed. Right? Wrong.

Mystery solved—problem fixed. Right? Wrong.

~

When I went to work for the Wisconsin Department of Health-Care Facilities in 2008, Jimmy's was one of the first stories told to me by a nursing leader. It was a case story used at a conference for Intermediate Care Facilities for Individuals with Intellectual Disability (ICF/ID) administrators. Jimmy's story was true, but it actually occurred in a facility on the east coast. I have added some details about the current RIIT process at the Center but stayed true to the story. The workshop topic addressed the subtle nature of abuse, and attendees then broke into groups to discuss and share their questions and proposed solutions. When I later asked the nursing leader to tell me some of the ideas the group came up with, she said, "Basically, Tim, they fell into two categories: improve how you check and do more training."

At that time, Brent, the facility's improvement coordinator, and I were new to the department. He'd come from manufacturing, and I had worked in private-sector healthcare. We had reducing patient injuries and improving the RIIT process on our radar early. We saw it as an opportunity to improve and a way to kick-start our quality improvement (QI) program.

Brent called me after attending his first Resident Injury Committee Meeting at the facility. "It was odd, Tim. There were twelve people—one professional from each care unit. The committee leader, a lead nurse, called on each person to report. The first reported two falls, three bruises, four minor scratches, and one minor injury of unknown origin. The rest of the reports were similar. There were no details related to date, time, location, body area of injury, corrective actions, outcomes. I asked the nurse if I could review past committee minutes. She said the previous Center's Director had informed her that this committee was a regulatory requirement and that they just need to meet this requirement. No written reports were produced. I could tell she wanted to do more."

I could tell she wanted to do more.

The Center Director was also new and a champion of continuous improvement, so Brent and I sat down to report our initial assessment, which included:

- The staff cared deeply about the safety, dignity, and quality of life for all the people they served.
- The RIIT process focused on analyzing the root cause of each injury EVENT. They treated each injury like it was a fire, and they understood their job was to put out the fire.
- There was no systematic approach to assess the PATTERN of events over time. They were not systematically identifying the sources of the various fires.
- There were no actions to address the FORCES or ROOT CAUSES that create those EVENTS and PATTERNS. In other words, there was no systematic effort to suppress fire sources or do any fire prevention planning.

Since injury events were already being addressed, Brent's and my efforts began with the injury committee. First, we had them summarize data from the detailed RIIT reports to identify patterns. Brent started to graph the injury data such as type, time, location, body area, etc. We got them to apply the Pareto Principle that "some type, place, time, person, etc. will account for the majority of injuries." Almost immediately, the staff began to see patterns by unit, specific locations, individual residents, and more. They could see injuries trending up or down on their unit or by each resident. And now, they could theorize why these patterns were occurring and begin to take improvement action.

An early example was a noticeable uptick in the category "scratches in the Fall." The team did a Fishbone-Root Cause Analysis to ask why more scratches might be happening during the Autumn months. It took some time to identify possible causes. However, a nurse's aide hypothesized that the Fall's scratches might coincide with the facility turning on the heat. Bingo! So before heating the buildings that Autumn, the caregivers started proactively applying moisturizers for the residents. Lo and behold, the usual uptick in scratches did not occur that Fall. The team continued addressing pattern after pattern like this with some success and failures.

The committee took on more and more responsibility. Brent and the nurse leader became good friends. She and other team members said they had never felt so empowered. Down the road, members of this committee became some of our biggest supporters of quality improvement at the facility. We would need their support for our next effort, which was improving the efficiency of the RIIT process itself.

She and other team members said they had never felt so empowered.

The RIIT process took weeks to complete and a sizable amount of staff's time. Individual work areas would regularly select "fixing" RIIT as a "QI" project. The aim was always the same—reduce the time it took to complete the reports. The Center even assigned two lead workers to facilitate the paperwork. However, these efforts would only make casual changes to the process. These projects achieved minimal results and often added more complexity, variation, and time.

But because of some of the initial success, people now had the energy and will to change a big part of their day-to-day work. So, we created a new team at the facility and set an audacious aim for it: reduce RIIT time by 50%. The team started by value-stream mapping of the process with time data for all essential steps. The team looked at the policies guiding the process and asked if we might be able to vary RIIT reports for different severity levels (minor, moderate, severe). They even took a field trip to benchmark what other health centers were doing. One place, for example, had underground walkways tying all buildings together. They had staff come to the paper in a binder kept where the resident lived. We started thinking—bring staff to the paper, not paper to the staff. "This will never work; we don't have tunnels" was the initial reaction to this idea.

We started thinking—bring staff to the paper, not paper to the staff.

But Brent liked the option of bringing staff to the paper. Maybe we could do this electronically? We ran the idea by DHS's technology department, but it didn't get very far since all we had was a loose concept. Brent had experience with Microsoft Access, so we decided to try out this idea using a simple database. Brent's nurse leader friend from the injury committee said we could try it on her unit. So we began testing the prototype with a few residents on a single unit. For months, the team would fine tune the data base, eliminate errors, and make it more user-friendly—one cycle of improvement after another. Eventually, we added more computers, more residents, and then the entire population of that unit. It worked! The staff came to the paper.

It would be a year or more to overcome resistance to the status quo before the team could implement this database across the entire facility. But within two years, with support from the Wisconsin Department of Health IT department, all residential health centers across the state rolled out the new "Incident Injury Tracking System."

This new tracking system reduced the time spent reporting and tracking injuries from weeks to hours and, in some cases, minutes. The Center's leaders could instantly see who, where, when, and how injuries were occurring. Managers could see what work was required and ensure that staff took corrective actions. All areas could now review and graph data instantly to understand injury patterns and take proactive steps to reduce injuries across the Center. They now had a way to make things better. It was no longer just checkers checking checkers.

~

And now the rest of the story.

A year or more had passed, when on a Monday morning after a weekend off, Janet woke Jimmy to see once again a dime-sized bruise on his forehead. The bruise was above the bridge of his nose and squarely between his eyebrows—exactly where it had occurred before. She checked the padding – everything was in place—that's odd, she thought. She'd report to the nurse, and they'd repeat the RIIT process.

The lead worker read statements from staff and investigated. Nothing. While exploring potential causes and solutions, however, Janet reminded the group that this had happened before about a year ago. Same person, same bruise, same time, same place, same size. Was this really coincidence? Let's look at the past RIIT file and compare them, the group suggested. The initial RIIT reports were not systematically filed but kept on the units they occurred, and Janet thought the first bruise happened in late summer, but they found it in early April's files.

It took some time, but eventually, they noticed that the person who cared for Jimmy on these two weekends was Paul L. On both occasions, someone had called in sick, and it was his turn to float. After talking to Paul, they were suspicious. This changed everything. The rule is that when there is suspicion of abuse, you turn the case over to a patient advocate trained to investigate abuse. Paul was assigned to non-resident duties immediately.

Annetta, the social worker, reviewed the past RIIT reports and meet with staff who worked on Paul's unit. She discovered others who Paul cared for had shown the same telltale bruise. What she found was worrying. Staff had witnessed that when Paul asked a resident to eat, sit up, etc., he would occasionally punctuate his demand with a poke of his index finger. Annetta asked why this happened. Paul's fellow workers said the poking never seemed serious, but they hadn't seen the pattern.

Tim Hallock has over thirty-five years of experience applying quality methods in service, healthcare, education, and government organizations. His career as a quality leader included the Wisconsin Department of Health and SSM Health Care. Tim has supported Baldrige Performance Excellence and the Wisconsin Forward awards as an applicant, examiner, instructor, and judge.

Questions for Reflection and Discussion

1. Tell a story from your own experience or one you observed where rather than checking for "fires" a plan was devised that eliminated a source of the "fires." How was this accomplished?

2. Are you actually improving your processes, or do you just have "checkers checking the checkers" in your organization or institution? Identify a process that might be improved by looking for patterns. Explain your answer.
3. Many quality improvements start small and include multiple cycles of improvement. But then how can you go big with what you have learned? What are one or two you might like to scale up eventually?

"Cancel the Meeting!"

by Kevin Little

My friend and teacher, Yukihiro Ando, told me what to do: "You have to call Mary back and cancel Monday's Quality Council meeting."

Yuki, a Japanese quality engineer who learned under Dr. Noriaki Kano in Japan, came to Madison in 1989 to spend a couple of years at Joiner Associates. Joiner Associates was founded by Brian and Laurie Joiner in 1983. They aimed to apply insights from W.E. Deming to help for-profit and not-for-profit organizations improve their operations, products, services, and customer satisfaction.

By 1989, the Japanese Total Quality Control experts had accumulated practical knowledge and theoretical insights from forty years of dedicated study and practice. When Yuki came to Joiner Associates, he had already worked for several years as a consultant to companies that were considered regularly for the Deming Prize, an annual Japanese award for excellent management. I had started work with Joiner Associates a few years earlier in September of 1985. I met Brian when he was a professor in the statistics department at the University of Wisconsin–Madison, where I finished my Ph.D. under George Box in 1983. I was assigned to be Yuki's partner. "Just take notes about what he does," Brian said. We would somehow distill my raw observations into something useful.

I had a lot to learn to help anyone improve their quality. Coaching organizations to transform their management using Deming's advice had little to do with my statistical course work. Monday Night Beer and Statistics sessions at George Box's house, where scientists and engineers presented challenges that might be helped by statistics, were more in line with what I needed to know. Still, most of the organizational challenges we faced with clients at Joiner Associates involved people, with all their motivations and quirks. Why would they want to change how they were running their organizations or institutions? What methods would they be willing to adopt to help them do it better? As Brian's partner Peter Scholtes told me, "This quality improvement stuff would be easy except for the people!"

"This quality improvement stuff would be easy except for the people!"

Brian had the idea that we could learn faster if we could watch Yuki in action. I could tag along while Yuki applied his skills and wealth of experience. While I wouldn't add much consulting value, I could at least help mitigate language challenges as Yuki navigated our upper-Midwest American English.

One of our consulting adventures involved factory floor observation and analysis at Placon Corporation. Following a successful consulting visit by Brian Joiner, President Dave Boyer invited Yuki and me to visit a specialty area where the staff made ant traps. The traps were small plastic containers filled with peanut-butter-based insecticide. This should have been a perfect opportunity for me to apply principles and tools to improve quality. The work involved machines and repetitive cycles, with a physical product as the endpoint. Bread-and-(peanut)-butter quality improvement! (See Dave Boyer's story on this project in this book.)

I remember one day at Placon when we piled up mashed packaging and misshapen containers that had gotten produced along with the desired output. All that waste represented a "mountain of treasure," a phrase from another Japanese master of continuous improvement. The waste and broken pieces gave everyone a clear view of our improvement potential to capture more ants. Translate the waste into dollars and add the cost of the wasted time of people and machines—and we indeed had a mountain of treasure.

All that waste represented a "mountain of treasure."

~

Yuki and I also had an engagement with Meriter Hospital in Madison. Thirty years ago, Meriter, now part of Iowa-based UnityPoint Healthcare, was an independent organization. CEO Terri Potter had agreed with Brian that Yuki and I could drive across town to help with Meriter's efforts at creating substantial improvement in a healthcare setting.

Following advice that Brian must have offered, Meriter had formed a Quality Council. The Quality Council included the top twenty or so senior managers—the top of Meriter's organization chart. The head of the company's Quality Improvement office, Mary Zimmerman, served as the internal council planner and agenda keeper. The Quality Council was formed to focus senior management's attention on policies and projects that would improve quality of hospital services.

Yuki proposed that several members of the Quality Council look at their areas of the hospital and report on problems and improvement opportunities. Mary proceeded to schedule a Quality Council session for a Monday. The plan was that Yuki would get their report materials first thing on Friday morning to prepare for the following Monday session. I would help interpret the reports.

Yuki's proposal used a learning cycle that forms the basis of all systemic change. At Joiner Associates in the early 1990s, we called the steps Plan-Do-Check-Act, following the lead of our Japanese teachers.

"Study" also suggests that you don't know all the answers and might meet a surprise.

(Note. Dr. Deming thought that the word "Check" did not capture the spirit of the improvement cycle he had derived from Walter Shewhart, the inventor of statistical process control. Deming preferred the word "Study," which implies an attitude of inquiry. "Study" also suggests that you don't know all the answers and might meet a surprise. For the past 25 years, I've used a version of Plan-Do-Study-Act developed by my friends at Associates in Process Improvement (API). Ron Moen and Cliff Norman of API concisely summarized the history of Plan-Do-Study-Act in a *Quality Progress* article titled "Clearing up myths about the Deming cycle and Seeing How It Keeps Evolving." Yuki's use of Plan-Do-Check-Act and my current understanding of Plan-Do-Study-Act are close enough that Yuki's lessons still shape my views and understanding of the entire improvement process.)

Specifically at Meriter Hospital, Yuki wanted the executives to first study their current situation. With his help, they could plan one or more appropriate actions or changes to try. Each action would require its own Plan. Then people would try to convert each plan into reality (Do). The executives and staff next should reflect on problems and successes (Study). Then the executives and staff would need decide what to do next (Act): adopt the change as regular practice, modify what they tried, or abandon the changes.

~

On the Friday before the Quality Council meeting, the day Yuki expected to get the first set of reports, I got a call from Mary. The reports weren't ready. I told Yuki we had a problem. He replied: "Call Mary back and cancel Monday's Quality Council meeting." Yuki said I was the native English speaker, so it was my job to convey his message to the Meriter team. I wasn't sure what to do, but I knew I didn't want to tell Mary to cancel the meeting.

But Yuki insisted. He said we needed to investigate the failure of our own little reporting plan if we were serious about Plan-Do-Check-Act. The plan was very clear to everyone: Executives would prepare reports and submit them by Friday morning. The executives and staff had failed to carry out that plan. There was no point to having the proposed Monday meeting if the ingredients for "study" were not ready. More importantly, according to Yuki, we needed to devote time to studying the failure of this first step. We needed to find out which executives had failed to prepare and why.

Yikes! I resisted. I didn't want to invent an agenda for Monday that would put executives and Mary on the defensive. I lacked the confidence and experience to weave a productive meeting out of our broken plan. Yuki pointed out to me, however, that we and the Quality Council had a plan. We were responsible for the plan. Taking responsibility meant that only the two of us and the council could study the failure. "If the bosses don't practice Plan-Do-Check-Act, then people in the organization might interpret PDCA to mean 'Please Don't Change Anything.'"

People in the organization might interpret PDCA to mean "Please Don't Change Anything!"

Reluctantly, I called Mary on Friday to politely explain Yuki's position. I was not bold enough to schedule an in-depth study of the failed plan. I waffled. We agreed not to cancel the Monday session just yet. Mary worked over the weekend to extract information from Quality Council members that would meet their plan commitments. We limped through the Monday session. We did not address the failure of our plan directly. Thus, we missed the opportunity to study and improve the way the Quality Council worked with us. Looking back, I could have followed Yuki's direction if I'd have had more skill and confidence. (Spoiler alert: Meriter's story of improvement has an enormously successful next chapter.)

~

My friends at API, working with Dr. Deming 30 years ago, connected the Plan-Do-Study-Act cycle to three preliminary questions to form the Model for Improvement.

- The first question addresses your aim: What are you trying to accomplish?

- The second question addresses measurement: How will you know that a change is an improvement, where improvement means you are closer to your aim?
- The third question addresses what you will do: What change can you make that will lead to improvement?

With answers to these three questions, you are set to test your change idea and measure whether the change brings you closer to your aim.

The Model for Improvement works whenever you are trying to reach a destination and you don't quite know how to get there. That is a common situation when trying to lead changes in any organization or institution! So long as you know your aim, a way to measure whether you are getting closer to the aim, and the ability to choose and test different paths, you've got a reliable method to help you improve.

I've learned that the aim question, all by itself, is a great place to start in work with any client or project. In the Meriter Hospital work, imagine if our first aim with the Quality Council had been stated explicitly as "Develop the Quality Council's skill and experience in Plan-Do-Check-Act thinking and applications."

If we had stated that aim, it would have been easier for me to follow Yuki's direction. I could have pointed out the failure of the initial plan and modified the Monday agenda to directly address that failure. Just like Placon's mountain of treasure, we would have seen the plan's failure as a bit of treasure to celebrate and learn from.

Yukihiro Ando helped me understand that serious application of Plan-Do-Study-Act starts with facing plan failures right here, right now. The good news is that we all have plan failures; they are all around us. The mental reframe we need is to change our view of failures from things to ignore, skate past, or downplay to treasures we are happy to find.

It's important to note that once begun, the subsequent improvement projects at Meriter netted outstanding results in key areas such as patient safety and satisfaction and staff retention. Even board operations were systematically improved, and Meriter became recognized as a pioneer in improving healthcare both locally, nationally, and internationally. See the story in this book by former CEO Terri Potter, "Leading with Powerful Questions."

Reference

Moen, R. and Norman, C. (2010). Clearing up myths about the Deming cycle and seeing how it keeps evolving. *Quality Progress,* 43 (11), 22-28).

Kevin Little, Ph.D., of Informing Ecological Design, LLC, is a statistician and improvement advisor who applies system design and analysis methods to solve practical problems. Over the past twenty-five years, he has worked to improve performance in health care and promoted sustainable buildings and communities. He worked as a senior consultant with Joiner Associates, Madison, WI From 1985 to 1995, coaching managers and project teams to improve quality and productivity. He earned his Ph.D. in statistics from the University of Wisconsin-Madison.

Questions for Reflection and Discussion

1. Give one example of a failure you have ignored, skated past, or downplayed. Why? What was the result? In retrospect, what did you learn from that?
2. Take one problem in your institution or organization and ask these three questions:

- What are you trying to accomplish?
- How will you know that a change is an improvement, where improvement means you are closer to your aim?
- What change can you make that will lead to improvement?

3. Have you had a mentor? If so, who was it and what did they mentor you on? If you wanted someone to mentor you on leading change, who might you ask? Check out some of the people and resources at BendingGranite.org.

You Get What You Measure

by Ben Reynolds

"A big thank you to Ben for creating this report," the plant manager said, and over 100 employees at the all-hands meeting turned to look at me. I, an intern at a distribution center, had not been listening and needed to rewind the meeting in my head. What report? When I saw the graphs on the screen, I realized it was a report I had finished weeks earlier, sent to my bosses, and forgotten about as I moved on to the next one.

The report linked the internal product picking data (at a distribution center) to the quality numbers shared by dealers. Prior to this report, the company could not link the picking errors identified by our dealers to specific employees, making post-delivery quality improvement impossible.

Over 100 employees at the all-hands meeting turned to look at me.

The plant manager had not warned me about this public recognition, or that this report had already led to both positive and negative performance reviews. As a distribution center, productivity remained a primary driver of pay and performance reviews. The more orders "picked" to be sent to dealers, the better the compensation.

A few employees had learned to "game" the numbers. The data showed that they had learned they could skip taking the time to actually count lightweight items—such as washers, keychains, bolts—if they just guessed on the quantity they included in an order. Their productivity numbers would improve, and since the items were light weight they would not flag the scale for a weight audit. Some of the most respected employees had learned this game and now found themselves facing negative consequences based on my report, which had found that other employees had honestly met their productivity numbers and were now receiving praise and raises. (Throughout the rest of my internship at this plant, I could tell how people landed on this spectrum based on my interactions with them, which was a very unpleasant experience for a twenty-year-old.)

~

I had expected the report to contribute to quality improvement, not to individual performance reviews. It solidified in my mind, however, that (as I later learned quality-guru W. Edwards Deming often said) the vast majority of workplace problems are system problems not individual worker problems. The system that had been in place unintentionally incentivized cutting corners and gaming the system, and the rookie intern had unwittingly discovered it simply by measuring what was actually being done on the plant floor.

I went into the internship as a database novice and came out slightly bruised but skilled in Microsoft Excel and Access. This helped greatly throughout the rest of my undergraduate classes, many of which provided continuous improvement case studies with clean datasets that contained clear answers if you knew how to approach the data. After graduation, I returned to work for my family's moving company, Reynolds Transfer and Storage (Reynolds), and crashed back to reality.

~

When I started at Reynolds in 2011, we were 100% paper. My goal was to change all that. We had Netscape email and an accounting system that could only print, but not export, reports electronically. Both were hosted on a server that used tapes—yes, literal tapes. The "system" we had for dispatching our fleet of dozens of trucks, cranes, vehicles, and 70-80 employees, was simply to print the job packet and put it in a wooden cubby on the wall.

So where do you start? Luckily for me, management had started the migration to Gmail. As my senior capstone project, my student group had recommended using Google Calendar, specifically the "resources" function (think projectors, conference rooms, etc.) to schedule the company fleet and personnel. This prevented double-booking, as the scheduler could only see the available assets and personnel and received real-time updates when a job changed. This eliminated the biggest issues with the paper cubby system: double booking, over booking, and lost jobs. (If you lost the packet, we usually forgot about the job until a customer complained). I had the whole company set up in about a week, trained everyone the next week, declared the switch-over date, and congratulated myself for completing my first successful process change.

Months later, however, not much had changed. It seemed that no one actually used the calendar. The job bookers were still using the paper system. The workaround was that the dispatcher had to manually add all jobs from the paper packets just a day or two ahead of time. This short lead time made it difficult, if not impossible, to coordinate the use of costly equipment and people across all the jobs for a given day. Frustrated and confused, I learned that an influential manager had told everyone they could ignore me; the system was not actually going to change.

It seemed that no one actually used the calendar.

I was able to sit down with that manager for an extended one-to-one training session. It turns out he had ignored my emails giving him access to the system, and therefore could not see the schedule. In his whole career to that point, he had used the cubbies on the wall to access the schedule, and he was not about to change because of some snot-nosed upstart—even if I was part of the family!

Upon finding himself locked out, he had set about undermining the new system. After my one-to-one, live training session with him, however, he realized the benefits of electronic scheduling. With him finally and really on board, the company fully migrated to the new scheduling system within a couple of weeks. In the years since, we have tested several other systems for dispatching and scheduling, but we remain on Google Calendar a decade later.

~

Several years went by. I switched roles at Reynolds to sales, helped with dispatch, drove a semi around the country hauling furniture, then worked as a consultant in Chicago for another company for eighteen months. I returned to Reynolds for several months before starting work on a master's degree in Manufacturing Systems Engineering at UW-Madison. Having unfortunately forgotten the lessons from my previous experiences, I figured starting a large process change in late November that would give me plenty of time to complete it before classes started in January. The target this time was obvious: our paper filing system.

On many levels, this filing system had glaring inefficiencies. Besides creating tons of paper (literally), it also caused delays in information transfer at many levels of the organization. Billing for jobs would get delayed because someone forgot to move a physical file to the next desk. People printed emails and calendar events and put them in the physical file, despite the existence of a permanent electronic copy. Since most of our files existed electronically at some point in the process, we basically backed up electronic copies with paper ones!

We already had access to Google Drive, so the switch seemed easy. According to my plan we would simply train everyone to use Google Drive, set up an electronic filing system, create some work instructions, and watch the company efficiency improve exponentially.

We tried this for about a month, and everything seemed to work. However, according to my data our paper consumption (and the noise from the printer) barely dropped. It turns out that people just continued the old system, and then scanned the whole paper file in at the billing phase. I was mad. This made no sense. Why were my fellow employees refusing to make this change?

I finally figured it out. I had failed to fully understand how people used the physical files. In addition to their use as an information deposit, they served as a tool for communication via sticky notes, which were then often removed before filing. They also served as a reminder of a task to complete—a visual to-do list in piles on desks throughout the office. I had made a costly mistake. People were *mad at me* for not recognizing how the physical files were really being used and building these capabilities into my new system. After a series of apologies from me, employees agreed to a reset and to try the same strategy on a different software system.

Why were people refusing to make this change?

A friend recommended Trello, which turned out to solve these problems in an elegant manner. In this project-management software, each job received a "card" which housed all the information for the job. Employees could chat with each other on the cards, attach documents, and move the cards left to right through "lists" at each stage of the information flow. People quickly saw the benefits.

By now it was April, which presented an additional challenge. May through September is our busy season, and no one wanted to change until the following fall. I knew, however, that the clunky paper system was costing the company substantially because of the inordinate time required to bill clients and bill them accurately. It took about two months of my asking, cajoling, and mandating, but we finally fully switched to Trello by June (2015) and still use this system years later.

~

After changing the two systems at Reynolds described above (and several other smaller ones), I finally had access to the datasets I had craved for years. Using the Microsoft Access skills learned as an intern, I combined the datasets from Google Calendar and Trello with our fleet tracking, timekeeping, and accounting systems. This allowed me to study productivity. We could also assess the profitability of individual customers. We cut ties with some, while investing in capital improvements to better serve others. We analyzed our cost data and embraced energy efficiency, waste reduction, and solar power for environmental and business reasons. However, it all felt reactionary to me, as if people made decisions to avoid getting in trouble instead of proactively thinking of ways to improve.

As management, we realized we had a serious weakness—Human Resources—so we hired an expert to fill this role. She quickly identified a major leverage point: We did not regularly communicate our company's values. If people did not know what we valued, how could they help us grow as an organization? How could we expect people to perform as we expected if we did not clearly outline our expectations? It seemed obvious in hindsight, and my family (the owners) agreed to prioritize this change.

How could we expect people to perform as we expected if we did not clearly outline our expectations?

As a family, we brainstormed what we valued in the company, and gradually reduced the list to the following three: Safety, Service and Sustainability. The following descriptions come from the first page of our re-written company handbook.

- **Safety.** We evaluate every decision with safety as the highest priority: the safety of ourselves, our customers, our community, and the items in our care.

- **Service.** We commit to providing the highest quality service to our employees, our customers, and our community through respectful and effective work.
- **Sustainability.** We strive to improve the sustainability of our planet, our community, and our company through environmentally and socially responsible business practices.

With this framework, we began to ask our people to make decisions by evaluating their options using the values above, with safety as the primary criterion. Upon reflection, our team (myself included) could have avoided many mistakes by slowing down and considering the company values prior to acting.

I now try to keep my message consistent. Mistakes happen, and as long as we learn and adjust future actions, we consider the resulting costs an investment, not a waste. At the writing of this reflection, we have not implemented this strategy long enough to evaluate the results, but we remain hopeful that it will guide our company and our people through decisions large and small.

The articulation of our company values aims to correct two mistakes I have repeatedly made and witnessed others make throughout my career: over-reliance on data and inadequate communication. It took years before I recognized the root cause of my internship issues at the distribution center—the management had incentivized productivity without the ability to measure quality. At Reynolds, I sought data through system changes without fully understanding the ways that people relied on the existing systems. Once we had that information, it helped us understand the root cause of many issues, but only after the event.

Given the variability of work handled by our crews, we have to help people make better decisions on their own. Can teaching safety, service, and sustainability continue to improve our organization? We think so, but either way we will learn and move forward.

Ben Reynolds is Director of Operations at Reynolds Transfer and Storage, a successful family-owned business with a 100+ year history in Madison, Wisconsin. A graduate of UW-Madison, Ben studied with and was a teaching assistant for Professor Mark Finster, where he learned and applied the connection between quality principles and sustainability. Ben has also been active in board service at Sustain Dane and Wisconsin Manufacturers Extension Project (WMEP). WMEP recently merged with the Wisconsin Sustainable Business Council where Ben also serves as a board member.

Questions for Reflection and Discussion

1. What three (and only three) single words would you give to summarize the values of your organization, institution, community, or family? Explain each word. How could you communicate these values more effectively and regularly? To whom?
2. Tell one story about yourself or someone you know well where a basic mistake led to real learning.
3. What do you think W. Edwards Deming meant when he said that the vast majority of workplace problems are system problems not individual worker problems? Give an example of this from your own experience or something you have observed.

Never Waste a Crisis

by Michael Williamson

Things were bad. Really bad. A municipality, the unit of government closest to the people, delivers services based on three things—its policy-making, its workforce, and its equipment. Some would argue that the most important of these is the equipment. And good working equipment was hard to come by in 1983 in the City of Madison. And it was becoming an issue, a big issue. If you are the Chief of Police and you have one, two, maybe a half dozen squad cars broken down and out of service, then your ability to put patrol officers on the street is reduced and you have a problem.

And if you are the Parks Director and a number of your mowers will not run and you have 200 city parks to keep mowed and presentable to the public, and it's the rainy season of June and July, you have a problem. And the same goes for the Streets and Sanitation Department, the Forestry Division and every other city department. Yet vehicles were sitting in the staging lot at the city's First Street Garage for days before a mechanic could even take a look at them. And then it was over a week or more before they were back on the street.

In the public sector, a rather small problem becomes a big problem much faster than it does in the private sector. At least that's my impression from a career in public service. That's part of the job you sign up for when you become an elected official or a civil servant. When parks are looking shabby and calls to the cops are not being returned in a timely manner, it doesn't take long before there is hell to pay.

So back in the early 1980s, being the empathetic humans that we are, we city officials in Madison, Wisconsin, immediately looked to who or what was to blame for the vehicular repair crisis. And in November 1983, a city audit identified several factors: less than desirable productivity, struggling labor management relations, and fragmented communication. The light was quickly thrown on the mechanics in the city garage. You know, they were, after all, "union" mechanics. So that had to have been at least part, if not all, of the problem.

For every complex problem, there is a simple solution. But it is almost always wrong.

~

A common approach to problems—back then, not now of course—was to try to throw more money at them: There were just not enough mechanics at the garage to keep up with the workload. In fact, Madison's Motor Equipment Division had permanently lost six staff positions over the past decade while the number of vehicles that needed servicing had grown from 546 to 725. To top it off, the city's preventive maintenance program had been completely eliminated due to budget cuts. One quick solution to the vehicular repair crisis might have been to add more positions in the division. But that is not what we did.

Lesson #1: For every complex problem, there is a simple solution. But it is almost always wrong. Debate intensified among the City Council members and across city government as to what to do. And as often happens, folks settled on the Mayor's Office to solve this problem, as he was our *de facto* city manager. So, what did the mayor do?

David Miller, an Assistant to the Mayor for Economic Development, had an idea. David was exploring new approaches to management that were rumored to be working in the private sector and in the process had heard about W. Edwards Deming, so he went to the University of Wisconsin-Madison campus for one of the famed two-day Deming seminars. After Day 1, he called Mayor Joe Sensenbrenner and said, "You better get down here, Mr. Mayor." To Joe's credit, he went.

When the two came back, we all met. Like Miller, I was one of the mayor's four assistants, but I had the most experience working in the public sector. The mayor walked into my office, plopped down in a chair, and told me about the basic principles he had just learned. Then he said, "Mike, I think this stuff can revolutionize how we manage city government." I considered his statements for about two seconds and said, "Mr. Mayor, this *#@! will never work in government." Today, Joe would say to me, "Do you want some ketchup with those words, Mike?"

A crisis is definitely an opportunity.

Meanwhile, the problem of the backlog of broken-down city vehicles continued to rise to the top of the pile. But the Deming seminar was hanging heavy in Mayor Sensenbrenner's mind. There had to be a different way to look at this situation, but what was it? All we had were translations of Japanese private sector implementation examples. No one, I mean, no one had tried these techniques in government, not even in Japan. But we were determined to try because it was the only solution that made sense to us. Our philosophy of government was (and still remains): If you want to change the status quo in an organization, you never pass up a crisis. Driving change in an organization is always tough, so why not use everything at your disposal, even—and I know this sounds somewhat unorthodox—new ideas.

So, our strategy on the vehicular repair crisis was to use the tools of quality and process improvement, which are summed up nicely in this one quote:

> Quality improvement, whether in public or private sectors, demands three major changes. First, it calls for a total transformation of management philosophy so all employees can focus on the never-ending improvement of quality. Second, quality improvement means making decisions based on data, not just on hunches and guesses. All employees must scrutinize all key processes in the organization to determine where and how they break down and how they can be improved. Third, improving quality requires an almost fanatical devotion to customers (Hunter and Wallen, 1986).

Lesson #2: If you are a leader or a change agent, you look for any crack you can use to create a different future. And a crisis is definitely an opportunity with lots of cracks. Therefore, do not, and I emphasize do not, let the crisis get away from you. The stakes in city hall were high on this one, but that's what made the situation an opportunity. That's what Mayor Joe saw. And fortunately, that's what Peter Scholtes saw. Scholtes, a city employee with organizational development experience, reached out to Bill Hunter at the University of Wisconsin-Madison.

It is great living and working in a university town, most of the time anyway. It happened that about this time, there was a group of university professors who were equally, if not more so, interested in this new approach to management. Their names included Brian Joiner, George Box, and Bill Hunter. They were looking for a place to pilot these new concepts. But Madison city government, I mean really? Professor Hunter volunteered for the challenge. Mayor Joe accepted.

Bill Hunter, a white-shirt-and-tie-wearing professor educated at Princeton and now on the esteemed statistics faculty at the University of Wisconsin-Madison, went down to the city garage to meet with the greasy-handed, blue-shirted mechanics, the workers. His aim was to discuss with them how they could improve their performance. Normally, this would not have been a good conversation. In these situations, one side is often self-righteous and the other side is usually being blamed. But not with Bill. That is not who he was. Rather, he met the workers where they were—trapped in a process over which they had little control.

~

Lesson #3: The 85/15 rule exists. It suggests that only 15% of the improvement opportunities rest in the hands of the workers, while 85% reside with management who have the power and the ability to control the process. (Deming said that as much as 94% is typically out of the control of workers.) Bill listened to the workers and they heard what he was saying. Terry Holmes, the president of the union, was in those early meetings, and he responded to Bill Hunter when he suggested that together they look in depth at the process. As Terry put it to Bill: "You are not telling us anything new. We understand what you are saying. The system is broken. And they are blaming us. Do you think you and this new idea can help us?"

Ah, we were blessed. Bill Hunter was not just any statistics professor. Of course, he understood all too well the 85/15 rule. More importantly, he was a man who understood and cared about people, no matter where they sat in the organization. The mechanics at the First Street Garage saw that and decided to trust him and this new-fangled approach he was touting.

The data will set you free.

A process improvement team was formed to study the repair issues using the new approach. They created two sub-teams—one to better understand the needs of the customers and one to study downtime on the job. After the customer team surveyed the customers, the result was confirmed: "Duration of downtime" was the primary concern to everyone. The downtime sub-team set out to gather real data on that.

Lesson #4: In God we trust; all others must get good data. One of the primary tenets of quality and process improvement is, "The data will set you free." Professor Hunter knew this. He asked the newly created improvement team to gather information on the downtime problem, and the team quantified what everyone had suspected: Average time to return a vehicle or a piece of equipment to active use was 9.5 days.

Not a desirable timetable for your customers, who in this case were the city departments who relied on the garage. For example, the Police Department had begun lobbying to use private sector businesses to do the oil changes and regular maintenance to speed up the return of their squad cars. But the reality was that the city mechanics did more than change the oil; they inspected the vehicles sent to them and found other items that needed to be addressed to prevent future failures. But each maintenance event took a lot more time because of this approach.

Closer analysis of the data, however, also revealed that much of the equipment was just plain old. It turned out that vehicles were being kept in use way longer than in the past. Non-police vehicles were getting replaced, on average, every twenty-one years rather than every ten years as had been the case a decade before. It was therefore taking more repairs to keep the fleet on the road.

Another cause of the delays in repairs became evident in the data on replacement parts. When you purchase equipment based on the lowest cost, you have no consistency in your supplier chain and get your equipment from a wide range of manufacturers. This means you cannot possibly keep all the parts on hand that you need. You must order them (sometimes even putting out a bid first) and then wait for delivery, which was inconsistent according to which vendor you chose.

But most surprising from the data was the delay that bureaucracy from City Hall was causing in the vehicular-repair wars. Approval for purchasing was slow and, it turned out, not really needed. The purchase of a part required 28 separate steps and the largest percentage of the time in this process was spent waiting for approval of the purchase of the parts from City Hall! As leaders in the organization, we were surprised and chagrined when we received this data.

~

Lesson #5: Watch for unnecessary approval steps that slow processes. Such approval rules usually are there to satisfy someone's need for control and/or as the result of an earlier misstep by someone (sometimes years before) that led to the addition of extra steps and therefore more complexity and more delay. The alternative we developed was to flowchart the entire process of vehicle maintenance, collect real data that could identify the problems, and then fix the real causes of downtime—all without creating new hurdles for the workers to jump over.

The "true" causes of the situation were starting to come into focus. The team made several key recommendations. One, the city should adopt a more effective replacement schedule that made newer, more reliable equipment available to the departments from trusted and accountable suppliers. Two, the city garage, working with its customers, should implement a priority system that identified the most urgent repairs and get those vehicles back on the street first. Finally, purchasing decisions should be delegated to the managers of the garage except in special situations.

But how did these three outcomes happen? Well first, a formal improvement process that was put in place. Second, useful data was gathered. Third, employees were listened to regarding the environment and processes in which they did their daily work.

~

Lesson #6: The line employees in any process understand the process better than any manager ever will. So, ask them, and then listen to what they tell you. (That is not always the case, but as Joe Turner, a garage foreman quipped after the changes were made, "Now there's less cussin' and more discussin'.") Always listen to people who know more than you. Never be embarrassed that people on your team have a better idea; be thankful they do.

Line employees in any process understand the process better than any manager ever will. So, ask them.

How did the vehicle repair crisis turn out, you might ask? Well, with the improved processes, the response time dropped—in some cases all the way down from 9.5 days to 48 hours. And the number of steps to purchase a needed repair part for vehicles dropped from 28 down to seven. The annual savings from these improvements was estimated to be $750,000. How's that for results?

More importantly in the long run, quality management had been birthed in the City of Madison, possibly the first governmental unit in the country, even the world, to do so! The First Street Garage became an example of what was possible in government. The story made it into Dr. Deming's next book. Bill Hunter took Terry Holmes, the union president, with him around the country to share their story. They even presented at Ford Motor Company—fancy that, the private sector learning from the public sector! What had been an unsung but critical department in city government, the First Street Garage, was now a model for the nation, and the workers beamed with a sense of well-earned pride, accomplishment, and recognition that had never existed before.

What a shame it would have been to have wasted such a crisis.

Epilogue: The bond between Bill Hunter and the mechanics at the First Street Garage was more than professional. They truly respected each other and enjoyed one another's company. When Bill Hunter died in 1987 at the much too young age of forty-nine, the two head union mechanics at the garage requested to pay their final respects in a special way to the man who believed in them. Their request was honored. And in January of that year, Terry Holmes and Joe Turner dug by hand the grave that was to hold Professor Bill Hunter's casket.

References

Hunter, W., O'Neil, J., and Wallen, C. (June 1986). *Doing more with less in the public sector.* Center for Quality and Productivity Improvement, University of Wisconsin-Madison.

Michael Williamson recently retired after forty-one years of leading complex public sector organizations in various fields, including local and state government, pension management and investment, environmental regulation, and university administration. He helped create the groundbreaking Quality Initiative in the City of Madison, founded the Office of Quality Improvement (OQI) at the University of Wisconsin-Madison campus, initiated the OQI for the State of North Carolina, and applied continuous improvement concepts in a wide array of other organizations. Michael co-founded the Public Sector Network in the American Society of Quality and has served on numerous national and state boards, where he constantly tries to make order out of chaos and never allows a good crisis to be wasted.

Questions for Reflection and Discussion

1. Tell the story of a good crisis you were involved in or observed that was not wasted. What happened and how did it happen?
2. Why is it sometimes difficult to listen to others in the workplace? Identify a group or unit it would be beneficial to listen to and gather data from. How might you best do that?
3. What can the private and public sectors learn from each other? Why should they want to?

Chapter Five

Managing by Facts

Introduction

Cutting through the Fog

Without data, you're just another person with an opinion.

W. Edwards Deming

"How did our girls win the regional and sectional soccer tournaments this year?" all the parents wondered. The school had not been among the strong teams historically, and now they won both the region and the sectionals. Each win was a surprise, even for the team. They kept winning, until they were standing on a podium with a monster-sized trophy in their collective hands. The team eventually took second in the entire state championship and has been regarded ever since as the biggest winner in the school's soccer history.

Ian Hau had been their coach. Yes, he was a professional soccer player, so he knew something about the game. He was also a graduate student at UW-Madison studying statistics and quality improvement. He started collecting data throughout the season. Using dots on a soccer field diagram, he showed the players where they were positioned on the field when they successfully passed and scored goals. Likewise, each goal they lost was analyzed and used to determine how to "error proof" and eliminate the chance of those "mistakes" in the future games.

In preparing for the state competition, Ian realized that if there was a tie, which happens frequently in soccer, they would go to penalty kick shoot-out and that would determine the winner. No ties were allowed! The girls were not the strongest team among those in the playoff, so instead of just using his soccer intuition the coach designed a scientific experiment to collect data to see which five players on his team were best at penalty kicks. Everyone expected the five best kickers to be those who were regarded as the best players overall, but to everyone's surprise two players who were mostly on the sidelines turned out to be among the best five penalty kickers. Because of this one change, the team won every penalty shoot-out game in the playoff, and the reserve players who did not have much playing time during regular matches became the team's secret weapons for penalty kicks.

Ian later went on to work in the pharmaceutical world, rising to the top of a major pharma company by radically reducing the time for getting new drugs to market and expanding distribution globally. And then he started his own company, guiding efforts to improve health care for the fast-aging population in China that is expected to grow from 200 million currently to 500 million in the next twenty years or so. In the face of these unprecedented challenges, data-based care is more important than ever.

~

A core value of the Baldrige Performance Excellence model for systemic, continuous, quality improvement is that leaders manage decisions by factual evidence. Leaders select, collect, and analyze data to inform and support them in making decisions. Does the information make all their decisions crystal clear? Of course not. Do leaders ever make quick, intuitive decisions? Of course they do. "Be sure you're right, then go ahead," said Davey Crockett. Relying only on your gut, however, is like driving blind in a thick fog. Facts are like high-tech fog lamps: with time and experience they can cut through the fog. Making decisions based on facts, often called "metrics" in the organizational improvement biz, is the only real long-term strategy to success. Like Coach Ian, successful change leaders use facts to determine the "best" way to accomplish their aims.

To support leaders in managing by facts, Baldrige asks two fundamental questions: What do you do? and How's it going? Your answers to those questions need to be grounded in facts about your goals, objectives, methods, and results. The stories in this chapter are about how you work to get from one point to the next. Using metrics keeps it real and can even reveal truths that may have gone unobserved without them. Ian didn't suspect free kicks would be a game changer until he gathered the data.

Organizations that crave to do things with quality as their goal use facts to answer critical questions, such as: How do we achieve our mission? What do our customers require? What are our goals? How do our processes perform? What are the risks? What have our failures taught us? How are we doing? How are our competitors doing? And more. Managing by facts guides them and provides a heads up for all their actions. As Dr. Deming used to say, "It is not enough to do your best; you must know what to do, and then do your best."

A question to consider: What story is *your* organization trying to tell, and what metrics are *you* using to do so? Here are four stories that answer that question by John Wiley, Matt Albert, Greg Simmons, and Kurt Southworth.

Working 99 to 5

by John Wiley

The book put me to sleep the first time I started to read it. I was waiting to board a plane to the West Coast and saw *The Deming Management Method* by Mary Walton in the airport bookstore. I had been hearing about Deming and Quality Improvement and needed something to read on the plane, so I plunked down some cash, took the book, and got on board. The plane made a nice takeoff, and I settled in to learn something about quality and how to achieve it. But at twenty pages in, I was bored and more than a little turned off, put the book in the seat pocket in front of me, and went to sleep. When I awoke, though, I picked the book back up and this time read it through cover to cover, and then I read it again. As a physicist/engineer, I saw an alignment with the scientific method. Suddenly, quality improvement made sense to me.

It was 1989 and Donna Shalala, our new chancellor, had just appointed me as dean of the graduate school, responsible for research and graduate education at the University of Wisconsin-Madison. I already knew UW-Madison and the graduate school as an associate dean in Engineering.

Donna was committed to students being treated like customers—a radical idea at that time. And we had the support of the Madison community, where public and private organizations were launching continuous improvement efforts right and left. As I considered how the Graduate School might make needed changes, so many of the principles in Walton's book seemed to have practical potential. So, when the plane landed I stuffed the book into my briefcase and set out to give it a try. My new staff and I identified two projects, and I decided to participate as a team member on both. As it turned out, one of those projects became a classic improvement project and helped launch UW-Madison's culture of continuous improvement that thrives to this day. That project was the graduate admissions process, and here is the story.

One thing kept eating at me: We were constantly losing some of our best applicants.

As the new dean, one thing kept eating at me. About 15,000 people applied each year to come to the university to earn a graduate degree, but we were constantly losing some of our best applicants. Although UW-Madison is a highly-ranked research institution, the competition among universities then and to this day is fierce. One of the first data points we discovered was that some of our graduate applicants were choosing to accept offers at schools that we clearly outranked! What was the problem? Turns out, it was us. "Us" as in The Graduate School. As individual departments scurried to make offers to top students, they had to wait for "Us" to complete our part of the process. The second data point was that it took an average of ninety-nine days for an applicant to hear back from UW-Madison. In the meantime, many of the best students had already been tied down—lock, stock, and barrel, so to speak—by peer and smaller or less prestigious institutions.

The competitiveness of our institution was at risk. We needed to reduce the time it took to make an admissions decision—quickly, by a lot, but also in a way that actually improved the excellence of our institution. As in most organizations, no one wanted to hear we were doing something poorly, so it was helpful to be able to use an approach that resembled the scientific method. Turns out, it *was* the scientific method.

We formed an improvement team and went to work. Joanne (Nagy) Berg was head of the graduate admissions office and led the team. We dove in immediately and learned systemic process improvement approaches as we went along, guided by a facilitator from our newly formed Office of Quality Improvement. Here are a few of the highlights from this classic project.

After mapping our process—literally creating a picture of what we wanted to happen at each step—each team member contacted three or four peer institutions to ask a few key questions. My call to University of California-Berkeley was transformative for me. It turned out that their admissions process was *all* about the process. Instead of their graduate office calculating all applications and the departments waiting to do anything, their departments did the first screening and prioritized students they were interested in recruiting based on their individual priorities each year. With this approach, UC-Berkeley was able to turn around a top priority application in five days. This let us think about completely flipping our own process. And five days became our audacious goal (although a bit daunting given our embarrassing 99-day starting point).

We had met the enemy and it was us!

We had always calculated and compared grade point averages of all applicants. After our conversation with UC-Berkeley, we wondered if departments really needed that information. So, we asked them. They said "Yes! But faster, please. A lot faster!" But given our new mindset, we wondered, "*Why* do they need these at all?" We went back and asked, and the departments said because the graduate school's fellowship office required that information. Well, the graduate school fellowship office was fifty feet down the hall from the meeting room where our team was having the discussion; so I got up and walked down the hall and asked our people there about it. Guess what they said? Yep, they said, "We don't need that information. Quit sending it to us!" There we had it: the first fruit of our quality initiative. We had what is called a "closed loop of assumptions" that resulted in a huge amount of wasted work and was one of the primary causes for our long admissions process that was losing us some of our best candidates. We had met the enemy and it was us!

Once we realized this, the departments started screening and prioritizing their applicants. We could then turn around their top selections in one or two days, allowing them to get back to their top candidates promptly. As outrageous as this example may seem, I guarantee that there are processes in your organization just like this. You just need to walk down the hall and ask someone "Why?"

Armed with additional information, our team continued to examine our process assumptions. For example, it turned out we were calculating the GPA of applicants only after we had *all* transcripts from *every* institution an applicant had attended after high school. (Think about trying to get *that* information on a timely basis.) We collected data and developed a "Pareto" chart. The Pareto principle says that you spend 80% of your time on 20% of the cases. In this case, we realized we were spending 80% of our time waiting for 20% of the transcripts, primarily from the first two years after the applicant left high school. We then redefined a "complete file" as only needing to include the last two years before application for admission. This cut out enormous wait time and dramatically shortened the time for response. Another breakthrough!

Once we mapped our admissions process as a team, improvement opportunities became clear. Traditionally, all applications had been due on the same day, for example. This created an unmanageable workload peak for our own staff. So we staggered application deadlines and spread out the work. Also, we discovered that our own forms, entry screens, and database for institutional codes were unnecessarily complicated, wasting time and leading to errors, which wasted more time. The screens were redesigned for easier processing, which led to reduced errors, which led to faster response to applicants, which led to a much higher positive response rate by top applicants.

Individualism is a hallmark of higher education culture, so standardization is a challenge, but we standardized as much of the process as we could. In addition, we held campus forums on admissions to inform and educate departments about the changes, their vital role in the new process, and the carrot of potential for securing their top choices.

When you start at ninety-nine days, (hard to make that figure up, much less admit it), you hope you can show big improvement. And we did. In fact, we hit our audacious goal of any applicant to the graduate school at UW-Madison being able to be admitted within five days. The graduate school's part of that process went from twenty-six days to three. Our backlog of work went from six weeks to zero. The costs for temporary help during the peak season were reduced by 40%. But far and away the most important impact was our ability to respond to, make an offer, and successfully recruit many more of the best and brightest students who had applied to us for admission.

While that last impact is difficult to measure statistically, it's intuitively obvious that a quick response is essential in our competitive landscape. We also saw tell-tale signs of success all around us: plants on windowsills instead of stacks of hundreds of non-alphabetized applicant files and transcripts, full cases of calculator tape now being used as a footrest by happier employees.

Plants were on windowsills instead of stacks of hundreds of non-alphabetized applicant files.

We learned to challenge the culture of "We have always done it this way" and realized that the consequences of not taking a risk are often worse than doing nothing. In order to take risks, you have to be allowed to fail; so we made a game of it. We held meetings where each person had to tell one "improvement" they had tried that had failed. It became a competition for the biggest or most embarrassing failure, and I was a frequent winner! I always say, "If you aren't failing, you aren't trying hard enough."

If you aren't failing, you aren't trying hard enough.

In 1990, we were launching our QI office and exploring whether this corporate approach might be useful, or not, in higher education. There was great skepticism, especially among us academics. The "99 to 5" graduate admissions project impacted every academic unit on campus. Graduate students are the lifeblood of a department's research success and for building future generations of faculty. Every department depended on graduate admissions to help them build a strong graduate student base for their department. So this project's results were widely visible and enormously consequential. The campus-wide forums and training sessions further leveraged visibility and awareness of the power of this scientific approach to improvement. After participating myself on quality improvement teams on this and other projects, I often spoke at various campus sessions, being careful not to oversell but allowing the power of the example to speak for itself. All our departments began fully realizing the benefits of achieving quality results as they were able to make offers to top graduate applicants within a few days. We published the story in the national magazine *Change* (Nagy, et al., 1993), and the project was recognized as a finalist by the USA Quality Cup Award program.

While we were bold in demonstrating the process, however, we were cautious in other respects. We used common language, not the jargon of the QI movement. We had to be careful to not say the "C" word (customer), as it was viewed as a "corporate concept" (two "C" words). As we expanded, we worked with the willing and never required anyone's personal engagement. We expanded to strategic planning, setting the example at the campus level, led by then Provost David Ward, and integrated it with the university's reaccreditation process. Colleges and departments at UW-Madison began requesting help in developing their plans in alignment with the campus priorities. Deans of schools and colleges at UW-Madison shared their plans with one another, which illuminated many opportunities for collaboration.

Improvement efforts expanded into housing, police and security, facilities planning and management, the UW hospital, educational innovation, global health, and more. The History Department used quality and systemic process improvement approaches to transform their administrative systems, setting an example that Zoology took to another level of departmental effectiveness Over the next decade, over 200 academic units requested help in their strategy and improvement efforts.

When you are starting something bold and new to a culture, you can cajole, require, and argue. Or you can invite, show, and convince. We were deliberate in looking for good early demonstration projects, and we were very lucky to find one we could "work" from "99 to 5."

Reference

Nagy, J. Cotter, M., Erdman, P., Koch, B., Ramer, S., Roberts, N. and Wiley, J. (1993). Case study number three, *Change: The Magazine of Higher Learning*, 25:3, 36-40, DOI: 10.1080/00091383.1993.9938457.

John Wiley had a long career with UW–Madison, with nearly forty years of involvement as a student, faculty member, and administrator. From 2000-2008, he served as Chancellor. Before that he was Provost and Vice Chancellor for Academic Affairs. He was also the university's Vice Chancellor for Research, Dean of the Graduate School, and Associate Dean for Research in the College of Engineering.

Questions for Reflection and Discussion

1. What is the most memorable change you have made in your work life? What did you learn from it? Describe a moment when something seemingly obvious provided a breakthrough. Describe a moment when you failed, and what lessons you learned from that.
2. How do you try to "bring people along" in your efforts to achieve excellence in your workplace? Be specific. How do other people you observe try to do it? Which tactics are most effective? Why? Which don't seem to work? Why not?

3. What is one thing that is simply not working in your workplace? If you were to form a team to improve a work process, whom might you approach to join, support, or monitor your efforts? What data might be helpful? What other organizations might you benchmark to learn best practices?

It's in Our Hands

by Matt Albert

I leaned forward eagerly, demonstrating intense interest as I waited for the answer to my question about the hospital's priorities and areas of greatest opportunity for the coming year. I anticipated that the implications of his response would be significant: The founding nuns of the Sisters of St. Mary (SSM), with their population declining each year, had recently announced their intention to hand over the business reins of their SSM Health system. This would put the responsibility for delivering on our mission and strategy squarely into staff and management's hands.

The hospital president's eyes peered from beneath his shock of white hair, out the massive bay windows overlooking the St. Mary's healing garden until they fixed on some unknown point away in the distance. What wisdom would he share? What insightful vision would he cast before me to motivate us and inform our vital few goals? What beacon of light would beam forth to pierce the gloom of lowering reimbursement and the increasing health system complexity? The words left his mouth with an even pause between each utterance, without emotion, from an almost trance-like state. He continued staring into the distance as he spoke to a spot beyond the edge of the hospital campus, somewhere toward the frozen shore of Lake Monona and the ice fishermen on Wingra Bay and said: "We need improvement on all fronts...."

I realize now the importance of an ongoing dialogue around priorities, the need for evidence to support the priorities we select, and the key element—the opportunity for the entire team, myself included, to be able to speak our minds about what the priorities should be and how to meet them. I realize now how a systematic approach can help an organization identify and focus on its priorities and, had I been more self-aware and cognizant of this at the time, might have taken that perfect opportunity to introduce some well-researched and influential ideas toward the immediate and then continuous improvement of our institution on several important fronts. At the time, however, I just remember feeling uneasy, uncertain, and a bit overwhelmed. For, as you all know, the more goals you have, the less likely you are to be able to achieve those goals effectively.

The more goals you have, the less likely you are to be able to achieve those goals effectively.

~

While we did end up with too many goals that year, as an organization we also achieved some important breakthroughs. We learned how to work together in cross-functional teams. We learned how to focus on one critically important issue at a time. We learned about human motivation and the psychology of change. We learned that we could achieve specific goals. We learned how to get back to fundamentals.

A month or so after the aforementioned one-on-one with the hospital president on priorities, Chris Baker, our Quality and Safety Systems leader and my manager at the time, proposed an improvement initiative. When she asked me to pull together a team to improve our hand-hygiene practice, the first words from my mouth were, "You want me to do what?" Surely the esteemed improvement methods like Six Sigma were not needed for this problem. Surely, we didn't need to pull a special team together. "Can't we just tell people to wash their hands?" I opined about the merits of focusing on a problem of greater worth (with more juice to the squeeze so to speak) that would inspire health care workers everywhere to embrace improvement science as their own. I was certain hand washing was not it. How wrong I was!

"Can't we just tell people to wash their hands?"

I was fortunate that Chris was willing to educate me on the importance of clean hands for both our employees' and patients' health and the health of our organization. "'Matt," she would say, offering me a squirt of hand sanitizer, "Washing your hands is the easiest way to prevent infections in the hospital." She would go on to expound on the virtues of cleanliness and the importance of sterile fields. And this was before the Covid-19 pandemic ever reared its ugly head.

Chris introduced me to the work of Florence Nightingale, who worked as a nurse during the Crimean War and discovered the majority of soldiers' deaths were due to infection and disease exacerbated by poor hygiene—rather than the direct result of battle. Melinda Reppen, another hand-hygiene mentor and one of the hospital's infection prevention nurses, shared the tale of Ignaz Semmelweis, who identified a link between poor hand-hygiene practices and higher mortality rates from puerperal fever in postpartum mothers. This was specifically the result of medical students and physicians handling cadavers without hand washing prior to deliveries. In spite of being ostracized and demeaned by his colleagues for publicizing and promoting this information, Semmelweis continued to raise the importance of clean hands and implement hand washing protocols. His ideas were not accepted until after he died, but they have saved countless lives and are even more relevant today.

In spite of my initial misgivings, my wiser (and cleaner) angel prevailed, and I was soon involved deeply in conversations of hand sanitizer placement, infection rates, and whether or not people really knew how to wash their hands. We ensured a cross-functional team with representation from nursing, infection control, patient safety, quality assurance, front-line providers, and administration.

As we developed and refined our problem statement and clarified reason for action, one of the more impactful moments of improvement culture came during a leadership meeting of all of the hospital directors and administrative council. We had pulled together the hand-hygiene rates (percent successful, before and after patient contact) for the previous year from across the SSM system. This bar graph showed St. Mary's Hospital-Madison—our specific institution—as the hands-down worst-performing location at a success rate just about 75%, while most other facilities were above 90%! I had just shared the data with the leaders and opened the floor for comment when the president, who usually presided, came into the conference room from another meeting.

Frank Byrne is an animated figure and a well-loved leader in the line of presidents of St. Mary's Hospital, the largest in the SSM system. Rarely did anything other than a positive word come from his lips. He had a knack for delivering even painful news in an inspiring and uplifting manner. That day, however, he was the only one calling things exactly as he saw them, and speaking out on a topic that lit a fire in him. "I don't know about the rest of you, but this is not acceptable!" Clearly agitated, he strode purposefully to the front of the room and seemed to make eye contact with every person in the room. Pointing accusatorily to the results on the screen, eyes never losing contact with his audience, he continued "Please let me know if you disagree, but this is not acceptable for our patients, our staff, or for St. Mary's Hospital. We *can* do better, and believe me, we *will* do better." Frank had put a flag into the hilltop, and there was no public dissent. We had done a lot of work already—pulling together a team, developing our charter and goals—but make no mistake: That moment marked the official kick-off of the improvement project and the point at which hand hygiene became a key priority for the hospital.

The following weeks and months were filled with many formal meetings aligned within the Define-Measure-Analyze-Improve-Control framework for meaningful improvement, as we sought first to understand the nature of our hand-washing problem and its root causes. Ultimately, we learned about ourselves and the very nature of leading improvement efforts. My preconceived notion that culture would naturally follow a good process was wrong—culture is an entity unto itself and requires the "soft" skills of human relationships that are so much more difficult than the "hard" statistical and tools-based skills one usually thinks of in improvement science. We used many Six Sigma tools, to be sure, and applied statistics and analysis to turn data into information. It boiled down, however, to people believing in the importance of what we were doing and having their hearts swayed as much as their minds.

The real change happened when the team felt personally connected to our goal.

The real change happened when the team felt personally connected to our goal. Personal accountability grew from their relationships with other people in the hospital. Remember those "formal" meetings I mentioned? Turns out those were less important than the impromptu hallway conversations we had. Usually these were with subject-matter experts (they are everywhere in health care, and probably where you work too; you just have to listen). These informal discussions usually started with a topic (seemingly) unrelated to the project at hand. In one particular case for me, it was a conversation with Ellen Smith, another of our infection prevention nurses. Ellen was fond of telling me how she had built up her immune system by walking barefoot in cow manure as a child on the farm. She swore there is no feeling quite as pleasant as warm manure squeezing between your toes!

After reminding me of this story again, Ellen started to tell me about her teenaged son, Brandon, and their upcoming plans to head to Disney World. I was always amazed at how much Ellen and her family, and specifically her son, Brandon, loved Disney and the Power Rangers. They structured their vacations around visiting Disney World, and their family became personally known to the Disney staff and performers there. I appreciated hearing about their joyful and playful experiences, and it gave me a glimmer of understanding of how special each moment was because Brandon faced many serious health challenges. In fact, their ability to go to Disney was often in the balance because of these health challenges. As a patient of multiple heart surgeries, Brandon also grasped this. Even as a 15-year-old patient, he was his own best health care advocate, asking each person who entered his hospital room, "Have you washed your hands?" and rewarding them with candy if they had. He knew better than most that hand hygiene defends against the spread of infections by eliminating or minimizing the human hands as a vehicle of their spread. From nurses to family members, no one (including the surgeon) was spared his pointed question and expectant look and everyone—I mean everyone—complied with that expectation. Everyone knew that failure to do so put Brandon's very life at risk, and his withering gaze would shame anyone right out of the room otherwise.

As Ellen shared this story about her son, I could feel the weight of meaning and importance behind the work we were doing, even more compelling than when I learned about the huge impact of the efforts of Semmelweis and Nightingale. It was this strong impulse and desire to protect those we love and care about most deeply that suddenly revealed itself in that conversation. This was why we were trying to improve hand hygiene! How could we get others to feel this?

Melinda Reppen, my teammate and the one who had educated me about Ignaz Semmelweis, made the connection with our data and came up with the idea of a question that would make it personal for everyone in the organization. We knew our compliance rate was just below 75%. We had surveyed over 500 health care workers to test their knowledge of the hand washing process and, contrary to popular belief, 95% knew the appropriate hand-hygiene process.

Applying the pareto principle to determine the 20% of causes that were driving 80% of the problem, we also gleaned from the survey responses that the majority of people just accepted that they were not going to wash their hands every single time simply because they felt they did not have time. In effect, our health care team had resigned themselves to hand washing only *some* of the time!

"According to our data," Mel said, "Our staff are essentially admitting they only wash their hands for three out of four patients! What if we asked people the question: Who is it okay for us not to wash our hands for?" As we mulled this over, she refined her question in this manner: "You have four family members in the hospital. For which one of them shall we tell the care team not to wash their hands?"

When Mel asked this question at what we called our "hand-hygiene champions" meeting, the team not only embraced the realization of hand washing as foundational to effective healthcare but also became downright indignant. There are none of our family members that it's okay to skip handwashing for! This was the moment we had been waiting for, the moment the unit champions stopped saying, "Just tell us what you want us to do." This marked the moment of collective personal ownership of the possibilities, the stakes went up, and the scales started to tip in our favor.

From this point forward, the ideas from the team, the champions, providers, and the front-line staff flowed prodigiously. We had a notion that a hand-hygiene toolkit would be helpful, and this newfound ownership filled the Improve phase of that project with impactful and meaningful solutions. The team developed a hand-hygiene pledge, accompanied by the image of a raised hand. These pledges were overlaid onto the palm of the raised hand and blown up to poster size. The posters were then signed by all front-line staff and providers and posted publicly in each unit.

Everyone was provided with a pin-on button featuring the upraised hand and the statement "Ask me if my hands are clean." Prompting this question from our patients and visitors was at first opposed by many physicians, who claimed opening the door for this query represented an abdication of our own responsibility to simply wash our hands. Because our data showed providers too often have the lowest rates of compliance across roles, their resistance was not surprising. This actually convinced the improvement team of the potential of the buttons to engage other stakeholder groups, including patients and visitors, in the crucial process of hand hygiene. After all, like Brandon, patients need to be their own best health care advocates, and who are we to question their right to question us?

Raising one's hand actually became a non-verbal signal adopted across the hospital as a way to quickly alert someone, including physicians, if they had missed a hand washing opportunity, especially before or after patient contact. We developed new hand-hygiene promotion posters every month and implemented a contest for the best hand-hygiene videos and posters. We trained hand-hygiene champions and practice observers; every unit's data was shared on the intranet. The champions developed checklists to assess a department's approaches and support for hand hygiene, touching on everything from the pledge to the placement of sinks and hand sanitizer dispensers.

Our rate of compliance at St. Mary's became an eagerly awaited result each month, and departments were eager to see the impact of the changes they had made. All of these approaches collectively became our "hand-hygiene system" that steadily helped improve hand-washing practice. Staff from across the street at our clinic started to notice and ask for hand-hygiene buttons and toolkit resources. Patients and visitors started to take notice and were empowered to ask us if our hands were clean. Hand washing became an organizational imperative, and the results followed.

Not only did we improve to climb out of last place, but St. Mary's Hospital became the highest-performing ministry in the SSM system, with a hand-hygiene rate of 99% before and after patient contact. This level was sustained for years after the hand-hygiene team disbanded. We also identified a correlation to a statistically significant reduction in our infection rate.

St. Mary's Hospital became the highest-performing ministry in the SSM system...

~

At St. Mary's Hospital, we focused on one of our most important fundamental health care goals and obligations. We learned about the importance of making change and improvement personal in order to positively impact the culture. (Sorry my improvement compatriots, a good process just isn't enough!).

Remember this story the next time you are faced with the need for improvement on all fronts, or when you are presented with an improvement opportunity that doesn't seem quite compelling at first, or when someone tells you something's important to them but seems unrelated to what you're asking about. Somewhere in the morass of opportunity there is a fundamental imperative crying out for your attention. It may not move you at first, but inspiration is often a matter of perception. Everything is related, and this connection is not the least reason that when someone shares something with us, we must listen.

Finally, ask the questions that make the vision of change personal for those implementing it. Ask the questions that, when answered, help people understand the ability and responsibility to change is in our hands. Purpose connects people to the process; this human connection generates the change. And yes, in case you're wondering, my hands are clean.

Matt Albert is a member of the SSM Health Continuous Improvement team, serving in the Wisconsin region since 2008. His guiding objective is to create and foster conditions for improvement and innovation in life and work. Matt has spent the past twenty years developing quality management and improvement systems with service, government, military, and health care teams. He has an MBA in Health Systems Leadership from Edgewood College, has served as a Baldrige Examiner, and is a Certified Six Sigma Black Belt (ASQ).

Questions for Reflection and Discussion

1. What steps can be taken to ensure an optimal balance between accurate metrics and the human and cultural ingredients necessary for any successful change effort? (Look back at what the author's team did.)
2. Why is informal human interaction so important to successful change efforts? Give one or two examples of how this worked from your own life or that of someone you observed.
3. Name a process that you would like to improve in your own organization or world. What metrics would you collect to help understand the process and identify potential improvements? Which of these metrics would be compelling to people in your organization, like the metrics on clean hands in this story?

From Inspection to Improvement

by Greg Simmons

Hey fellas, it's the bastard from WIPRO!

Anonymous, circa 1985

That day I drew the shortest of the straws. It was the mid-1980s. Our board president, a local radiologist, had triple-booked himself for speaking engagements that night. He took the most attractive venue, made apologies to another, and handed the third (and most fraught) to me. The Milwaukee County Osteopathic Association (MCOA) was having their monthly meeting on the south side of the city and wanted to hear from someone from the Wisconsin Peer Review Organization (WIPRO), later renamed MetaStar. More accurately, they wanted to pillory someone from WIPRO for what they considered to be our intrusion into their osteopathic practices. I called the association's president to get the logistics—time, place, other expectations. I had been warned that he was difficult to deal with, but when I asked what to expect, he joked, "Cocktails at six, dinner at seven, castration at eight, and crucifixion at nine."

That didn't sound at all encouraging, even as a joke. At the same time, I knew I had to represent our organization, so I prepared for the evening the best I could.

I arrived that night part way through the cocktail hour. From across the bar, someone yelled: "Hey fellas, it's the bastard from WIPRO!" I had never been introduced that way before in my life—and I was pretty sure that my parents' marriage had been well-documented for fidelity—but there was little doubt that the osteopath in question was referring to me.

"Cocktails at six, dinner at seven, castration at eight, and crucifixion at nine."

After some polite conversation and a few somewhat more polite introductions, we moved to the dining room for the remainder of the evening's festivities. I was sweating like a proverbial pig. I sat at the main table and engaged in some small talk as one does. I happened to notice one of my own board members sitting a few tables away and seized on that fact as a way of making some positive connection between myself and the group. I mentioned this to the MCOA president, "Oh, there is Dr. C! He is on our board." Without a pause, the president informed me, "Dr. C is an idiot!". That further lowered the level of collegiality I expected that evening, and while the event actually wasn't the most acrimonious I attended in those days I was very glad when the meeting ended with my scalp intact. To this day, I don't remember what I said to the semi-hostile crowd.

~

Some dozen years before that convivial event, the U.S. Congress had come to a realization: The two healthcare programs launched in the mid-1960s, Medicare and Medicaid, were spending way beyond what had been forecast. Also, there was no way to tell whether or not the services being rendered were of good, bad, or indifferent quality. In response,

Congress created a national program that would be run by physician peers and would judge the need for and quality of care given to those patients. Originally, several hundred local peer review organizations were established across the country to assure that medical services—chiefly hospital services at this point—met professionally-recognized standards. By the mid-eighties there was one such organization covering all of Wisconsin, the Wisconsin Peer Review Organization (WIPRO).

WIPRO reviewed hospital medical records by the thousands—up to 70,000 a year at the peak—looking for lapses in care that could raise questions about the quality of the medical services being provided. If one of our physician reviewers had questions about the care, a letter would go out to the attending physicians asking for further information and sometimes an explanation for why they had provided the care in the way they did. Since these letters were literally questioning the skill, knowledge, and follow-through of doctors, they felt confrontational. If you got a letter from WIPRO, it was akin to getting one from the IRS—a comparison we heard over and over. There was also the potential for Medicare to deny payment for a hospital stay that was judged to have involved poor quality care. This created a lot of bad feelings toward WIPRO among doctors and hospitals. Steve Laking, our chief operating officer, and I would joke about carrying flak jackets in our cars, and I only half-jokingly extolled the virtues of having a back-corner office, thinking I could be more easily forewarned of the appearance of an irate visitor who might have breached our security.

As time went on executives from WIPRO became "popular" additions to the meeting agendas of hospital medical staffs and groups representing hospitals, doctors, medical records professionals, and hospital financial officers—such as the Milwaukee County Osteopathic Association. We were all deeply lodged in what we called a "Quality Assurance" model. First, experienced nurses on our staff would screen medical records. Their results were then presented to peer physician reviewers to render professional opinions regarding other doctors' care—without seeing the patients themselves, of course. An appeal to a second physician reviewer after a negative review was also available. That resulted in three levels of checking. Ultimately a practitioner who didn't agree with a ruling could appeal to an administrative law judge who was not bound by the findings of previous reviewers, adding yet another such level. Inspection upon inspection upon inspection. Defects were occasionally found as a result of this drawn-out process, and sometimes they were serious. But most of the time, they were not.

Defects were occasionally found as a result of this drawn-out process, but most of the time, they were not.

~

In the early 1990s, because of concerns raised by the American Medical Association and others, the federal Institute of Medicine (IOM) did a thorough review of this program, by then known as the Peer Review Organization (PRO) Program. The IOM concluded that the program was unnecessarily confrontational in its design and that, while it could uncover an occasional case of egregiously poor quality, it was not set up to systematically improve care for large populations of patients. This was their way of saying that looking for defects was less effective in protecting patients and the Medicare Trust Fund than a broader plan for improvement. This led the national Health Care Financing Administration (HCFA) to embark on a redesign of the work to refocus on systematic improvement of medical care as opposed to relying on inspection of potential outlying bad apples.

This shift in vision created new opportunities for improving healthcare. The first experiment was an effort entitled the Cooperative Cardiovascular Project (CCP). The idea was to base collaborative learning on established science-based indicators of cardiac care and collect data on trends in those indicators over time. WIPRO was chosen as one of four initial state-wide organizations to test this methodology. Officials at HCFA had been influenced by Donald Berwick, MD, and others who had begun to adopt the teachings and tools of W. Edwards Deming and his disciples. Statewide PROs, including WIPRO, accessed in-house instruction in systemic improvement to support this new effort. Physicians with backgrounds in public health and preventive medicine joined PRO staffs to recruit physician champions to work with local participating hospitals. For example, Jay Gold, MD, joined our staff to fill the role. Measurable improvements in care began to be achieved. Data indicated that lives were saved and further disease prevented as hospitals adopted expert systems of more reliable care. WIPRO itself established a company-wide training plan in continuous improvement and introduced these tenets into all parts of our operations.

In the following years, HCFA sponsored more hospital projects in improving the quality of care, including efforts in surgical site infection reduction, early treatment of stroke and heart attack in emergency departments, and many others. WIPRO found eager participants among many professionals in Wisconsin hospitals, and tangible improvements were implemented, decreasing suffering and death for many patients. In one project focusing on central line-associated bloodstream infections, we documented substantially fewer deaths experienced by the patients at participating institutions than otherwise would have occurred.

As the continuous improvement approach to healthcare was catching on nationwide, local supportive organizations arose, the Madison Quality Improvement Network (MAQIN) being one of the earliest and most successful. Through a fortunate set of circumstances WIPRO became MAQIN's landlord and began to learn from and to collaborate with their members and staff on our own improvement training.

Local supportive organizations arose.

Dr. Berwick and others founded the Institute for Healthcare Improvement in Boston and developed a design for collaborative learning known as The Breakthrough Series that incorporated the Model for Improvement based on Deming's original work with refinements by Tom Nolan and others. Many PROs, including WIPRO, made wide use of these techniques in leading improvement efforts. As an unaffiliated and therefore non-interest-conflicted convener, WIPRO was able to bring potentially competitive institutions together to share best practices and accelerate improvement. During this time, following the IOM's advice, HCFA dropped the widespread and much maligned review of medical records as a way of inspecting for quality defects. Continuous improvement in WIPRO's work—internal and external—was off and running! We weren't wearing the black hats anymore. We were providing technical assistance and support that actually helped providers improve their outcomes and, at the same time, also increased their satisfaction with their healthcare delivery in a noncompetitive and blame-free environment. The transformation of our work from inspection to improvement was near complete.

The transformation of our work from inspection to improvement was near complete.

In 1996, in recognition of its transformation to a quality improvement organization, WIPRO embarked on a process of restructuring its governance, its internal culture, and its public image in order to maximize its effectiveness in the larger community. We took a traditional board of trustees of twenty-one doctors, very much patterned after a medical association board, and reconstituted it as a total of twelve people—physicians, nurses, business representatives, and public members who were beneficiaries of the healthcare programs on whose behalf we worked. Staff were guided by the work of writers like Alfie Kohn and Peter Block, which gave us guidance on the type of workplace culture that would best support continuous improvement in collaboration and empowerment. A thorough review of our own personnel programs resulted in the removal of counterproductive practices such as rating, merit pay, and annual evaluations. Senior leaders committed themselves to developing an environment of trust, openness, and respect that would remove barriers to improvement. As a final and more public acknowledgement of the organization's transformation and new role in the community, we adopted the new name, MetaStar, a word meaning "guiding change." The federal government officially (and somewhat typically bureaucratically) changed the designation of contractors like MetaStar from Peer Review

Organizations (PROs) to Quality Improvement Organizations (QIOs). New life in the continuous improvement industry had officially begun.

~

In the late 1990s, additional opportunities for applying MetaStar's expertise in healthcare improvement began to emerge. HCFA–now the Centers for Medicare and Medicaid Services (CMS)—saw the value of using QIOs and their experience with hospitals to help achieve better care in nursing homes. Consequently, HCFA contracted with places like MetaStar to provide collaborative improvement assistance to long-term care facilities. This turned out to be great news for nursing homes. For decades the only outside stimulus for improving the nursing home industry had been the heavy hand of a survey and certification process that was the most stringent of inspection regimes. Inspectors from state government would look for violations of rules and codes that could result in the levying of significant fines, penalties that many facilities could hardly afford and which, arguably, could cripple their ability to marshal the resources necessary for the very improvement that was being called for. MetaStar's contracts with CMS received the enthusiastic support of the nursing home associations in Wisconsin: Wisconsin Homes and Services for the Aging (WHASA) and The Wisconsin Health Care Association (WHCA). In collaboration with the Wisconsin Department of Health Services, MetaStar has provided improvement learning and technical assistance to the vast majority of Wisconsin's 400 nursing facilities for over twenty years.

The first decade of the new century introduced MetaStar to the outpatient setting. CMS contracted with MetaStar and other QIOs to offer technical assistance to small physician offices in the adoption and "meaningful use" (read: for quality improvement) of health information technology—i.e., electronic medical records. After a successful pilot program, the national Department of Health and Human Services (HHS) offered contracts to organizations to be extension centers for this work. MetaStar, with the encouragement of other Wisconsin statewide healthcare organizations, took on this additional role. The Wisconsin Health Information Technology Extension Center (WHITEC) was formed and enrolled physician practices throughout the state in programs using continuous improvement approaches for the adoption and use of IT in healthcare. Our experience, neutrality, and lack of a specific healthcare sector constituency made MetaStar the natural choice to spearhead this effort.

As MetaStar's reputation as a systemic improvement partner grew, we took on more community responsibility as a neutral convener not only of healthcare organizations but of the wider business community as it, too, dealt with improvement issues. As a tenant in the MetaStar building, MAQIN shared resources with MetaStar—meeting rooms, a librarian, eventually administrative staff. As businesses became aware of the fact that continuous improvement was an extensive change process and not an instantaneous fix, however, some began to curtail their investment in their improvement efforts and local support organizations like MAQIN began to lose members and needed more support. MetaStar provided office space and other services pro bono. I joined the MAQIN board and served as chair for a number of years.

~

When patient safety arose as a new emphasis in healthcare quality, MetaStar agreed in 2009 to staff and support a newly reconfigured collaborative workgroup known as Patient Safety Wisconsin.

In the meantime, MAQIN had transformed itself into the Wisconsin Center for Performance Excellence and was responsible for the Wisconsin Forward Award. (WFA is the program for recognition of business excellence based on the Malcolm Baldrige National Quality Award. The WFA was launched in 1997 by then Governor Tommy Thompson.) MetaStar provided a home and a staffing arrangement for the WCPE. MetaStar staff have served on the organization's board and as WFA examiners. MetaStar completed four WFA award applications over the years, all winning recognition, culminating in the highest designation—Excellence—in 2017.

Focusing on processes has proven to be both more satisfying and more effective than inspecting for defects.

MetaStar has, in the 2000s, branched out into a number of additional activities including healthcare data auditing, oversight of state programs for community-based services, and provision of continuing medical education events. Continuous improvement is the core of our organization's approach to supporting those we serve. Focusing on collaborative learning and continuous improvement thinking and processes has proven to be both more satisfying and more effective than inspecting for defects. It has led to the formation of strong partnerships of mutual trust for MetaStar staff, its customers, and those who benefit from its services.

For MetaStar and those it serves, the new approach to continuous improvement truly has turned out to be good news. And, as far as I know, none of our employees has ever again been threatened with crucifixion or called "The bastard from . . . ." At least not to their face!

Greg Simmons was the CEO of MetaStar, a nonprofit healthcare quality improvement consulting firm, for thirty-two years. During his time there, he took on national leadership positions in his industry and chaired a learning collaborative comprised of colleagues from similar organizations. In addition to his work at MetaStar, he has been active in his local community as a trustee of numerous social service agencies and educational institutions. He has a master's degree in Health Services Administration from the University of Wisconsin-Madison.

Questions for Reflection and Discussion

1. To which approach do you personally respond best: Inspection or Improvement? Explain your answer with examples.
2. What do you think is the proper role of outside consultants and supportive organizations in the process of creating positive change? List three or more things that they can do that "insiders" cannot.
3. In your experience, why do people fear or at least suspect change? How can you begin to help overcome resistance at a local institutional level? Tell of one time when you have seen this happen successfully.

Faster, Less Costly, More Effective

by Kurt Southworth

Growing up, I had always aspired to become a helicopter pilot in the military. As a son in a family with a rich military history, I often dreamed of one day having the opportunity to serve as my father had, and his father before him.

Having just returned from a deployment to Iraq and serving as a newly promoted Major in the Wisconsin Army National Guard, I was attracted to continuous improvement and wanted to leave my organization in a better place. I shared my vision with my fellow Majors, and we decided to tackle an issue that had been hanging over us for some time—helicopter pilot readiness.

When pilots return from flight school to their unit, they are designated Readiness Level 3 (RL3)—the basic level of readiness. They receive base and advanced mission-task training when they return to their assigned unit, including multi-ship, external loads, and combat maneuvering flight. Through training and evaluation, pilots eventually achieve Readiness Level 1 (RL1) status after demonstrating proficiency in all assigned mission tasks. This process can take up to two years for National Guard aviators. Unlike active-duty Army pilots, they return to their civilian employment upon graduation from flight school, and their remaining flight training competes with their civilian and family commitments.

In 2011, the Madison-based helicopter battalion had just returned from a one-year tour in Iraq. Large deployments are a heavy lift in the lives of everyone involved. On returning home, people start to question their future commitment and you see an uptick in retirements. On the flip side, you see an influx of new pilots to fill existing positions. These changes increased our pool of pilots undergoing RL progression training by almost 300%, and our pilot readiness at the time had declined from the Army standard of 75% to well below 50% over the previous ten years. This decline had a direct and negative impact on the state emergency response and federal mobilization readiness standard of 85%. We knew we had to do something to improve.

Each year, however, we spent the same or more dollars in training and logistical support without improvement to our aviator readiness. My fellow Majors and the State Aviation Officer felt there must be a better approach to training our pilots. We decided to form a team to apply the principles of systemic improvement we had learned in a shared Master Program in Quality Systems Management from the National Graduate School of Quality Management to see if we could make a difference.

Dan Russ and I, along with a guiding coalition, created a charter to look at the problem. As is the case with many improvement initiatives, we were met with many skeptics and those who felt that, as they put it, "If there were a better way to get this done, someone would have thought of it already." Others simply assumed the current training was the most efficient and productive way to produce highly trained helicopter pilots—otherwise "someone else" would have let us know the process needed to be changed. But senior leadership finally saw the value in making this improvement project a priority for the state, and they overruled the skeptics.

"If there were a better way to get this done, someone would have thought of it already."

~

The Wisconsin National Guard was no stranger to continuous improvement. We had a Total Integrated Management System (TIMS) Team to work on improvement, and we were dedicated to its continuation. TIMS was a nationally recognized group of soldiers applying Baldrige principles. TIMS efforts included an organization self-assessment, strategic planning, tracking goals and objectives as part of our Strategic Management System, and seeking out quality improvement projects like this one to improve pilot training.

We began by defining the problem and quickly developed a process map to portray the current or "As Is" process of training helicopter pilots. We found this process had continued in the current state for well over a decade with little or no refinement. Although a basic tool, the process map spoke volumes and highlighted areas ripe for improvement. We also noted that the current training process is standardized throughout Army National Guard Aviation, making it easy to implement our project within the National Guard should we find areas to improve. We found that even though the training was standardized, the timeline in which to complete the training varied greatly depending on a soldier's status upon his or her return from active-duty flight school.

Realizing the training timeline was critical, we were able to use the current pilots in the training program to collect some basic measurements. We captured relevant metrics, to include the time needed to complete the training for Guardsmen both with and without conflicting civilian occupations. We also analyzed hundreds of flight records for current and retired pilots. We found that the timeline was very "ad hoc" and "Ill-defined," which significantly impacted our helicopter pilot readiness.

We quickly developed a process map to show us the current or "As Is" process of training helicopter pilots.

In addition to the timeline, we also analyzed the financial impacts of the various training timelines. To be as effective as possible, we chose to test a few variables in the training timeline and measure the results. Would they help or hurt what we were trying to accomplish?

~

A National Guard soldier's time is limited. The military seldom keeps you in a position for more than about two years, so we needed to get things off the ground quickly. We landed upon three different target groups and applied different strategies to accomplish the training goal for each of them:

1. Some trainees continued with the "As Is" process, flying Additional Flight Training Periods (AFTPs) when it worked out with their civilian employment.

2. Others used a mix of AFTPs and the two weeks we referred to as our "Annual Training" where we conducted fifteen consecutive days of training.
3. The final group of pilots stayed on active status for thirty consecutive days following flight school to facilitate their readiness level progression.

After ten months of collecting data, the analysis said it all.

1. Group one, which consisted of pilots who used just AFTPs, had the highest number of flight hours used, the highest number of days to progress, and the highest total cost.
2. The group two pilots who used Annual Training and AFTPs used 10-12% fewer days to progress, 20% fewer flight hours, and 25% less total cost than those in group 1.
3. Finally, the pilots who used continuous orders took 50% fewer days and 30% fewer flight hours to progress, and we showed a 35% reduction in total cost.

After ten months of collecting data, the analysis said it all.

Although the numbers were clear that group three demonstrated the improvements we were looking for, we needed to consider the impact on soldiers. We worried, for example, that—for soldiers returning from a year or more away from home for initial flight training–extending the duty for an additional month could impact them and the organization in ways we might not understand. Accordingly, we surveyed current and former pilots who had participated in the various training scenarios. All agreed that the continuous orders had no negative impact on their family or civilian employer. The consensus was that since they were already away from home for at least a year, an additional thirty days was no issue, especially considering the return on investment for the rest of the organization.

With the data compilation and analysis complete, we approached our sponsor and presented our findings. Within weeks, we worked out the funding stream and the instructor pilot availability to begin training new returning pilots in the 30-day continuous orders method.

When good people apply the basics of continuous improvement, results tend to take care of themselves.

Over the next five years, we cemented the changes in our Standard Operating Procedures and clearly documented the defined and repeatable process for future commanders to follow. We averaged a $3,500 reduction in training cost per pilot, $12,000 in saved flight hours per pilot, and a 50% reduction in training time for progression from RL3 to RL1. Together with other improvement efforts, we have drastically reduced the time and money required to progress new pilots for RL3 to RL1 and have attained a sustained readiness level well above 75%. Our past performance was at or below national standards, and now we showed at or above performance—the highest we have ever been. Now our program is a benchmark standard for other states to follow. As you can see, this results from great people applying quality principles to make a positive difference in the world and, in particular, a difference in the readiness of Wisconsin Army National Guard helicopter pilots.

These strategies and lessons learned have been shared with aviation organizations around the United States to increase readiness for all. When good people apply the basics of quality and continuous improvement, results tend to take care of themselves. As it turns out, it makes no difference if you are in the military, business, health and social services, education, community organizations, or elsewhere; you can use the practical principles of continuous improvement to make a significant difference in the world.

Lt. Colonel Kurt Southworth serves as the Director of Quality for the Department of Health Services within the Division of Care and Treatment Services for the State of Wisconsin. He also serves as the Deputy Commander for the Wisconsin Army National Guard's 64th Troop Command.

Questions for Reflection and Discussion

1. What arguments against making change do you hear in your organization or institution? How do you respond to them? Be specific.
2. What kind of data would you need to make the change you want to lead? How would you get it?
3. Lt. Colonel Southworth compared his unit's pilot readiness and training costs to national norms and so jump-started improvement. With what state, national, or industry norms do you or could you compare your unit's outcomes?

Chapter Six

People, Culture, Community

Introduction

Creating a Wave!

Imagine a room full of workers, all having their own individual job instructions; no one seeing the others' instructions. The boss in the room says, "Start," and the room begins popping, people standing up and sitting back down, randomly, all over the room.

The boss asks the customers who are watching through a one-way mirror, "Is this what you were looking for? Are you satisfied?" The customers are clearly disappointed. The boss tells the workers to try harder, their jobs depend on the customers being happy, and she again says, "Start!" The room starts popping again, only with more energy, people popping higher, making more grunting noises. The employees are trying hard! The boss notices one worker who is really trying hard and invites him to the stage to be awarded Worker of the Month.

But the customers? They're still not happy. "Not buying it!" says one.

Finally, the boss pushes the pause button and asks the workers what they need to do their job to the customers' satisfaction.

"We don't have any idea what we are trying to create," says one.

"We only know our own piece of the puzzle," says another.

Then the boss invites the customers into the room to explain to the employees what their expectations are. They say, "We came here to see the wave."

The workers look again at their instructions: "Wait until the person next to you stands up and then starts to sit down. Then you stand up and then you sit down." Everyone has the same instructions. "Oh, you want us to do a wave like at a baseball game. We know how to do THAT!".

Now that the employees realize what the end product is supposed to be, suddenly their instructions have context. They can adjust their actions to those of people around them. Their combined efforts can create the "wave" that the customers "came to see."

The boss says, "Start!" and the employees work interdependently to create a wave. The customers clap and cheer. Some of them even join the wave!

~

Next, the boss asks the employees how they might improve their product for the customers. They talk among themselves and decide how they can make the wave smoother and more fun: throw up their arms as they stand, put the wave to music, and lots of other ideas—some good and some not so good! When the boss says, "Start," the room becomes a thing of beauty—a rolling wave of human beings set to music from *The Nutcracker*.

The customers begin to come back and bring others, because they have been delighted before and want to be delighted again.

~

Most workers try to do a good job. They take pride in their work. They want to go home at the end of the day and feel they accomplished something. If workers only know their own piece of the puzzle, however, they have limited ability to act interdependently as part of a team, and ultimately to produce an outcome that meets the needs of their customers, whomever they might be. Here are six stories about creating an environment that enables people to do their best work, leading to delighted employees and customers alike by Maury Cotter, Tom Mosgaller, Karen Crossley, Kathleen A. Paris, Denis Leonard, and Anonymous.

Pull v. Push

by Maury Cotter

A line of students wrapped around the block and marched right across the front page of the city's newspaper that Chancellor Donna Shalala opened that morning at breakfast. Students were unhappily waiting to pay their tuition bills at the Bursar's office as they arrived for the fall semester. Chancellor Shalala wasn't happy either. She was quick to contact the Bursar's office, calling for a more efficient process and no more lines! An employee team from the Bursar's office used newly developed quality improvement tools to streamline the payment process quickly and successfully, resulting in no more lines. And so, began another way of looking at achieving excellence at the University of Wisconsin-Madison.

After this impromptu beginning, I was hired to help form, and later lead, the university's Office of Quality Improvement. Focusing on non-academic aspects of student life, like the Bursar's project, provided quick gains, low hanging fruit so to speak, without confronting the academic traditions so sacred to colleges and universities. Our focus was on reforming and improving, using common sense ideology, a framework that did not arouse suspicion or opposition from a more traditional academic culture. In other words: It was a "pull," not a "push" approach.

And this became our approach to introducing quality improvement in higher education culture. In the words of Robert Pater in his book *Leading from Within:*

In the martial arts, the most effective way to move people is to:

first make contact with them,
then join with their direction of movement,
and finally,
to steer them to the desired course.

We needed to understand the culture and work with it.

To do what we needed to do to achieve quality excellence at UW-Madison, we needed not to focus on trying to change the university culture, but to understand it and work with it. To listen and understand. To help people move toward what they cared about. This concept is summed up for me in the phrase "Pull v. Push." You can see this play out at the macro level as leaders set a tone and direction; and it plays out at the micro level in individual, everyday interactions. Culture is everything you do, how you do it, and even why you do it. That isn't just true at the UW-Madison. Every organization has a culture; and understanding that culture is essential to successful change efforts. It was true then and it is true now. Think of Push as directing, requiring, judging, perhaps even ordering with consequences. Think of Pull as inviting, inspiring, clearing paths, and perhaps even incentivizing with positive recognition.

As I reflect on our efforts to make change inside our university culture, what stands out to me is not some clearly defined and followed path, but "Aha" moments. Moments of wise leadership. Moments of crisis. Moments of serendipity. Here are a few of those stories.

~

This is a story of sustained momentum, largely due to an extraordinary succession of aligned leaders. When Chancellor Donna Shalala moved on to become part of the Clinton cabinet as Secretary of Education in 1993, David Ward became Chancellor and John Wiley became Provost. When David left and became President of the American Council on Education, John became Chancellor. A few years later, David returned to serve as interim chancellor for two years. This provided nearly twenty years of amazing continuity: three leaders who were aligned in values and priorities (although wildly different in style). That continuity of strategic leadership, each committed to improvement, enabled sustained focus and progress, netting major advancements in research and education, infrastructure renewal, philanthropic growth, (and even multiple Rose Bowls).

Of course, this was about more than just simple continuity of leadership. Coming from the outside, Donna had promoted David and John as insiders respected in the academic community. She had also chosen other people who shared her values and priorities. There was a sense of mutual respect among them. Also, as they passed the baton, each did not feel a need to put his/her/their own identity on things, or discredit previous paths. Instead, they built on each other's shoulders. This approach to succession from Shalala as an outsider built a foundation that was sustained for over twenty years at UW-Madison and continues to this day in many ways.

Donna said she planned it that way, appointing David and John as two young, respected, and progressive future leaders. David agrees, but John says it was all an accident!

~

When David Ward became provost, he realized that there were a few important things that should be prioritized and advanced.

Consultant Brian Joiner helped us realize how important a strategic plan could be. But David knew it wouldn't work in our academic culture for him to declare a set of priorities. As it happened, a couple of years earlier, UW-Madison had completed its ten-year accreditation review by the Higher Learning Commission, including a faculty-led self-study. David Ward read their self-study summary, *Future Directions,* a document that presented six priorities for the future. These priorities were almost exactly aligned with his own thinking. Here was an instant "strategic plan" from a document that had been sitting on a shelf. He didn't call it that, though. He added a couple of priorities, put them on an overhead projector slide and used that outline as he talked with audiences ranging from faculty governance groups to donors to students. He put resources behind the priorities and shaped key positions to be responsible for implementing them. Major initiatives were usually led by faculty.

As tangible outcomes emerged, one day it was time to write it down, and the university had its first ever written strategic plan. Over the next two decades, we kept strategic planning integrated with the reaccreditation process and also expanded engagement in the planning process with over 6000 faculty, staff, alumni, donors, and community members. But I would argue that David's one-page overhead slide was perhaps the best plan we ever had. It was clearly communicated, well resourced, and actively executed. By building the plan based on priorities identified in a faculty led self-study, and always co-owning it with the faculty, David had created a powerful "Pull." As he often said, "The most radical thing I did was to take a plan off the shelf and implement it."

"The most radical thing I did was to take a plan off the shelf and implement it."

~

As John Wiley said recently: "Changing culture was never foremost in my mind; just doing things better." Although I didn't try to change the culture at UW-Madison, I did get eaten up and spit out several times for not understanding it! Having come from outside higher education, it was new to me. But I worked with colleagues to listen, learn, and honor it, and to understand what aspects of the culture pulled people to act. They included: new knowledge, discovery, truth; educating the next generation; application of knowledge to solve local and world problems; and clearing the clutter to be able to do those things as uninterrupted and unimpeded as possible. The more we learned, the more we appreciated not only what this culture had to contribute to improvement of our institution, but also how it could impact the world. How could we use quality approaches to help advance what was already most valued? "Just doing things better." Another Pull.

Sometimes, doing things better was urgent and necessary. For example, as described so well in the story "Working 99 to 5" by John Wiley earlier in this book, a student applying to graduate school waited an average of 99 days to receive a response. A team focused on process improvement helped shorten the admission response process to less than five days.

This graduate admissions project was a powerful demonstration. The purpose was clear—to recruit and enroll the best grad students. The results were dramatic. It was led and championed by credible leaders and was eventually recognized nationally. Those who most benefited from the improvements included the biggest initial skeptics. This one project provided a breakthrough moment. Another Pull.

Another example was Time-to-degree (TTD). TTD is an outcome metric that most students and parents care a lot about. In fact, it was a big public issue. TTD was seen as a failure for universities nationally in the 1970-1980s, with average TTD around six years. This could not continue. Today, UW-Madison's TTD for an undergraduate degree regularly hovers just below four years. This dramatic level of improvement was not accomplished by a forming a stand-alone improvement project team, but the TTD goal was itself an urgent driver across the university. We took a systems-improvement approach to the problem across multiple fronts: advising, timetables, addition of classes in gateway courses, residential halls as learning communities, summer orientation, policies that protected space for freshmen in key courses, etc. All these were contributing factors to the TTD problem and were all addressed simultaneously and systematically.

These types of changes could be made in alignment with the academic culture, and everyone understood it was important to think systemically. They were addressed through a Pull, and the successful outcomes then became a Pull in themselves.

~

The chair of the History Department, Professor Ken Sacks, asked for help from our quality improvement office to improve the administrative operations of the department. Early on he knew that the department staff had been notoriously problematic for over twenty years.

Then he realized that the staff had turned over many times in twenty years. "Maybe it's not the people. Maybe it's the systems," Professor Sacks told me.

All the staff members in the History Department did their own jobs—scheduling classrooms, managing hiring, budgeting, advising—separately. If they were on vacation, their work was on vacation too. With Ken's leadership, the staff worked together as a team to transform how they provided the administrative support to the department. In the course of the improvement project, they established systems, streamlined processes, identified backups for critical functions, redesigned the office space to facilitate handoffs, collaborated to level workload peaks and valleys, and helped shape the roles of their incoming supervisor. This became an example for other departments and their chairs. Another Pull.

If they were on vacation, their work was on vacation too.

After the History Department experienced success in improving their administrative processes, I suggested to Ken that he talk with Professor Warren Porter, chair of the Zoology Department, who was interested in considering quality approaches, but Ken was reluctant. "History is so different from Zoology," he noted simply. He and I talked about how all departments have budgets, schedule classes, hire faculty, manage space, conduct research, etc. So he finally agreed to talk with Warren. Ken and Warren clicked, and an improvement effort was off and running in the Zoology Department. This time, the effort engaged the whole department, including all faculty and staff. Zoology had become a bifurcated department, with two distinct groups at odds with each other. To help identify their shared purpose, Professor Porter focused on guiding principles and strategy. Zoology defined their shared identity and aims and began collaborating across the two competing sides. Standing committees were revived and aligned. Faculty who embraced planning and process improvement went on to become department leaders. Today, thirty years later, the department is continuing to operate as a more integrated whole.

The History Department example illustrated how quality approaches can improve administrative operations. Zoology illustrated how values and strategy can strengthen the academic missions of education and research. History inspired Zoology, and they both went on to inspire many other departments. We created venues to facilitate those connections, including what we called "Chairs Chats" and an annual showcase of improvements. Throughout, we focused on willing pioneers, helping them attain success, rather than trying to convert the skeptics. A Peer-to-Peer Pull.

When colleagues from other universities visited to learn about our approaches, invariably they would ask, "How do you get everyone on board?" My response was always, "We don't." The culture of higher education is not conducive to everyone agreeing on everything. A key value in academia is to challenge ideas, to think critically, to seek truth and new understanding—not to join hands and walk in lock-step.

I would explain our thinking, and then visitors would often ask again, "Yes, but how do you get everyone on board?" David Ward came up through faculty ranks and understood the academic culture intimately. As a leader, working to advance major initiatives, he came to believe that you often only need about 15% to be on board. (Of course, it helps if that 15% includes thought leaders, or at least that most of the thought leaders aren't in the 85% and completely opposed). If you are working to get everyone to agree on a concept that you haven't yet demonstrated, it just becomes a target for critical shots. You will spend an inordinate amount of time trying to convince the tail end of the curve. But if you have about 15% willing to engage, you can build momentum and success. Then others will see it's possible and it can become a Pull.

If you have 15% willing to engage, you can build momentum and success.

One example was the creation of cluster hires. Complex problems often involve more than one area of knowledge. For example, a new energy concept might involve engineering, agriculture, biology, sociology, and more. To help address this, David Ward used a good chunk of the political capital he had built up and started a new initiative called "Cluster Hires." For these initiatives, three or four faculty would be hired to form a "cluster" to focus on a complex problem or new area of knowledge that crossed disciplines and departments. The cluster hire model was designed to engage faculty in inter-departmental collaborations.

To do this, David created a competition for new faculty appointments. Faculty across campus were invited to submit proposals for research into a new area of knowledge that crossed disciplines, and the proposals needed to be submitted in collaboration across departments. Those selected would receive three to four new faculty lines to share.

I am convinced that had this idea been put out for discussion and approval, it would have been severely criticized and taken months or even years to be approved, if ever. Imagine in your organization asking people to hire across existing major units! Even David's leadership team was skeptical of the idea. But he made it big enough to be compelling, small enough that it didn't disrupt or take too much from other initiatives, and fast—the first proposals were due in a few weeks. Over ninety projects were submitted, representing what we called "a critical mass of the willing." The idea gained favor of the governor of the state, who gave the university nineteen new faculty lines to use on biological clusters. And the state legislature liked it and awarded another hundred new lines. Before anyone could Push back, cluster hires had become a Pull.

Over ninety projects were submitted, representing "a critical mass of the willing."

Of all the tools available for improvement, I believe the most powerful is the question. If you go in as an expert and *tell* someone what they *should* do, there is a natural resistance. If you go in and ask thought-provoking questions and help facilitate deep consideration, they will own the questions... and the answers. We used this method to help units develop their strategic plans. We began by asking our clients at the university, "When your plan is completed, what questions will it answer for you?" Doing this helped energize the group and provided ownership of the planning process and the completed plan. It helped get a critical mass on board. A "question-based planning approach." A Pull.

~

In all organizations, we often stay focused on our own jobs. In academia, this is amplified by the very mission and roles of faculty—to dive deeply into a specific area to discover new knowledge, which you then "defend" and are awarded with your advanced degree. Many of the moments and opportunities for change occurred as those silos were cross-wired. Here are a few final examples:

Dr. Ian Hau was a statistics professor who used quality approaches to improve his teaching, soccer, and anything else in his path. He went on to become an executive vice-president at GlaxoSmithKline. There, he improved the process for getting a new drug to market, where each day saved a minimum of $1M. We invited him to talk with us about his approaches. One thing he taught us was how to get as much done in a process as early as possible, versus in chronological order. He showed us how they prepared a final report for a new drug approval by having the report well developed before the final data came in, ready to drop in the findings and move it forward quickly. This, in contrast to gathering all information and then starting to write the report. Sue Riseling, chief of UW-Madison police and security, took this concept back to her leadership team. With the same tools, they shortened the time to produce their annual report from months to a few weeks. And then they tightened the time to hire new recruits, which gave them a huge advantage in hiring the best new candidates in competition with university police departments across the nation. In the end, a pharmaceutical company's practices helped improve our police department.

The School of Business and the College of Engineering brought their respective advisory boards together to address the following two questions: What do Business majors need to know about Engineering? What do Engineering majors need to know about Business? Their answers were used to help redesign curricula in both Engineering and Business.

Similarly, when the School of Medicine was developing an online course for medical professionals to learn how to use big data to help leverage discovery and development, a major challenge was the size of the potential audience to make the program cost effective. We took the question "What do medical professionals want/need to learn about technology" and added "What do data experts want/need to know about medicine?" We more than doubled the potential audience by adding the inverted question.

Health is a complex world problem that a comprehensive university like UW-Madison is especially equipped to help advance. We created a Global Health institute with an open door to any discipline, and we developed venues to encourage and support collaboration across traditional silos. We started by identifying the most obvious disciplines, like medicine, population health, and pharmacy, but soon learned that nearly every discipline had something to offer in addressing health globally. Think about the roles of education, law, sociology, nutrition, and so many more. How could we facilitate connections across our broad campus to identify useful collaboration?

One approach was to sponsor "Ted Talks," short presentations on a range of global health efforts. One researcher told how they were addressing a problem of dying banana trees, which provided much needed sustenance in a third world community. A sociologist recognized that the local people listened to soap operas on the radio. They worked with radio shows to build into the stories a simple method that people could use to save their banana trees.

Another approach we used was "Speed Talks." Each person had two minutes (a bell comes in handy) to share the essence of their global health work, followed by an open reception for people to connect. Researchers from medicine, social work, engineering, education, law, population health, and more gathered to explore collaborations to impact health globally. Among the productive connections from these was one that stood out to me. A pediatric medical researcher used his two minutes to talk about efforts to vaccinate children in Africa, sharing the challenge of reaching and convincing parents. A psychology researcher then shared her efforts focused on exactly the problem of parents' reluctance to vaccinate. The two connected during the open reception to explore potential collaboration.

These simple methods helped people collaborate across traditional lines to address complex world problems, like global health. A Pull.

Greg came into my office and closed the door. "I just want to know... is this the way things are done around here?" he asked politely. He was a new associate vice chancellor, and he was getting his first dipping into our culture after having worked for a national bank. I don't remember the circumstances, but his was not an unusual reaction. I always tried to connect with new people, especially those coming from outside higher education, as they provided "fresh eyes" to help us see ourselves. New deans were particularly enlightening. "What is a divisional committee anyway" one new dean asked, questioning a key element of our revered but often complex governance structure.

It's so easy to assume that something must be the way it is. By looking outside, sometimes you realize that something you think is a given, is not. You don't necessarily learn a better way, but at least you realize it can be different. It allows you to ask new questions. Not just, "How can we *improve* this process?" but perhaps "Do we even need to *do* this process?" Fresh eyes open us up to bigger, bolder ideas.

In addition to listening to new people, we actively sought to learn from many on the outside, including our City of Madison public and private sector colleagues, peer institutions both locally and across the globe, and corporate America. We partnered with Fortune 500 companies through the TQ Forum. And we helped found a national network for sharing quality approaches, the Network for Change and Continuous Improvement in Higher Education (NCCI). Recently, we benchmarked with a dozen universities to help boost our efforts to build online educational options to reach new audiences.

If you are looking for breakthrough ideas, you might need to break free from the confines of your silo and cross-wire with people and places where you least expect to find solutions. A Pull.

Peter Drucker was right when he said that culture eats strategy for breakfast.

Peter Drucker was right when he said that culture eats strategy for breakfast. After the culture ate my breakfast, lunch, and dinner a few times, I realized how much power there was in honoring and working with and within the culture. Start by seeking to understand what people value and what drives them to act. Design approaches to help them connect and take action. And, when you feel like pushing, create a Pull.

Reference

Pater, R. (1999). *Leading from within: Martial arts skills for dynamic business and management.* Park Street Press.

Maury Cotter was a founder of the Office of Quality Improvement (OQI) at UW-Madison and served as director for over 20 years. Working with top leadership, she coordinated the development and implementation of the campus strategic framework and led a staff of consultants, providing consultation services for cross-campus initiatives, academic and administrative units throughout campus. Maury was a founder and past president of the Network for Change and Continuous Improvement in Higher Education (NCCI) and continues to consult with universities and companies internationally.

Questions for Reflection and Discussion

1. Describe one time you were pushed to change. Now tell of one time you were pulled to change. Which was more effective? Why?
2. If you are in academia, how do you respond to the author's descriptions of the culture there? If you are from another sector or type of institution, what are the similarities between that culture and that of academia?
3. Which of the many examples in this story hit you between the eyes? Why?

Good Enough for Government Work

by Tom Mosgaller

During the American Civil War, "Good Enough for Government" was declared a performance standard for suppliers of goods for the northern troops.

"Are you the new guy the mayor was talking about at the management team meeting this morning? The quality guru that is going to improve things around here?" His voice dripped with sarcasm and his posture was menacing.

"Yes, I'm new to government and thought it would be good to introduce myself. I was told you were a straight shooter who might have some advice for me as I start this new job." His answer:

> Well, I have been a department head with the city for over twenty years, came up through the ranks. Didn't get to be a guru by going to college. Frankly, I don't know why the mayor thinks we need a Quality and Productivity guru. You know the City of Madison is always ranked in the top ten on everything. We'd be ranked even higher if we didn't have snow and ice to contend with six months of the year. Can you do something about that as Q&P guru? Don't take this personally but I think we could have better spent your salary on something like a groundskeeper at one of our golf courses or even another cop, but I wasn't asked about my opinion on this one.

As I was about to leave this painfully unproductive meeting, the man closed the door, leaned across his desk, and said something I will never forget. "Mayors come and go. They each have their pet projects. This Quality and Productivity thing is one of this mayor's projects, so as a department head I played along. In the end, the mayor will feel like he got something he wanted done, we get our department budgets passed, and the city will be no worse for wear. Just don't expect anything to change, guru. The buck stops here with the department heads. We make and break mayors."

"Mayors come and go."

~

That was my "welcome to the city" introduction from one of the most powerful department heads on my first morning as the Q&P director for the City of Madison, Wisconsin.

In reality, I didn't know what the director of Q&P was supposed to do any more than he did! I surely didn't feel like a "guru." I hadn't worked inside a large city bureaucracy. My previous work was as a community organizer in the rough and tumble inner cities of Chicago and Philadelphia. I had also organized farmers during the farm crisis of the 1980s. I'd never even had a real office before, and now I was two doors away from the mayor of a city with 3000 employees, fourteen labor unions, 30 different departments, and hundreds of services ranging from snow plowing to animal control that needed to be done right...and usually "right now."

The mayor, Joe Sensenbrenner, told me that I was the first Q&P director in the public sector—ever, anywhere—as far as he knew. And therefore, there was no roadmap. They were not hiring me because I was a quality expert. He knew that changing the entrenched city culture would require someone who could roll with the punches, even when there was resistance (and maybe deliver one once in a while). And who could roll with the punches better than an experienced community organizer? The mayor said there were "some of the best people around" in this "new thing called Quality Improvement" right here in Madison. He said he knew I would find them and learn what we needed to do to make it happen.

I started my job like any organizer worth his or her stripes would, going out and immersing myself in the daily work of the city. I held over 200 one-to-one meetings with department heads, union leaders, city council members, middle managers, and front-line workers. I rolled up my sleeves and picked trash, rode with the snowplow drivers, walked the neighborhoods with police officers, attended well-baby clinics with public health nurses, road the actual buses that people took to work in the morning and rode home again the same night, and sat in on fire-call debriefings with the fire fighters who actually fought the fires. I worked, I listened, and I asked a lot of questions of the real gurus—the people who did the actual work of making the city work—or in some cases—not work.

I asked a lot of questions of the real gurus, the people who did the actual work.

~

While I was doing my work, I was also witnessing the rapid emergence of the quality movement all across the country. American companies were finally waking up to the fact that other countries were eating our lunch in the marketplace, particularly the Japanese. Their commitment to quality was threatening "Made in America" as a global standard for quality and productivity. The performance of Toyota, Honda, Mitsubishi, and other global companies was forcing American manufacturing companies to rethink quality. Mayor Sensenbrenner simply figured that as American companies like Motorola, Ford, IBM, and 3M were committing to systematic improvement in quality, why couldn't we adapt the same principles to the governmental sector to make a good city even better? "Here, improvement matters" could become the mantra or the motto of the City of Madison.

The Madison community already was home to many of the early quality pioneers. The University of Wisconsin-Madison had globally recognized leaders on the faculties in statistics, engineering, and business who were more than willing to share their knowledge and practical experience with the city. These faculty members including George Box, Søren Bisgaard, and Bill Hunter, who along with Joiner and Associates' founders Brian and Lori Joiner and Peter Scholtes, were among the experts who pitched in to help the city. They, in turn, introduced us to many of the global quality luminaries including W. Edwards Deming, Joseph Juran, and Myron Tribus, who gave of their time and talent to see how quality principles they had helped develop for industry could be adapted to government.

Dr. George Box held a class on statistics at his home on Monday evenings called "Beer and Stats." He encouraged me to attend as a way of brushing up on my own statistical acumen so I could support our improvement teams in collecting data. In truth, I went for the beer and ended up lapping up the stats.

A citywide network was organized called the Madison Area Quality Improvement Network (MAQIN) that served as a model for a community approach to quality. The annual Hunter Conference, sponsored by MAQIN, was named after the late Professor Bill Hunter, who had been working with the city's first improvement project in vehicle repair of the city's motorized equipment. The annual Hunter Conference brought together thousands of local, national, and international students to learn from one another how to achieve excellence in the functioning of government and not-for-profit agencies.

As Michael Williamson told in his story "Never Waste a Crisis" elsewhere in this book, some of the city's first quality ventures addressed practical problems like turnaround time for repairing and maintaining the city's over 700 vehicles. Data showed it was taking an average of 9.5 days to get a vehicle repaired. Department heads complained to the mayor that they couldn't have important pieces of equipment out of service that long and that he should do something about the "lazy mechanics" in the City Garage.

As Michael relates, a team of motor equipment employees systematically looked at why it was taking so long and was able to reduce turnaround time down from sometimes 9-10 days down to two. They reduced the number of steps to get parts from twenty-eight down to seven. They estimated the annual savings would be$750,000. A few months later, that same team revisited the process and was able to reduce the steps from seven steps to three with the implementation of a preventive maintenance program.

Even more important than the reduction in time and the cost savings was the realization that the mechanics were *not* the problem. They worked under an outdated and ineffective purchasing system but were being blamed for the lack of productivity. Leaders from this team were later invited to Detroit to share their story with leaders of Ford Motor Company. Today if you went over to the new motor equipment facility you would see what twenty years of continuous improvement can do. The new facility is state-of-the-art and recognized nationally for everything from its use of technology, professionalism of its staff, and energy efficiency, including the first prototype electric fire truck.

Another team of Madison public works employees was working on improving the buying process for large city trucks. Historically, trucks were bought on low bid and very little attention was paid to long-term quality. The team recommended a set of criteria for evaluating bids based on life-cycle costing that included vehicle repair records. Criteria included resale value, driver preference, quality, safety, and productivity. It was revolutionary to have front line workers using data and making buying decisions. (One unexpected long-term benefit was that the staff took better care of the vehicles they bought and therefore they lasted longer.)

The staff took better care of the vehicles they bought and therefore they lasted longer.

A team from the radio shop looked at the buying process for portable field radios, which were constantly being repaired. They field tested a variety of radios and developed a set of specifications for buying radios that included operator preference and long-term reliability. The result was better radios that didn't mysteriously end up under a truck tire or getting dropped in the lake because they functioned so poorly. When end users were engaged in the purchasing process, they bought the highest quality (not necessarily the most expensive) equipment. Who'da thunk, indeed?

A team of Madison Metro Transit drivers and administrators looked at how we hired city bus drivers and realized that the process had fifty-four steps, which discouraged many qualified people from applying. No one had ever flow-charted the process to see how many steps there were. They only knew that the process was long and discouraging. The team was able to reduce the process down to fifteen steps and cut the time for hiring in half. Applicant numbers went up, and the quality of drivers improved.

In the first five years of Mayor Sensenbrenner's six-year tenure, we had hundreds of employees engaged on teams working on problems that they or our "customers" had identified as bottlenecks or barriers. As time went on and trust increased, many departmental teams asked to have members of other departments on the teams, and some even asked to have citizens on their teams to make sure they were getting direct feedback from the people affected by the city's services. We worked hard to make improvement a part of everything we did. No fancy language of "quality" and "productivity," and definitely no gurus!

At the same time, other Madison organizations were ramping up their systems-improvement work. The University of Wisconsin-Madison, American Family Insurance, Home Savings and Loan, Madison Area Technical College, CUNA Mutual Insurance, the State of Wisconsin, St. Mary's and Meriter Hospitals, and various veterans' hospitals all caught the spirit. As momentum built, hundreds of other businesses, cooperatives, and service organizations began adopting quality principles and practices in their own work.

I loved to hear of people visiting Madison taking the cab from the airport and talking to the driver about the improvement project they were working on at the Madison Cab Company. I remember the city Parks Department employees hanging satisfaction surveys on citizens' doors to get feedback on their tree trimming in the neighborhood. And Zimbrick Automotive, a private Madison company, separated itself from the competition by introducing quality principles as fundamental to their service philosophy.

One of my all-time favorite stories is about a team of garbage truck drivers trying to figure out why at 2:00 p.m. every day there was a long line of trucks queued up to dump their trash at the recycling plant. The wait could be fifty minutes to an hour. Skeptics would charge that the drivers caused the problem to avoid working, but—like so many of the problems we tackled—the problem was with the system, not with the people.

The problem was with the system, not with the people.

The employee team that tackled the disposal-waiting-time problem began by collecting data. Butch, a veteran driver, and Bill, a relative newcomer, volunteered to create a spreadsheet and collect data for two weeks showing how long trucks sat in line waiting to dump their loads of trash, and how long it then took them to get off the tipping floor and back on the street. Armed with a stopwatch and their clip boards, the two men began observing the process and documenting what they saw.

I vividly remember the meeting where Butch and Bill shared their data. They also gave a verbal walk-through of an average day for drivers, beginning at 7 a.m., making 500 stops, and heading to the recycling facility around 1:30 and then sitting in line waiting to dump their loads.

The thinking in the public works shop was that we had to build a bigger recycling plant to accommodate the time it took to dump the loads of trash—a solution that would have cost millions of dollars. Butch and Bill's data, however, showed that it only took an average of three minutes to enter, tip, and get off the tipping floor. This was not causing the queuing problem.

The team continued to pore over the data trying to figure out where they could improve the process. Wheels were turning, ideas were being thrown out (along with some very colorful language), and every single idea was being scribbled on the blackboard. Then Buck, one of the quieter team members said, "We all start at 7 a.m., both on the east and west sides of town. Right? What if we tried spreading out the starting times so we wouldn't all get to the recycling plant at the same time?" This was a moment of truth. Would the garbage truck drivers reject Buck's idea because it would mean a change in the way they had always done things, or would they see it as a possible solution worth testing? It meant half of the drivers would have to start work at 6 a.m. Would it be those on the east side or the west side of town? Or would they throw the idea out completely because they were all part of the same union and didn't want to break rank with their fellow trash collectors?

After a brief silence, Butch looked at Bill and they both agreed that they would go back to their own east side team and see if *they* would be willing to pilot the idea for six months. Bill told me later that part of the incentive they shared with their fellow east side drivers was that they could be done by 3 p.m. and get to go fishing earlier!

Ultimately, the pilot test worked, and the new process was adopted. More importantly, the drivers owned the solution and continued to adjust the recycling process to make it even better. The immediate savings in fuel from trucks idling in a queue was estimated at $30,000 per year. This, combined with eliminating the cost and long-term disruption of expanding the recycling facility, was worth millions of dollars to the city coffers.

~

Twice a year there were public presentations by our city improvement teams of the projects they had been working on. These gatherings were hosted and attended by the mayor, city council members, and city employees; and the general public was invited to attend and learn how their tax dollars were being used and—better yet—saved. The city cable channel captured the team's presentations, which were then made available to all city residents.

I arrived early at the Edgewater Hotel, where the first improvement team presentations would be held. As I walked into the hotel, I saw a big man with a long ponytail standing with his family by the big windows looking out over Lake Mendota. I didn't recognize him until he yelled for me to come over and meet his family.

It was Butch, his wife, and their three children, and Butch's mom and dad. Butch was wearing a suit and tie, and his whole family was dressed like a million bucks. After introductions I reminded Butch that the presentations didn't start for an hour. He gave me his big grin and said, "I know, Tom, but when would my family and I ever get to come to the Edgewater Hotel? I pick up the trash in this neighborhood, and I always wanted to see what it was like inside a fancy hotel like the Edgewater."

Butch's answer took me back to the advice the department head had offered me on my first day five years before, "Just don't expect anything to change, guru."

Butch offered me the best comeback to that guy anyone could ask for: "Tom, can I buy you a beer?"

Tom Mosgaller is past president of the American Society for Quality (ASQ) and the Madison Area Quality Improvement Network (MAQIN). Tom's work experience includes being Director of the Office of Organizational Development and Quality for the City of Madison, VP of HR and Organizational Development for the Marshall Erdman Company, and a Director of Change Management in the University of Wisconsin-Madison College of Engineering. In addition, Tom has served on numerous community boards, including as chair of the Badger Rock Middle School and the national Public Health Foundation (PHF) board.

Questions for Reflection and Discussion

1. Tell the story of a time when you or someone close to you felt real pride in an improvement or excellence they achieved in their workplace.
2. Why do people "on the ground" usually know what they need more than those who supervise them? Does it surprise you that the workers in the story who got to buy their own radios purchased higher quality (not necessarily higher priced) products? Give an example from your own life when you did exactly that.
3. When it comes to change and/or improvement, are there any reasons why people who work for not-for-profit or governmental organizations would be less interested or more resistant to change than those in the private sector? If so, what do you think those reasons are? Discuss your perception with others in both fields. Later: What did you learn?

One Family at a Time

by Karen Crossley

We believe that change happens when inspired people take action.

Sustain Dane

"Why does Grandma use paper towels to wipe up spills when she could use rags?"

"Isn't it wasteful to use so many paper napkins when we could be using cloth ones?"

"Aren't we sort of cool when we walk the mile or so together to school—rain or shine, fall/winter/spring—when our friends always get rides from their parents?"

"Shouldn't we carpool to get to soccer practice?"

"Turn off those lights! Remember how much electricity that lamp used up when we measured it using that cool gadget we borrowed from the library?"

"Don't you dare throw that in the garbage! It can be recycled!"

"If it's yellow, let it mellow. If it's brown, flush it down."

These are off-hand observations from children as they participated in Sustain Dane's EcoTeam program. Sustain Dane grew from earlier experiences with creating positive change across organizations, nurtured by Brian Joiner, a leader in the quality improvement movement mentioned frequently in this book. The group works to improve the environment and all the systems that impact it. In the 1990s, Sustain Dane (https://sustaindane.org/) offered an innovative program to the Dane County, Wisconsin, community. It was rooted in the belief that *change happens when inspired people take action.* EcoTeams were introduced to the greater Madison area and a welcoming invitation was extended: Come one and all—convene a small group of people and participate in an intimate, shared learning community supporting high-impact, lasting, behavioral change.

EcoTeams originated in the Netherlands with over 150,000 people participating worldwide. An EcoTeam is a group of households or other collection of people—e.g., members of a faith community—who get together once a month over a five- to six-month period to follow a step-by-step process of manageable actions on sustainable living. Team members measure their household's environmental impact, share their experiences, and agree together on implementing practical lasting changes in their lives. Key themes include: Waste & Recycling, Shopping & Consumption, Energy Use, Transportation, and Water Use (https://www.thensmc.com/resources/showcase/ecoteams). My highly positive experience with EcoTeams resulted from Sustain Dane's offering. Thank you, Sustain Dane! Here's my story.

~

Once upon a time, there were six young families living very close to one another on two adjacent blocks in Madison's Tenney Lapham Neighborhood. Twelve adults and fourteen children composed our happy, very close-knit bunch. As an early supporter of Sustain Dane, I learned about the EcoTeam program and got excited about participating. Having grown up as a baby boomer in the 1950s and 1960s, and developing an ever-increasing environmental sensitivity related to caring for our precious planet, I was intrigued by the opportunity to learn and do more. I was motivated to challenge myself in new ways.

Further, the idea of engaging in a learning journey with dear friends and neighbors was an appealing bonus. So, I carefully drafted what I hoped would be a compelling invitation to five other families asking them to consider joining us (my husband and our three young children) in the EcoTeam adventure. Thankfully, it didn't take much persuasion. All invitees were enlisted. Bravo! I was thrilled. Despite unbelievably busy family lives (with all parents working outside of the home and myriad kids' activities), we all committed to the six-month journey together. We buckled our seatbelts, and the rewarding ride began.

We buckled our seatbelts,
and the rewarding ride began.

~

Opening act: A meeting was arranged whereby a volunteer EcoTeam facilitator trained by Sustain Dane joined us for our introductory session with all the grown-ups and children together at one of our homes. The curriculum was outlined. Workbooks were distributed. Roles and responsibilities were described. A schedule and calendar were created.

We were launched and became a dynamic, self-directed, learning community and EcoTeam. We even came up with our team name—*Jambachakaladist* (or something like that). It was a creative, difficult-to-remember and pronounce, combination of syllables that included letters from all fourteen of our children's names. Even today, the mention of our EcoTeam's name among this special group of friends that has remained very close over the several intervening decades, triggers a smile, perhaps even a laugh, and a sweet memory.

The journey: We met all together, crammed into one another's homes, six times over the span of roughly six months, for a two-hour, themed session. And then we finished at the end of the ride with a final celebration, inviting other friends and neighbors to extend our EcoTeam's reach. A typical session was hosted and led by one family. There was pre-work—e. g., readings and research, meeting preparation, post-session homework, and accountability to one another—guided by each other and our workbooks.

For example, my recollections of the "Water Use" session in our home includes the following. First, my husband led an opening warm-up exercise. He created and taught us a new version of a well-known spiritual song *Wade in the Water* that we all sang together in spontaneous harmony and as a round. Nice!

Second, we presented and exchanged data and findings related to individual and global water use, availability and how to reduce consumption and pollution.

Third, we offered hands-on demonstrations. One involved all jamming into our small bathroom where my husband showcased several simple ways to reduce water use in our toilet (who knew you could add a brick to the tank?!) and various low-flow faucet gadgets.

Fourth, we each were expected to time our showers prior to the gathering (pre-work) and then share with the group the duration of our typical showers. (Pals were in shock and awe that I could get clean in under a minute.) We discussed new info and tools related to water use, and strategies for reducing it. And finally, we each created and shared goals for individual, family, and group action, committing to hold one another accountable and report in during the intervening weeks and at our next session together.

Our journey unfolded. We learned a lot together during each session when we gathered and during our conversations in between. We nudged one another to keep on track and on task. We talked a lot among the group, sharing ideas and resources formally and informally, as well as discussing the environment with our wider circles of families, friends, neighbors, and networks. We committed to take action, actually did it, tried out new practices, and indeed changed some of our lifelong behaviors. Of course, we often slipped up along the way. Friendly reminders from our EcoTeam members provided support and gently nudged each of us keep on track. We wrote about our EcoTeam in the neighborhood newsletter and talked about it at formal neighborhood meetings. We even hosted a dynamic, hands-on, interactive, public workshop with each of the six families hosting an issue-themed station. (Our family's station once again focused upon water since we had become newly enlightened resident "experts" on that issue.) As a result of our experience, multiple additional EcoTeams were spawned among more of our neighborhood friends. The EcoTeam movement flourished in the

Tenney Lapham Neighborhood and throughout the entire Madison, Wisconsin community.

We committed to take action, actually did it, tried out new practices, and indeed changed some of our lifelong behaviors.

~

Creating and engaging with our EcoTeam was purposeful and powerful. We supported our shared learning and built community. We took tangible actions, measured results, and held one another accountable. We led by example and communicated with others. We've kept its spirit alive. And perhaps just as important, our friendships have deepened in new ways. And did I mention that we had loads of fun together along the way?

With deep gratitude, I and the rest of us in the program thank Sustain Dane for instilling the inspiration and providing the EcoTeam curriculum and support. I truly believe our six families were inspired to take action and that our action created some lasting and impactful (albeit not enough) change that continues in our lives and in our current communities far and wide.

Sustain Dane programs and services still include, and have expanded well beyond, growing awareness and action at the grassroots individual level. The portfolio of learning opportunities hosted by Sustain Dane now targets businesses, nonprofit organizations, educational institutions, municipalities, and more. Its reach is both deep and wide, with a wholistic approach that includes sustaining a healthy planet, a strong community, and a just economy—with the ambitious goal of creating collective well-being for all.

Isn't that what the sustained improvement described in this collection of stories is all about?

Karen Crossley's career focused upon natural areas conservation; higher-education fund raising; support of arts, culture, and local history; and civic engagement. Her volunteer service has targeted the environment and sustainability, public education, youth leadership development, entrepreneurship, and social impact. She served as a Peace Corps Response Volunteer in the Republic of Georgia in 2017-2018, supporting organizational capacity building. Karen has a master's degree in botany from the University of Washington, and an Executive MBA from the University of Wisconsin-Madison.

Questions for Reflection and Discussion

1. What is the value of pursuing positive change at the grassroots family-and-friends level? Tell one time when you tried it and what happened. Both the good and the not-so-good!
2. How do you move from individual action to collective action to create change? What are the obstacles? What are the resources you can use? Give examples of each.
3. What is the role of education—both formal and informal—in achieving excellence?

Disaster at the Ritzy Restaurant

by Kathleen A. Paris

That we are interdependent at work was a lesson I learned from Andy the dishwasher. During college, I worked as a server in a fancy hotel with an even fancier dining room. Guests at this dining room were treated to meals cooked right at their tables. My job was to make fresh Caesar salads and cook flaming Steak Diane, Bananas Foster, Cherries Jubilee, and other lusciously dramatic dishes.

Andy (not his real name) was a developmentally challenged adult from a nearby institution whose job was to wash dishes for the dining room. He was enthusiastic about his dishwashing job, showed up in freshly laundered whites every day, always on time. To anyone's memory, Andy had never missed a shift in the years he had been there. He would stop you in the kitchen and ask how things were going, "Were the dishes as clean as you wanted, Ms. Paris? Are you happy with my work?" People secretly smirked that Andy cared so much about his humble job of dishwashing. How awful is that?

One Saturday night, Andy didn't show up for work. No one had even noticed until the dishes started piling up. I hope I can adequately describe the disaster in brief. Those of us who were servers on this busy night were actually washing dishes for our own tables. Naturally our dishwashing meant less time to take care of our very discriminating customers.

People waited for their food while we hunted for clean soup bowls. The shrimp cocktails edged from crispness to limpness while we scoured dirty trays hunting for cocktail forks to wash. I staggered out at closing time exhausted, undertipped (of course, because our service hadn't been up to par), and dismayed at the pile of dishes that remained to be done by someone else.

One Saturday night, Andy didn't show up for work.

I never knew who cleaned up that mountain of dishes that night, but I know that the next time I saw Andy at his post, washing away with his smile intact, I was grateful. I realized in a very concrete way that the dishwasher and I needed each other to be successful.

That is what a successful organization requires: recognizing that we need others in order to be successful ourselves.

Reference

Edited excerpt from *Staying Healthy in Sick Organizations: The Clover Practice*™ by Kathleen A. Paris, 2008. Reprinted with permission.

Kathleen A. Paris, Ph.D., provides strategic planning consulting and leadership development in higher education, healthcare, nonprofits, and for-profit businesses. In addition to work on the U.S. mainland, she has provided consultation to the Organization for Economic Co-operation and Development (OECD) in France and has consulted in Guam, The Virgin Islands, Canada, Cyprus, Switzerland, and the United Kingdom. Paris has written numerous books and articles, including *Bringing Your Strategic Plan to Life: A Guide for Nonprofits and Public Agencies.*

Questions for Reflection and Discussion

1. Describe one time you realized the importance of a co-worker to your work. What did you do after the realization?
2. General Colin Powell said in his autobiography, *My American Journey,* that "all work is honorable." Do you think this belief is held in your organization? Why or why not? What changes do you hope to see in your own part of the organization around this notion? How could you help make it happen?
3. To be successful, all parts of a system must not only work well; they must work well *together.* Give an example from your own life or one that you have observed where that did happen. Give another example of an organization or institution in which the parts do or did not seem to work well together.

A Deeper Sense of People and Purpose

by Denis Leonard

> There is no power for change greater than a community discovering what it cares about.
>
> Margaret J. Wheatley

How could I know that meeting one person would ultimately impact the rest of my career? When I accepted a teaching position at UW-Madison in the late 1990s, I immediately focused on finding a community that I could connect with. I found one, as the famous Irish prayer says, because "the road rose up to meet me."

In Belfast, where I began my business career, I had experienced people passionate about continuous, systemic improvement. This group was centered on the Ulster Business School's quality research and the Northern Ireland Centre for Quality with its focus on the European Framework for Quality Management (EFQM) and its annual conference. These passionate researchers, trainers, assessors, and volunteers had created a community and formed me as a professional at the start of my career. It was perfectly natural that I would seek a similar community in Madison, where I found my community and more.

My search first led me to Professor Don Ermer. When I arrived at UW, the first thing I did was to telephone him. Typical of Don, the phone conversation was brief, because he wanted to meet. "I'll be right over," he said. He walked through the snow to come across campus to visit my tiny office in the UW-Madison School of Business.

Don wasted no time in volunteering me to be trained as an Examiner for the Wisconsin Forward Award, to speak at an American Society for Quality (ASQ) Madison meeting, and to advise the ASQ Student Quality Society that he had established! In between signing me up for a range of quality volunteer roles and telling me about his iceboat, Don would say, with a laugh and a huge grin, "I've got another quality story for you." I was to hear that phrase so often over the next ten years. Don was quite simply passionate about developing the next generation of undergraduates and graduate students to understand what the word "quality" means and how to lead the changes needed to make it happen. He was especially committed to developing and encouraging women as leaders of change in their organizations.

Over the years, Don told many fascinating stories, including those involving W. Edwards Deming and Joseph Juran. It engendered a feeling in me of being really connected to the top leaders of the Quality Improvement movement. Don's stories were mini case studies of just how focusing on improvement could make an impact. There were positive and negative examples, always told with energy and humor, and always provided valuable lessons.

Don also encouraged me to become more involved with the American Society for Quality (ASQ). I still volunteer in ASQ roles, including being on the Certified Quality Manager Exam development and scoring teams, the Editorial Board of the Quality Management Development's (QMD) Quality Management Forum, and others. I am still volunteering over 20 years after.

~

Being in Madison on-and-off for a decade provided me a unique opportunity to connect with key people in the continuous improvement community who worked at an international level. It began with Don, an ASQ Medalist and continued with regular opportunities to converse with Professor George Box. I met Dr. Val Feigenbaum, who is often linked with Deming and Juran as one of the leading experts on Quality Improvement. I am lucky that Val and I had time to talk, have coffee, and stroll together. He exemplified so many of the qualities of passionate professionals: courteous, unassuming, focused, full of stories, and exhibiting a real sense of energy that was palpable. Others, without their knowing it, were role models for me, such as Tom Mosgaller, the ASQ President for several years, and Tim Hallock, who was instrumental in St. Mary's Hospital becoming the first to win the Baldrige Award in healthcare.

All of these experiences came from the Madison community I tapped into and the training, opportunities and support that emerged from it. What impressed me most was the huge amount of time and energy these professionals contributed for free because they loved what they did, and they believed it made a difference.

What impressed me most was the huge amount of time and energy these professionals contributed for free.

I distinctly remember often driving to the university along the Beltline Highway to work in this lovely, bustling city with the blue lakes sparkling in the sun being very conscious of driving past the where the ASQ Madison Section meetings were held and where the annual Hunter

Quality Conference was held. I was surrounded by, and was part of, that community.

The lesson for me was that people were the foundation of my career. People—passionate fellow professionals—provided the core of my development by sharing their ideas and the lessons they had learned with this outsider from Erin.

~

Just as any transformation process must begin with the basic purpose or mission, sustaining a community of colleagues is similar. It is not just about getting your work done or furthering your career—there has to be a deeper sense of purpose. There is, of course, a direct correlation between people and purpose. My passion for quality was ignited by those I was involved with early on and with whom I am still connected decades later. And they are still open to sharing and supporting others in helping to make the world a better place. (For proof of this assertion, you need look no further than the stories in this book in your hands.)

Most improvement professionals focus on the workplace (where we all spend a large part of our lives) creating employee satisfaction, reducing stress, increasing motivation, encouraging collaboration, and celebrating engagement. Beyond a single workplace, however, a national and international impact of the movement towards quality is obvious. Benefits of systemic workplace improvement range from simply decreasing wasted time at work to developing better services and products that meet and exceed requirements and even save lives. But the people who can really change your career are those that don't just apply concerns about quality to their job requirements but expand their interest into other aspects of their lives. Such people have a deep sense of purpose. They exude passion and will enrich your life. I promise you.

In Northern Ireland, I had been introduced to the broad concepts and tools of TQM (Total Quality Management), ISO 9001, the EFQM Quality Award, and other resources. In Madison, however, the people with a sense of purpose came from an amazingly broad range of perspectives and expertise. Through them I was exposed to the Malcolm Baldrige National Quality Award program, the International Team Excellence Award, Six Sigma, Lean, and a deeper understanding of the fundamentals of Statistical Process Control. My work in America was in a broad range of industries, from higher education to manufacturing to environment to construction and provided me with an inclusive approach to quality that I maintain to this day. There is often a danger of becoming myopic or pigeon-holed as "the ISO person" or the "Baldrige Examiner" or "It's all about Lean." The unique community in Madison provided a broad perspective that allowed my expertise to be more strategic and integrated in nature, with full realization of the power of strategy, alignment, and integration of approaches to fully leverage quality improvement across the board.

There is so often the danger of becoming myopic or pigeon-holed as "the ISO person" or the "Baldrige Examiner."

~

As I said earlier, there has to be a *purpose,* and *people* are the key. For example, when I was asked to take continuous improvement to a new level at Madison's Veridian Homes construction company by David Simon, the co-owner and president, I worked for someone who had a passion for quality. David had personally led and inspired people for years and had seen the impact of systemic improvements. He was constantly full of ideas and energy, driving forward and bringing his team with him. Part of that drive was having a purpose—that is, what Veridian wanted to represent beyond just building homes. One purpose included building what David called "Green Energy Efficient Homes" and having a positive impact on the community.

When I arrived as a quality improvement manager, a company merger was already in process. A lot was going on bringing two teams together to form one culture while continuing to build approximately 500 homes per year across Dane County and beyond. It was a busy time. Before the merger, David Simon's company had used process maps and achieved the Baldrige-based National Housing Quality Award (NHQA), so attention to process was familiar to many in the company. It was a great starting point. Initially my focus was ensuring that the concepts for quality were sustained for those who had been on the continuous improvement journey so far, while bringing those new to the concepts along. This involved painting the big picture, using "Big Q" (as coined by Dr. Juran, focusing on companywide strategic issues) and also focusing on "little q" for the functional operational level issues such as improving cycle times, reducing defects, and improving customer satisfaction. It was also the time when I was supposed to get to know people across the company and find allies and champions.

The first phase of the job was all about learning and connecting. My approach was ad-hoc in that I didn't implement any new tools or approaches. Rather it was about keeping an even keel and using the time to better understand how the business worked and who the personalities were, and from this I was then to leverage everything I had learned about quality to implement the best tools for the greatest impact.

Key champions of my work were the VP of IT, Chris Luter, and the VP of Construction, Gary Zajieck, both passionate about their own professions and open to new ideas. As I said to both of them, "I have a toolbox, take a look and see which you would like to try out. Then show me where you want to work to fix or improve something and I'll show you how the tools can be used for that!" In that way we worked together as a team, and there was a great synergy.

"I have a toolbox, take a look and see which you would like to try out."

If I had not been able to find and develop the relationship with key champions like Chris and Gary, then "wins" we could build on may not have happened. The ad-hoc could have turned into a spinning of wheels, an aimless wandering of disparate initiatives. Things could have gone very wrong if this ad-hoc phase had gone on too long.

The second phase of the project was focusing on establishing *processes,* creating a *structure for change.* I was able to introduce the Baldrige Model quite smoothly since the company's National Housing Quality Award meant everyone was already familiar with Baldrige, and that allowed me to use a national/international model as the Big Q strategic infrastructure and take it beyond an industry-only focus.

I also introduced ISO 9001 systems and was then able to use its process mapping concepts to visually show the team key current processes and imagine improvement. To focus and support improvement teams, we successfully used the Six Sigma DMAIC (Define, Measure, Analyze, Improve, Control) concept. All of this was under the strategic umbrella of Baldrige.

As time went on, we used Baldrige Express to conduct two assessments and achieved three national quality awards for homebuilding. The ISO 14001 systems allowed us to then achieve Green Tier with the Wisconsin Department of Natural Resources and build on that to collaboratively create a Green Tier Charter.

The use of the tools and the impacts resulted in a real sense of pride among the team. This was not just about winning national awards. Gary came to me one day to tell me that his construction managers were telling him that the homes they were building had reached new levels of performance in Blower Door Tests. These are the tests that indicate how air-tight each home was. The team had not created any form of competition about this issue; it came naturally from a pride in their work and their own desire for quality in their product.

During a National Housing Quality Award site visit by a team of judges from around the USA, we created posters and displays around the walls of our main meeting room. Each department displayed achievements it was most proud of. This was the room the judges would meet in with the leadership team for a presentation on the company and to answer key questions throughout the three-day visit.

What I had suggested—posting a few key images and metrics—turned into a full scale "science fair" concept. Every department was so proud of what they were doing and achieving that they took the whole idea of "showing off" to a new level. It wowed the judges.

At this point I had been using the focus on purpose and people internally—that is, in my own thinking. While this was going on, I was constantly using the same concepts externally, by getting ideas, support, suggestions, and links to resources from the rest of my Madison quality community. But now, in the third and final phase of the project, I turned to more fully using the community at Veridian Homes itself. I had key leaders and managers attend the Annual Hunter Quality Conference and ASQ Section Meetings. I invited colleagues to visit the company as guest speakers, to run quality concept courses and facilitate Baldrige Express independently. We had benchmarking visits to the Trek Bicycle Corporation and St. Mary's Hospital to help get perspectives outside the homebuilding industry. I also presented what we were doing with a homebuilding company at ASQ meetings, WFA Conferences, and other events that provided two-way learning—my sharing what we were doing and then getting feedback and suggestions that I took back to the Veridian improvement team.

Veridian went on to achieve two Gold NHQAs, Energy Value Housing Gold Award, Builder of the Year, AVID Customer Satisfaction Award, Safety Award for Excellence, Innovative Housing Technology Award, *Professional Builder* Magazine's Builder of the Year, and many others.

Madison was and continues to be unique in the continuous improvement world, but you will need to build your own quality community! Indeed, all the lessons I learned can be adapted for your career and your community. Volunteering, sharing ideas, supporting each other, leveraging knowledge for others, making a difference can be achieved anywhere. I now have colleagues in Ireland, Iran, Greece, and India all who gravitate toward those with passion to share ideas, conduct research, and co-author. It doesn't matter where you are. Today's technology breaks down the barriers of distance and creates opportunities (even, it turned out, during a world-wide pandemic).

Build your own quality community!

Seek out and build your community of passionate advocates for quality. It will drive your career and life and strengthen your workplaces and your community. Get the right people together, clarify purpose, and improve processes. With this you can create success and sustain it. Again, I promise.

Reference

Leonard, D. "The Course toward Collaboration: Leveraging the Links between the EFQM Model and ISO44001 to Improve How Individuals and Organizations Work Together." 2021. *Quality Progress*, 54(11), 38-45.

Denis Leonard, Ph.D., is head of Integrated Management Systems for Graham Construction in the Greater Belfast Area of Northern Ireland. Denis received the prestigious 2020 ASQ Edwards Medal for outstanding leadership in the application of modern quality control methods. In 2021, he published the paper "The Course toward Collaboration" in the American Society for Quality's flagship scientific journal, *Quality Progress*. In 2022, he was awarded the ASQ Lancaster Medal for his contributions to the International Fraternity.

Questions for Reflection and Discussion

1. Name three current or potential colleagues you have for your own efforts in creating change. What do they have in common? How can you organize formal and informal ways to collaborate? Be specific.

2. What are other words for "passion." What are you passionate about? Why? Tell a story about trying to make change about something you care about.
3. How can you expand your view of what is possible in your work or personal life? Can you take a trip? To where? Can you read a book or join an Internet community? Which ones? Will you do so? When... or why not?

I'm Late, I'm Late, for a Very Important (Surgery)

by Anonymous

I'll never forget sitting in the pre-op room with Max [patient names and identifying characteristics have been changed to protect individual privacy]. I was assigned to co-lead a project to improve first-case, on-time starts in the operating room. That day, I was conducting current-state observations in the preoperative department, and Max was one of the first patients I followed through our preoperative processes. He was waiting to have an operation to remove cancerous tissue. As I was sitting with him, he told me about his cancer treatment journey. When he was originally diagnosed with cancer, he was hesitant to get on board with the doctor's recommended surgical treatment plan. The thought of surgery was too overwhelming, so he started looking into alternative treatment options.

I could feel his hopelessness, fear, and anxiety.

After months of unsuccessful "alternative" treatments and depleting his life savings, however, Max's cancer rapidly progressed. He returned to the traditional medicine route and eventually found himself sitting next to me, waiting in pre-op to be wheeled into the operating room.

As Max told me his story, I could feel his hopelessness, fear, and anxiety. He was facing an uncertain future in an unfamiliar environment.

Max mentioned several times that being in the hospital and waiting for the impending surgery was scary, that he didn't feel in control and didn't have a clear understanding of what was happening around him. Doctors and nurses were in and out of his room, asking him what seemed to him to be the same questions. He felt alone for long stretches of time.

Despite the best efforts by our preop and surgical teams, we were running fifteen minutes behind schedule. I could sense the additional wait time and anticipation intensified Max's anxiety. His experience that morning, like that of so many other patients facing serious surgeries and uncertain futures in our institution, would become my driving motivation for improving processes in surgical services and first-case on-time surgery starts.

Though our patients are the center of why we do what we do, they are not the only entities impacted by late surgery starts. Our doctors, nurses, nursing assistants, surgical techs, and many other staff members are also affected. One missing medication, lab result, or care order can start a chain reaction in scheduling that is hard to rebound from. For example, when the OR nurses arrive to pick up a patient for surgery and the patient isn't ready to be wheeled into the operating room, it starts the chain reaction. Surgeons and anesthesiologists often then run behind in seeing other preoperative patients or doing their regular rounds with patients on the in-patient units. These doctors, therefore, sometimes aren't there (at least on time) to anticipate patient questions, recognize their need for additional consultations, or just sit with a patient and their families to (once again) explain the procedures, the reason for the surgery, or the expected outcome.

The ultimate result of a system that produces late starts is the reinforcement of a culture that normalizes late starts.

Another downstream effect is that physicians become disincentivized to arriving at their appointed time to pre-op since the patient is so often not ready to be assessed. Normalizing late starts disincentivizes continuous improvement. (This is true in almost any institution you can name.) In surgical medicine, this normalization can lead to operating room utilization taking a significant hit, with cases going overtime or getting delayed or bumped to a different day. Thus, the institution is significantly impacted financially since surgical teams often work overtime. In addition, the operating rooms are sub-optimally utilized.

~

This kind of systemic delay was the driving force behind me gathering a cross-functional team in one hospital to conduct a week-long rapid-process-improvement effort. As a young continuous-improvement advisor, I knew the learning experience would be invaluable for me. I also guessed it would also be an opportunity for me to build new relationships within the organization, develop my leadership skills, and show the organization that had just hired me that systems improvement science really does work! (I was eventually proven right on all these counts.)

We first constructed a team of surgical services leadership, surgeons, anesthesiologists, pre-op and OR nurses, surgical techs, and other improvement advisors. For the eight weeks leading up to the workshop, the team conducted observations of patients from the moment they arrived in the preoperative department to what we called our "safety timeout," which was the hard stop to double-check to confirm we had the right patient, the right procedure, and the right site.

We performed and shared time studies and waste walks to create what we called our "current-state value stream map" during all our observations. It was extremely important that all members of the team observe the process from start to finish. This allowed them to experience various perspectives and appreciate the challenges that other colleagues were facing every day. Of the multiple cases we observed, only a small percentage started on time. This presented a huge opportunity for improvement, and I was excited to help lead the charge in guiding the team to make real quality improvements in the care we offered.

The first day of the process focused on assessing the waste in the current journey for patients through the preoperative process. As a team, we described any waste that we observed. Most of these fell into the category of some type of waiting: waiting for physicians to see the patient, waiting for lab orders, waiting for the surgical team to arrive, waiting for the history and physical to be updated, and many more "wasted-time" examples. The most valuable outcome of this exercise was in breaking down the silos within the organization and in team members recognizing how their individual work impacted the larger care-delivery system. These exercises also debunked many assumptions that team participants had about the work outside of their own department walls.

~

After the current-state situation had been confirmed, our team envisioned a future process without waste and tried to imagine a future-state value stream that would work for patients and staff alike. Everyone in healthcare knows that individual institutions and systems often struggle when called upon to challenge the status quo; and getting teams to think beyond current barriers and norms can be extremely challenging—or even counterproductive. There was lively discussion among our team members about what was realistic to propose that also constituted an efficient and safe medical process. When we focused on asking ourselves what achieving the best future state for our patients looked like, however, we were almost always able to come to an agreement. Reminding ourselves of our true north—our patients—was vital to having a successful process.

When we focused on asking ourselves what achieving the best future state for our patients looked like, we came to an agreement.

We used a fishbone diagram to identify the root causes of the gaps between our current and our desired-future state. Then our small teams worked together to brainstorm various improvement ideas. We made sure all the teams had representation from various roles and perspectives so they could keep all stakeholders in mind when generating ideas.

As a larger team, we then prioritized the improvements that our group could impact during the following week. We were able to produce ideas that would address waste we had observed, including setting time expectations for surgeon and anesthesia arrival in pre-op, creating a visual management board outside of the patient's room to keep track of their preoperative preparation status, adjusting the arrival time of OR nurses to allow for more set-up time for larger cases, and streamlining the questions that the surgical team asked patients.

~

Empowering our nurses, surgical techs, and other front-line staff to lead these tests of change was what brought me the most joy.

Often organizational change is simply rolled out on a large scale without front-line input or thorough testing of the change. During the events described here, we performed small tests for several different improvement initiatives. These small tests required just-in-time training and a little encouragement, but empowering our nurses, surgical techs, and other front-line staff to lead these tests of change was essential in the success of the improvements and was also what brought me the most joy. *They* were the ones who lived this work every single day, knew their departments, and could most effectively involve their co-workers in any change. Leading these changes also gave our team members the confidence needed to be champions of improvement in their own areas, which is ultimately what allowed the various improvements to be sustained.

That institution has experienced significant improvement for first case on-time-start rates since our process was implemented. While the outcome metrics are important to celebrate, many other wins came out of this effort. Walls were broken down between departments, with everyone able to appreciate the part they played in improving the larger system.

I wrote down this quote from an anesthesia team member at that hospital that I now have sitting on my desk: "It is important that we go and see one another's work." This practice has become extremely important in my work of eliminating assumptions, fostering a culture of cross-functional teamwork and systems thinking, and reminding everyone involved that we share the common goal of providing exceptional care for their patients. People like... Max.

Anonymous is a career systems-improvement professional currently working at a well-known medical center in the United States, which is the writer's reason for choosing to remain anonymous.

Questions for Reflection and Discussion

1. If your unit's work gets behind, does it impact the work of others? Does it result in a delay for the customer? Are you often waiting for another unit to finish before you can do your work? How might you make improvements to the overall system? Who would you collaborate with to do so?
2. Can you identify practices or behaviors in your organization that are dysfunctional but have become normalized over time? How might you begin to change that? Who would it be important to engage?
3. Have you ever experienced being part of a great change in a group or institution or system? If so, tell the story. What was the single most important element in making it work?

Chapter Seven

Leadership

Introduction

You Step Up, You Learn, You Get Better

What was the first time you were asked to lead something? Maybe you were the littlest kid in your first-grade class (I, Tom Mosgaller, was) and Sister Ursula asked you to lead the eighth grade graduation procession. (She did and I did.) Or maybe you presented your artwork to win the local Knights of Columbus poster contest on why you shouldn't mess with bulls. (I wasn't a good drawer, but my uncle was president of the Knights of Columbus.) Or maybe your whole family was in a bad car accident and in critical condition and you, at thirteen years old, were the only one left standing to organize your neighbors to help get the farm work done while your entire family was recovering in a critical care unit. (That happened to me as well.)

~

Rarely in life are we prepared to lead. Things happen, we step up, we learn, and–whether we want to or not–we get better. Then we teach others by our example. That's life as it is, not as we would like it to be. In life as we would like it to be, we would be provided a succession plan well in advance, be properly coached and mentored along the way, be reaffirmed or corrected when we do things right or wrong, and maybe even get a certificate in some kind in leadership skills that gives us the credentials that validate our readiness.

Instead, most of us are thrown into the deep end of the pool at some point. There is no manual, no instruction guide, no "Can I think about this?" You step up, you learn, you get better. We all know famous leaders who learned by being thrown into the deep end. Moses was a murderer, on the lam so to speak and herding his father-in-law's sheep in another country, when he got the call to lead the Hebrews out of Egypt. Abraham Lincoln learned to lead by being thrown into the crucible of the Civil War. Mother Jones organized the March of the Mill Children when she didn't know what else to do to fight child labor. Martin Luther King, Jr. was encouraged, despite being a very young and inexperienced preacher, to become a leader in the civil rights movement. You get the call, you do it, you learn, you get better, and in the process you teach others by your actions. That's life as it is.

When people are challenged and step up, over time they learn how to lead. Then they get better. Finally, they teach others how to lead. Every leadership situation is unique, but some universals endure the test of time—whether the situation was two thousand years, two hundred years, or two days ago. As the proverb advises, "Where there are no leaders, be thou the leader."

The compilers of this book know that leadership matters. Without leadership, organizations flounder, they lose purpose, their processes for getting things done unravel, and their people wonder where they are going.

~

The National Institute of Science and Technology (NIST) has codified the elements essential for organizations to achieve performance excellence. These seven elements are called the "Malcolm Baldrige Criteria." They are all important, but leadership is the most important element because leaders make change happen. For you, that might be your department or local branch, or it might be the whole organization. The principles apply at any scale.

Baldrige does not prescribe what *kind* of leadership is right for your organization or institution; but based on extensive research Baldrige provides a set of profound questions that help you gauge your organization's fitness, beginning with *your* leadership capabilities. All the other Baldrige essential criteria for excellence—strategy, customer focus, workforce engagement, process management, measurement, and the all-important getting of results—depend on leadership. Without leadership the other six criteria can languish in the desert of apathy.

Leaders are people who create or identify a shared vision powerful enough to lift people out of their preoccupations and focus them on things worthy of their efforts. Here are just some of the qualities of leaders. All of them can be developed. In you.

- Leaders stand for the whole and engage everyone in setting a shared direction that commits the enterprise to action.
- Leaders lift people up and reaffirm why their daily work matters.
- Leaders foster a culture of open communication and inclusion, encourage transparency, and champion continuous improvement in everything they do.
- People follow leaders, and leaders get results.
- Leaders take the long view and nurture other leaders.

Have you been called to lead? Are you ready to lead? Are you willing to lead? What do you need to learn to be able to lead? Who will help you learn to lead? When the stakes are high and you are called to lead, what will be your answer? Here are stories that can help you get to *yes* on these questions, two by Jim Bradley, and one each by Terri Potter, Joe Sensenbrenner, Paul Soglin, and Kent Lesandrini.

~

Compilers' Note. When Joe Sensenbrenner left as mayor of Madison in 1989, no one knew what the newly reelected former mayor, Paul Soglin, would do about continuous improvement efforts in the city. In addition to Mayor Soglin's story in this chapter, learn more on how we got started with him and his new administration (on the issue of tons of soggy leaves, ice, and a blizzard that Mother Nature had thrown at us) in a story by Tom Mosgaller, "Never Say Die," available free at Bending-Granite.com.

Also available on our website are additional stories on leadership development, including by Tom Mosgaller titled "Men in Black" and by Barbara Hummel titled "MAQIN: Developing Your Own Community of Practice."

Banking on Quality

by Jim Bradley

Do you do what you're good at or do
you do what makes you feel good?

Drew Howick

"What do we do now?" I began my search for guiding principles to inform my first formal leadership role when I was a young man in my early thirties. I found it humbling and more than a bit scary to have others look to me and ask, "Right, now what do we do?" My first reflex was "(pause) ... Well, what did we do before?" I knew, however, that this response was inadequate in a dynamic world and business environment. I sincerely desired to take successful action on improvement of our bank for my work colleagues, customers, and community. This isn't a story of once and done. It's a story of a journey that spans over thirty years and continues today.

We diligently pursued creative ways to delight our customers.

Fortunately for me, in the late 1980s the Madison area was on the leading edge of learning about and applying the concepts of quality management. It's often said, *When the student is ready, the teacher will appear.* I was a very willing student, and I am grateful to the skilled "teachers" active in Madison's large and engaged continuous improvement community. Together, they aspired to support a community of life-long learners. This book, including stories by many of my mentors, is a testament that our collective aspiration is alive and well thirty plus years later—with hopes to pay what we learned forward to the next generation of community leaders.

~

The guiding principles of what was called then the "quality improvement" movement offered a welcome answer to my question, "What do I do now?" These principles are firmly grounded in the concepts of customer delight and creating/nurturing a work climate that supports employees and other stakeholders in a company with the ability to have pride and joy in what they do. The very concept of quality requires a focus on work processes and how they meet and exceed customer needs and expectations. I learned that while it is not a total abdication of my responsibility to provide answers, it was reassuring to find an entire philosophy of change that begins with exploring internal and external customer needs. The approach was empowering for all the bank's staff, not just me. We became masters of the work processes we managed, we listened to the higher authority of customer needs, and diligently pursued creative ways to delight our customers and ultimately have a positive impact on our community.

Home Savings Bank was founded back in 1895 and is now serving its sixth or seventh generation of Madison and Dane County residents. For these 125 years, the bank has continually adapted to changing needs of our customers and community. Focusing on anticipating customers' needs has allowed us to answer questions before they were asked. As a result, we often had services in place before they were mandated by consumer protection regulations. For example, we developed systems to proactively eliminate a customer's private mortgage insurance, significantly reducing the ongoing cost of homeownership. When feedback from our customers told us they didn't appreciate surprises at the closing of a home purchase, through data analysis we worked on perfecting our estimates of the two or three costs that tended most often to be surprises to them. We paid particular attention to first-time homebuyers. Working with a local tax preparation firm, we developed a unique seminar helping first-time homeowners take full advantage of tax benefits using the timing and deductible costs of their home purchase.

We are one of a handful of banks statewide that have an Outstanding Community Reinvestment Act (CRA) rating from the Federal Deposit Insurance Corporation (FDIC) in recognition of our performance in meeting the credit needs of Dane County residents. We have held this rating proudly for over twenty years.

~

Foundational to the principles of systemic improvement is a clear understanding of your purpose or aim. Over many years we've crafted, revised, and refined various statements of our bank's purpose. Most efforts have been collaborative and shared both internally and externally. The exercise is simultaneously frustrating and enlightening, exhausting and exhilarating. In the end, by making our intentions clear, purpose statements served as valuable touchstones to guide both our individual and collaborative work.

Personally, I have had the wonderful opportunity to learn in small group settings with or led by Peter Senge, systems scientist and lecturer at MIT, and Michael Mucha, chief engineer and director of the Madison Metropolitan Sewerage District. Both taught me the value of crafting a personal vision and taking the bold step of sharing my own vision with others: moving from *guarding* it to *becoming a steward* of my life's purpose; acknowledging that I depend on the help of others. (My concept of a personal vision is that it is the driving force of your life's work, whether in the workplace, in the community, and in personal settings. Relative to Maslow's Hierarchy of Needs, it equates to self-actualization or self-transcendence.) I hope that in some small way this writing contributes to "enhancing local pride and well-being," which is my personal vision statement.

~

Among the most valuable lessons I've learned is the difference between an individual's skills and his or her strengths. Madison-area management consultant Drew Howick was instrumental in my understanding of the distinction. In an all-staff retreat at the bank, Drew asked us, "Do you do what you're good at or do you do what makes you feel good?" Drew stressed that a person's skills are most visible to any observer, but that people can find it exhausting and unfulfilling to be constantly asked to employ only their recognized *skills.* Their *strengths,* on the other hand, are known instinctively by the individual—areas of natural interest, personal inquiry and learning, activities that are energizing and fulfilling—and those they are willing to use whenever called upon.

As an example, a team leader may observe that a colleague is highly organized, a skilled negotiator, or a capable editor. With the best intentions, the leader may naturally assign work to align with those observed skills. Ironically, the leader may actually be contributing to the worker's job dissatisfaction and potentially creating a vicious cycle in which job success encourages more exhausting work assignments and ever-increasing dissatisfaction.

I have found that my one-on-one discussions to explore the personal visions and strengths of my work colleagues were among the most meaningful and respectful work-related conversations I ever held. The insights I gained from them enabled me to align position responsibilities and work assignments with individuals' strengths, nurturing a reinforcing cycle of increased pride and joy in their work. Contrast this approach with one-on-one meetings focused solely on tasks and metrics.

~

"All models are wrong, but some are useful," respected statistician and UW-Madison professor George Box wrote in 2005. This statement has informed my curiosity and humility when addressing challenges and offering solutions. It is remarkably powerful for formal and informal leaders to simply say, "I don't know, let's find out" or "Good idea, let's give it a try" or "How else will we ever know if it works or not?" Trial and error, building on what works and discarding what doesn't, uses the scientific method and helps flatten the hierarchy that often stifles creativity and discourages engagement.

Building on what works and discarding what doesn't helps flatten the hierarchy that often stifles creativity and discourages engagement.

At Home Savings Bank we developed a series of statements we titled *Assumptions for a Dynamic and Rewarding Workplace.* These statements related to business success, collaborative and respectful work practices, and how we enhance our community.

We used the term "associates" for those working in Home Savings Bank. As CEO, I always considered my work colleagues to be in a sense "paid volunteers," because they always have many options for other employment.

We tried to change the expectation that all information flows from the top down by empowering and encouraging our associates to seek information on their own. Associates were also encouraged to independently resolve issues. Clearly stating these and other assumptions showed our current thinking and allowed us to test and revisit them in a process of continuous improvement.

I found that recognizing systems and appreciating their complexity is a vital leadership competence. In my experience, one of the most puzzling questions is whether systems thinking is inherent or learned behavior; is it part of one's nature or the result of nurturing? As in all things, it is partially both and, in any case, I found it a discipline worth practicing and strengthening. How can staff members improve their own work if they do not understand what came before or what comes after their part of a process? Mapping the key steps in work processes–with special attention to the hand-offs from one worker to the next–can build systems improvement thinking and helps assure mutual respect among work colleagues and the development of quality work products that benefit customers.

How many leaders perceive that the decisions we make have ripple effects throughout the entire organization and possibly beyond? Systems at play in an organization, its work processes, and products mirror the complex systems in the natural world. Perhaps, the reverse understanding is more likely—that we see the complex systems in the natural world but not in our own organizations! For example, we all understand that the simple action of grasping something in our hand involves the complex connectedness of nerves, muscles, fingers, and thumb. Likewise, we know that a toxin dumped in a river will ultimately contaminate the lake into which it flows. In business, it may be harder to foresee that a single action will be felt far beyond one local site or office.

Recognizing systems and appreciating their complexity is a vital leadership competence.

And it's no surprise there is a strong overlap of quality practices and environmental sustainability—both disciplines are rooted in systems thinking. Recognizing this connection, and our commitment to having a positive influence on our community, Home Savings Bank built the first Leadership in Energy and Environmental Design (LEED) "Silver" bank office in Wisconsin in 2006. Much like vision/mission statements in an organization, LEED standards for energy and environmental design created a superordinate goal that fostered collaboration and decision-making among all parties—building owner, architect, general contractor, and subcontractors. We were able to make the most effective decisions using the LEED standards as our reference.

~

My professional role at the bank and the support provided by my very capable work colleagues have enabled me to serve on a number of boards for community-based nonprofit organizations. Through the years I learned how volunteer service, whether in the boardroom or in the direct delivery of service, comes from a very deep place in the volunteer. As a leader, I was never sure whether my work colleagues complied with my requests because of my position authority or because of their genuine agreement. In contrast, volunteer work requires true engagement and alignment with higher-order purpose. Volunteering is, perhaps, the best example of intrinsic motivation.

Volunteer board service for not-for-profit entities has been an invaluable practice field for developing my leadership skills as a banker. In my own organization, daily events and tactical decisions often made it difficult to step back to see the patterns and trends that are vital for strategic thinking. Nonprofit organizations, however, routinely revisit their mission and purpose for resonance with community needs and use compelling storytelling to engage donors and volunteers alike.

Collaborating with highly skilled executive directors and board colleagues to align purpose with strategic and operational plans, budgets, staffing models, and the delivery of their products and services has been a wonderful learning experience for me. Plus, the experience has been not only highly rewarding, but transferred easily and effectively back to my own organization. As an example of strategic focus, our lead lending officer and associates created and offered a seminar to help people "Gain Financial Stability, One Step at a Time." My colleagues had recognized that we were most often serving customers who were already financially secure and could be served by any other bank. They were interested in sharing their expertise in serving those that could benefit from help in getting started or back on track.

~

Leadership can be challenging. Taking time to reflect and center myself has been helpful, both personally and professionally. I have found the timelessness and grandeur of the natural world to be especially restorative. Seasonal cycles, the permanence of a mighty oak, the ebb and flow of a river or large body of water give a sense of grounding. This grounding reminds me that organizational structures and challenges/successes are human constructs. Ideally, the changes we make are also creations of goodwill, done with respectful treatment of all involved.

Reference

Box, G. E., Hunter, W. and Hunter, J.S. *Statistics for Experimenters* (2nd edition). (2005). Wiley-Interscience.

Jim Bradley, CEO of Home Savings Bank, Madison, Wisconsin, since 1985, knows the impact of clear purpose, valuing people, and focusing on processes. Understanding that a bank is a complex system nested in larger systems helped him and the many people he has worked with over the years create improved outcomes. Jim's board service with community-based nonprofits has provided him valuable learning opportunities, which are described in the last story of this book, "It's in the Water."

Questions for Reflection or Discussion

1. Name three banks or other companies you enjoy doing business with. Make a list of things they have in common.
2. What are your skills that other people notice? What are your strengths that others may not know about? Tell two quick stories

about being asked to use a skill and then a strength to help in a project to change an organization or institution you are involved in. Which was the most satisfying? Why?

3. Write your personal vision statement. Does it align with your professional work, your personal life, and your volunteer service in the community? If not, consider how to better align your activities with your vision.

Leading with Powerful Questions

by Terri L. Potter

When one is clear and constant in one's purpose, fear does not control the atmosphere (and thus the data), learning is guided by accurate information, and sound rules of inference. When suppliers of services remain in dialogue with those who depend on them AND the hearts and talents of all workers are enlisted in the pursuit of better ways, the potential for improvement in quality is nearly boundless.

Donald Berwick, M.D.

The hospital was strangely quiet that Christmas Eve Day except for the holiday music playing in the lobby. Most of the patients had been discharged. When I walked to my office, my footsteps echoed in the nearly empty hallways. I was clearing off my desk and making a few notes when I heard a quiet tap on my door. "Come in," I called.

It was an employee. In her hand she had a 5 x 7 frame. "I would like to give this to you," she said. On it was a poem she had written. The gist of it was this:

I am not just a parking attendant.
I am an employee who has much to give the organization.
Thank you for seeing me as more than a parking attendant.

~

I have enjoyed close to fifty years of leadership in healthcare and community organizations, and I kept that framed poem on my desk for many years. In my mentoring role, I have had the opportunity to speak to a number of young leaders. A common question they would often ask me was "How did you stay relevant?" to the issues of the day. My response often surprised them. I explained that I had to recreate myself four times in my leadership journey. In each of these situations, I needed to demonstrate an understanding of the needs of the people I served. I had to answer these essential questions:

- Who is your primary customer(s) today? Who do you anticipate your primary customer to be tomorrow?
- What are the primary needs of your customers today? What do you expect the primary needs of those customer needs to be tomorrow?
- How do your capabilities match up with their needs today? How do your capabilities match up with their needs tomorrow?
- Do we have any service gaps today? What service gaps might there be if we sustain our current array of services into tomorrow?"

An important key to effective leadership of any organization is not to know all the answers but to know the important questions to ask.

An important key to effective leadership of any organization is to know the important questions to ask.

My own quality improvement journey was jump-started by a national report. In November 1999, the blockbuster Institute of Medicine (IOM) report "To Err Is Human: Building a Safer Health System" was issued. A key finding in that report was the assertion that preventable errors were causing between 44,000 to 98,000 deaths every year and over a million injuries. Virtually every health professional and every health system said, "What do you mean we killed ten people last month? No not here!" The truth was that none of us knew the extent to which we contributed to those deaths. The IOM report was a wake-up call.

U.S. manufacturers, by then, had shown success with using the Total Quality Management (TQM) tools that had fueled Japan's economic boom. With the IOM report as a motivator, providers across the country began to adopt these strategies to improve clinical quality and safety in the healthcare world.

I knew we had a choice. Do we just sit back and let other people take pot shots at us and be defensive? Or do we step up and take this opportunity to answer those questions ourselves? I turned to local but internationally-revered consultant, Brian Joiner, to help us adopt the improvement tools to connect with our customers and reduce our preventable medical errors at Meriter Hospital in Madison, Wisconsin.

One of the first things we did was benchmark with other organizations. I decided that I wanted to see what a world-class continuous improvement organization looks like. Brian offered to serve as my host at Florida Power and Light (FPL). FPL was the only U.S. company that had ever won the Deming Prize, a prestigious Japanese quality control award. Thus, the path was laid out that would govern my work for many years.

I pondered these questions in preparation for the visit:

- Can we set aside practices that we have used in the past in order to achieve today's successes?
- Are we open to learning new ways to manage?
- What are principles that guide us?
- What measures do we use to determine success? Failure?
- What could a healthcare organization in Wisconsin possibly learn from a power company in Florida?

The visit did not disappoint me. I was captivated by the entire process to which we were exposed:

- Teams of managers and employees working together to attain targeted improvements.
- The role of management as facilitators, not decision makers.
- The role of team members as owners of the improvement process.
- The enjoyment and fun that team members had in their work.

As I reflected on what I had seen in Florida, I said to myself "I want to be part of a team culture that incorporates improvement processes into daily work the way FPL demonstrated." In a word, I was sold on the systemic improvement processes and realized that I needed help–a lot of help—in learning the skills and application of quality improvement (QI) tools to be successful.

Guiding us in benchmarking and laying the foundation for quality institution-wide was Mary Zimmerman. Mary was the very first Meriter employee to be exposed to quality improvement concepts and served as our internal quality guru. We never would have accomplished what we did without her. While playing a key role in Meriter's quality transformation, Mary was also one of the founders of the Madison Area Quality Improvement Network (MAQIN) and represented us with a variety of organizations.

We continued benchmarking best practices as members of the Quality Management Network headed by Harvard M.D. Don Berwick. This group included hospitals from Hawaii to Boston. We met several times a year to focus together on mutual problems.

We also became students of national Baldrige award winners. We noticed that winning organizations worked collegially with organizations in other industries besides their own. They willingly shared what they had learned in seminars and programs, and we willingly listened. Locally, we compared ourselves with a variety of these winning organizations. There was much to be learned about delivering quality healthcare by looking outside of healthcare.

Another early decision I made was to find a person with whom I could work and learn the QI tools and methods. Someone who would be my mentor. Someone who would critique me when needed and encourage me when I deserved it. I was fortunate to have someone living is my backyard who met this test. I hired Brian Joiner as my personal coach and trainer.

In the decision to reduce errors and improve patient safety, we first measured where we were. "How many preventable patient accidents that caused harm occurred in our hospital each quarter?" I was stunned to learn that we had sixty-four preventable accidents or errors in the first quarter of that year alone. We analyzed where the accidents occurred—whether on patient floors, or the pharmacy, or the O.R. or E.R., or elsewhere. We then took action across the entire hospital to reduce these preventable accidents. Over a period of years, we reached the perfect score of no preventable accidents. We continued to sustain significant improvement from that point forward.

I was stunned to learn that we had sixty-four preventable patient accidents or errors in the first quarter.

I realized early on that I had to model for the hospital's executives what I was learning from Brian. So, I became their teacher and coach. I required each hospital executive to select and complete a process improvement project which would foster their learning and understanding of process improvement.

These top leaders were paired with another executive of similar rank. Each leader was asked to observe the "Las Vegas principle" of confidentiality (you know, "What happens at Meriter, stays at Meriter"). The pairs would check in with each other on progress and ask each other questions using the Inquiry Model (see Scholtes, 1998) to move the projects forward. At first they didn't feel comfortable openly sharing—they weren't sure if they could trust each other. But the use of inquiry—asking the right questions—questions related to essentials such as purpose, customer needs, data, and what we were learning—greatly reduced the anxiety. Ultimately the Inquiry Model proved greatly beneficial. When an improvement project was completed, each leader made a presentation on the process and outcomes.

We reduced our critical-care nurse turnover rate from the typical 9-10% to 4%.

One of these projects, for example, addressed the problem of turnover among critical-care nurses at Meriter. By finding out from the nurses themselves what were the unique satisfiers and dissatisfiers for them, we were able to make changes to greatly reduce turnover. We reduced our critical-care nurse turnover rate from the typical 9-10% to 4%.

Another improvement project dealt with improving board operations. The project focus was "What can we do to reduce the time spent on non-productive conversations?" We used time as our metric, measuring how much time we spent in decision-making versus non-essential topics. We systematically got rid of agenda items that were mostly a time drag and focused on those things that were essential. That project dramatically improved the board's functioning, operations, and effectiveness.

~

A strategy that I found to be powerful as well as efficient is the designation of a Review Team in addition to a Project Team. The more cross-cutting the project is within the organization, the more important the Review Team becomes. In our model, a *Project Team* is composed of the people doing the operational work and is typically composed of staff and supervisors. A *Project Review Team* is composed of several upper-level executives who are not involved in the everyday implementation work of the team but play an essential role in the team's success.

The main responsibilities of the Project Review team are to ensure that the team has the resources to fulfill its mission, remove organizational roadblocks, serve as a reality check, and ask the questions that the Project Team needs to be able to answer. The two teams work in partnership. Some of the advantages of this design include these:

- Top executives on the Review Team can support the project without the time required to be on the Project Team itself.
- The Review Team can clear roadblocks and run interference within the organization in ways that cannot typically be done by the Project Team. We found that projects with a Review Team do not remain stuck or blocked for long!
- Project Teams can move ahead with confidence that they have organization-wide support.
- Review Teams can apply learnings from project they review to other projects they themselves lead.

~

All our process improvement projects were grounded in our strategic plan. With our core mission to "Heal, Teach, and Serve," we at Meriter identified the high-level key indicators that would tell us that we were making a difference: patient safety, patient satisfaction, employee satisfaction, employee retention, and others that reflected our strategic priorities.

We created our own Meriter Hospital tool kit for organization improvement which included guidance and encouragement for using these:

- Seven Total Quality Management Tools (Run Charts, Pareto Charts, Flow charts, Fishbone diagrams, Scatterplots, Control Charts and Tree Diagrams).
- Plan Do Check Act (PDCA) Cycle.
- Standardized Project Management Charts.
- Team Management Tools and Skills.
- Seven Planning and Management Tools (Affinity Diagram, Interrelationship Diagram, Tree Diagram, Matrix Diagram, Arrow Diagram, Process Decision Chart, and Priority Matrix).
- Inquiry skills.

As the leadership team was learning process improvement and quality management strategies, a similar process of coaching, teaching, and learning took place between executives and their department managers and between department managers and their supervisors. This cascade approach resulted a fully-engaged organization which showed:

- A high degree of alignment among all leaders.
- Creation of a resource pool of internal talent.
- Capacity-building for completing several large- and small-scale improvement projects at the same time.
- Circumventing the "rush to foxhole" approach common to introduction of new management methods. (It had been common lore among department managers that they could wait for the

"flavor of the month" improvement effort to pass while they hid in their foxholes!)

The lessons I learned throughout this transformation were these:

- Learning is an inherent element of continuous improvement.
- It is important to learn from every person and organization with whom we are associated.
- Cultural change often must precede organizational improvement.
- It was vital that a "safe learning crucible" be created for top leaders in the organization.
- Failure at any stage needs to be viewed as a learning opportunity.
- Inquiry—asking the right questions—is more effective than inquisition.
- An individual inside your organization who will be the repository of all improvement tools, concepts, and relationships will contribute immeasurably to your success.

Failure at any stage needs to be viewed as a learning opportunity.

~

For you—today's leaders of change—I would share this advice:

- Celebrate small victories. They matter to your people and will keep you energized as well.

- Insist that a top executive sponsor each institution-wide or cross-cutting improvement because resource and policy issues will inevitably arise. The more transformational the improvement effort is, the more imperative it is to have executive sponsorship.
- Assess the relevance of your organization from time to time: Those that do not do so, risk becoming irrelevant themselves.
- Use the quality improvement tools available to you (and described in this book). They are powerful and useful for understanding how processes and systems work and how to improve them.
- Be visible daily in your organization. Walk the corridors and the cafeteria and be ready to listen.
- Practice inquiry over inquisition. Ask the right questions.

Meriter Hospital achieved national and international recognition. For years, Meriter was recognized as a pioneer of quality in healthcare both locally and internationally. Meriter was named one of the nation's 100 Top Hospitals by Thompson Reuters for several consecutive years. In 2006, Meriter received a Wisconsin Forward Award of Excellence among many other quality awards and distinctions.

I was honored to share our story of transformation in Brisbane, Australia, with an international audience of physicians and healthcare administrators. These were all thrilling accolades, to be sure, but for me it was that poem on my desk that never failed to inspire.

References

Deming, W.E. *Out of the Crisis* (ninth edition). (2018). MIT Press.

Scholtes, P.R. *The Leader's Handbook: A guide to inspiring your people and managing the daily workflow.* (1998). McGraw-Hill.

Berwick. D.M. "Continuous improvement as an ideal in health care." (January 5, 1989). *New England Journal of Medicine* (320:53-56). DOI: 10.1056/NEJM198901053200110.

Terri L. Potter was president of Potter Consulting, LLC. For seventeen years, he served as Chief Executive Officer of Meriter Health Services in Madison, Wisconsin. Potter has been recognized with the Award for Excellence in Innovation by *Madison Magazine* and by the *In Business* Executive Hall of Fame. He passed away just prior to publication of this book, and his leadership will be missed but not forgotten.

Questions for Reflection and Discussion

1. Which of these pieces of advice from the author will you take to heart? Why? How?
    - Celebrate small victories.
    - Insist that a top executive sponsor each institution-wide or cross-cutting improvement.
    - Assess the relevance of your organization from time to time.
    - Use the quality improvement tools available to you.
    - Be visible daily in your organization.
    - Practice inquiry over inquisition.
2. What are three things that excite or intrigue you about the possibility of your becoming a leader of change? Be specific.
3. Write a three-line poem of thanks to someone who has helped you understand that you are more than your job title. If possible, frame it and give it to that person. If not, put it on a refrigerator or bathroom mirror at home or work where you will see it often.

It All Came Together

by Joe Sensenbrenner

There was no community on earth experimenting, learning, applying, and sharing new knowledge more broadly than Madison, Wisconsin, in the decade following a lecture there by Dr. W. Edwards Deming in 1983. This belief was widely shared by Madisonians and by well-informed visitors, including the nearly 1,000 attendees of an annual international conference designed, conducted by, and focused on local practitioners. And the belief was well-founded. Unprecedented application of new learning began happening in banking, high tech, the state legislature, the University of Wisconsin-Madison, healthcare, and–perhaps most remarkably—in local city government services including library, building inspection, police, motor equipment, streets, daycare, and interagency coordination. The interplay and expansion of these learning clusters occurred largely within a membership organization named the Madison Area Quality Improvement Network (MAQIN), founded in 1983. MAQIN was the organizer of the aforementioned annual Hunter Conference.

The range and depth of these activities and their interaction was the subject of "Quality in the Community; One City's Experience," the feature article of the magazine *Quality Progress* in May 1991 authored by four MAQIN founders (see Box, et al.). Its content, message, and invitation were noted by the American Society for Quality as the "Best Management Paper" of the year.

Additional national attention was drawn by the *Harvard Business Review* magazine that same year when it published "Quality Comes to

City Hall," framing for its readership the nation's first systematic application of continuous improvement principles to municipal government. By 1993, Madison practitioners were presenting/leading/consulting at conferences, retreats, and in-house settings for virtually every type of organization you can imagine.

In recognition of these same principles, the preeminent U.S. Department of Commerce annual award for best corporate practices had been initiated in 1988. The Malcolm Baldrige National Quality Award has recognized 106 business, healthcare, education, and non-profit organizations over the last thirty years, while training judges and recipients to recognize best practices in making organizational or institutional change.

~

Why and how did this happen in Madison, a city of 170,000—and that included about 42,000 students most of the year? As three-term mayor of the City of Madison (1983-89), a co-founder of MAQIN, and co-author and author respectively of the *Quality Progress* and *Harvard Business Review* articles, I had a unique vantage point from which to observe the depth and breadth of what was going on in those years. The purpose of this story is to respond concisely to this question. Why Madison? I believe there were seven principal factors which converged in those years.

Worry. The self-confident consensus of what has often been characterized as "The American Century" had entered a period of disquiet and uncertainty by the 1970s. Civil unrest, political scandal, gender-role challenging, assassinations, the rise of OPEC, and cultural fragmentation—all compounded by eroded economic security—was captured for me in a nationwide debate that was the title of a June 1980 NBC Special Report, "If Japan Can, Why Can't We?" It focused on the obvious inferiority of the entire American automotive industry—once the pride and engine of America's international ascendance in the early 1900s.

Giants became ghosts.

The loss of jobs, profits, and confidence in our manufacture, sales, and service of cars rippled across the country. Iconic American product-defining companies suddenly became unprofitable, shuttered domestic production, slashed pension benefits, and appeared to offer no strategies for a path forward. Giants became ghosts: Kodak, Xerox, Polaroid, Zenith, U.S. Steel, Alcoa, all gone the way of Timex. A major best-seller, *The Reckoning*, by David Halberstam surveyed the economic and intellectual landscape and found fault in American lack of inquiry, initiative, and rigor when contrasted with that of many Asian governments and companies.

Something New. When I asked Dr. W. Edwards Deming (whose important work has been well documented in this book) in 1983 to tell me where quality improvement was being pursued in the public sector, what literature on that subject I could access, and who the leaders of the movement were, his answer was characteristically succinct: "There is no such example, literature, or practitioner. And I am not sure it will work, because the motivator of going out of business is not present." However, we had many overseas manufacturing results to observe and ample local opportunities for improvement. These methods had never been adapted, tested, and evaluated in public-sector entities. The underlying stories of how whole industries had identified priorities, designed products, organized processes, and developed talent that resulted in market dominance had yet to be written.

"I am not sure it will work, because the motivator of going out of business is not present."

Many Madisonians, however, chose to see possibilities in adapting and reframing change that was open-minded, data-driven, team-based, system-recognizing, and respectful of everyone's input. "New" experiments grounded in strategies established elsewhere proliferated. And in circumstance after circumstance, we were the first. For example, Madison was the first city government to have an annual budget line item specifically to support continuous quality improvement. Police and other departments in Madison pioneered requiring employees and managers to demonstrate knowledge and skill in designing and facilitating actual improvement projects with outcomes as a requirement for promotion and advancement. Madison was the first city government to insist that all city units—from libraries to streets to human services—acknowledge those they served as their customers. This meant finding out what these customers needed and were expecting. We knew we were the first in these and many other innovations, and we were emboldened by that knowledge.

Pure Hunger for Better Things. As exposure to the potential and effectiveness of these ideas spread, longstanding conundrums and visionary possibilities came into focus with people of goodwill. These early adopters were motivated by a desire to improve their organizations and their communities.

People who had labored in dysfunctional systems stepped forward again and again from new and unexpected places. Among the early leaders: teacher David Langford at Mt. Edgecomb High School in Sitka Alaska; Dr. Don Berwick, founder of the now-global Institute for Healthcare Improvement; the AFL-CIO statewide in Ohio; Buffalo, N.Y. social services; Governor Terry Branstad of Iowa. They were almost without exception "the best of the best" in that they were seeking to do ever better work simply for the pride of its doing—not to make more money or build an empire for themselves. With motives that were widely recognized as noble, they could recruit and advance their projects in unencumbered ways. As experienced and knowledgeable workers inside impaired or destructive systems, they knew that things should be better and often knew how to make it so.

They were seeking to do ever better work simply for the pride of its doing.

No Organized Opposition or Alternative. A distinguishing characteristic of the newness of our efforts was the absence of a real "opposition" or alternative method: no one had yet observed the failure of continuous improvement anywhere. Usually social or practical new ways of doing something have a converse or natural opposition. Here, besides humankind's innate apathy, there was an absence of organized pushback. Of course, no change this significant would happen without some pushback, and internally there was resistance from some of the power brokers within city government.

But that skepticism did not result in an organized evidentiary or philosophical opposition, so progress in systemic improvement methods continued. We claimed the higher ground related to respecting employees, supporting front-line management, communicating organizational clarity of purpose, and continuously improving methods and outcomes. Careful examination of process, customer-defined metrics of inputs, and outcomes analysis and improvement theory were embedded in Deming's "Fourteen Points," one of which included improving organizational culture. Imagine: There was almost no debate on the basic tenets; our ideas advanced across a broad range of fronts.

Met the Operational Need. Any new movement needs multiple sources and methods of spreading the word and access to its tools. We delivered by sharing individually and at MAQIN's annual Hunter Conference, by authoring community-wide infrastructure and case studies and articles, and by establishing prototypes for outreach that included *people telling first-hand stories.* There were many occasions where MAQIN members were simultaneously presenting on multiple stages at a conference on quality practices in different sectors and industries. The expectations of different professions were varied—and our practitioners spoke the "improvement language" of each of their peers.

Any new movement needs multiple sources and methods of spreading the word and access to its tools

The Team Handbook, first published in 1988 and co-authored by local authors Brian Joiner and Peter Scholtes (who first learned about improving quality as a city employee), was named one of the "100 Best Business Books of All Time" in 2016). By the late 1980s, Joiner, Scholtes, and Professors George Box and Bill Hunter were figures of international standing. All of them lived and worked in Madison and directly participated in municipal projects.

Altruistic Practitioners and Structure. Madison's community-wide quality improvement efforts had ignited a spark nationally and internationally. As interest grew, other for-profit consultancies and freelance writers emerged with their new products and packaging. Osbourn and Gaebler, for example, wrote extensively in 1993 about Madison's improvement efforts and the enormous amounts of money saved while city services were continuously improved.

Improving government was part of the Clinton-Gore policy platform. In 1993, President Bill Clinton asked Vice President Al Gore to investigate how the federal government could be made more responsive to the American people. Gore's resulting report recommended the model proposed by David Osborn and Ted Gaebler. It was during this time that the national Baldrige Award from the U.S. Department of Commerce was being created.

Almost without exception, the most prominent supporting evidence for the success of these many movements was derived from projects or experiments rooted in the MAQIN networks. Front-line practitioners often agreed to share freely and welcomed more data. Eventually, various sectors began creating their own special learning platforms, and the demand for a central market for introductory learning about continuous improvement diminished over time. The methods, site organization, and community structure sharing became readily available as "public goods," especially with the advent of the Internet.

Leadership. "While I don't understand this and have misgivings, I am willing to go along with this small budget item," said veteran alderperson Warren Onken, leveling his gaze over his ever-present toothpick. "But next year I expect you to answer tough questions."

"I won't be back." I replied, continuing, "If the front-line and managers aren't here to speak on its behalf persuasively by next year, then you will hear no more from me." I write these lines sitting under an October 1984 newspaper photo of the thirty-three Madison city employees (including the heads of Police, Fire, Engineering, Streets, Library, Day Care, Planning and Development, as well as union presidents, beat officers, firefighters, secretaries, receptionists, and more) who presented a collective increased budget request to be used for their continuous improvement efforts. It passed unanimously, including Warren Onken's vote.

"If the front-line and managers aren't here to speak on its behalf persuasively by next year, then you will hear no more from me."

This dynamic captures my experience within many settings: a curious and slightly bold person creates an opening—a clearing—in the midst of a mess of dysfunction, and then good people step forward. By the 1990s front-line workers and people of influence (including the

UW-Madison Chancellor, the Dean of the Business School, hospital presidents, legislators, and corporate executives) sought and achieved membership on the Board of MAQIN. They exercised their "clearing" authority in their areas of impact.

The convergence of widespread experimentation was not the result of traditional, top-down directed activity. It was distributed and arose in multiple settings. No person or small group could be assigned to the outdated concept of the solitary heroic "leader." At that time, in the emerging field of systems thinking, the concept of "self-organizing" purpose-defined entities in chemistry, nature, and human affairs seemed to be operative locally and spreadable harmonically. Big ideas were abroad.

In sum, extraordinary learning and progress was initiated forty years ago in Madison. Today's question is whether another explosion of collaboration and progress is needed and possible now in our post-Covid pandemic world. We know from our efforts that improved results come from disciplined inquiry. What we don't know is whether there is another army of people who want to learn to lead successful change.

What actions might *you* take in your own organization? What is different now compared to the world in the timeframe of these stories? What are the supporting or restraining factors that exist today? What drivers of thought and action are relevant? What skill sets are needed to define and evaluate existing systems? What do the people need? These are the questions your organization or institution needs to be asking itself right now.

References

Box, G.E., Joiner, L.W., Rohan, S., and Sensenbrenner, J. (1991, May). "Quality in the community: One city's experience." *Quality Progress*, 57-63.

Covert, J. and Sattersten, T. (2016). *The 100 best business books of all time: What they say, why they matter, and how they can help you.* Portfolio.

Halberstam, D. (1986). *The reckoning.* William Morrow and Company.

Gore, A. (1993). *The Gore report on reinventing government that works better and costs less.* Three Rivers Publishing.

Osborn, D. and Gaebler, T. (1993). *Reinventing government: How the entrepreneurial spirit is transforming the public sector.* Plume.

Joe Sensenbrenner served three terms as mayor of Madison, Wisconsin, from 1983-to 1989. He was a founding member of MAQIN and served continuously as a board member. He has consulted with governments in the United States, Australia, and New Zealand, and authored articles on applying Total Quality Management (TQM) to communities and the public sector. He is currently engaged in philanthropic activities to promote community-building, environment, arts, and education. Sensenbrenner holds a J.D. from the University of Pennsylvania Law School.

Questions for Reflection and Discussion

1. Have you ever been part of a movement that seemed to have a life of its own? If so, describe the feelings you had. If not, watch a good movie on such a movement and then describe the feelings you have watching it. (For example, you could watch *Norma Rae,* or *Les Misérables,* or *Black Panther,* or *Dunkirk,* or *Sojourner Truth.)* What movie about a movement would you suggest others watch?

2. How are the private sector and the public sector the same? How are they different? What do you think might be the special concerns for each in terms of leading change? Find one person who works in each sector and ask them if your perceptions are correct.
3. Which of these stated reasons for the success of the continuous improvement movement intrigues you? Explain how they relate to a specific change or changes you might want to lead in your own organization or institution.
   - Worry.
   - Something New.
   - Pure Hunger for Better Things.
   - No Organized Opposition or Alternative.
   - Met the Operational Need.
   - Altruistic Practitioners and Structures.
   - Leadership.

The Harambee Collaboration

Paul Soglin

I returned to office as mayor of Madison in 1989 focused on numbers—the growing numbers of Madisonians living below the poverty line, particularly nonwhites. The two weeks between election day and inauguration day were packed with essential activities. I met with the twenty-two city council members, hired my staff, made over 125 appointments of citizens and council members to committees, boards, and commissions, and met with city department heads.

In the middle of these fourteen days of fourteen hours each, I was informed that several department heads committed to Total Quality Management (TQM) had arranged a meeting for me with the prestigious W. Edwards Deming and his associate Myron Tribus. I was not in the mood. My first focus was the growing inequity in Madison. I was too busy. It could wait. They insisted and I relented.

The meeting did not go well. I felt rushed and distracted by the rest of my pressing workload. Despite my own innate support for the principles of quality improvement—using data to make decisions and listening to the people who do the work—I was suspicious. Police Chief David Couper, Deming, and Tribus outlined the current Madison continuous quality improvement program and wanted my immediate support, which to me was a contradiction because I had no data, no evidence as to the effectiveness of the program. As I told Tom Mosgaller years later, "They wanted me to make a decision with the information they gave me, not the data I needed."

But what troubled me most was the experts' view of my city. I felt that, for these internationally-known TQM advocates, Madison was the first and most important city to implement *their* system. We were *their* project where they had invested both *their* time and money. All of my arguments—that we were a democracy, that I was elected by the people of Madison, and that this was their government, requiring me to make a thoughtful decision—seemingly fell on deaf ears. I felt that they failed to realize that my re-election, focused on poverty and race, was an imperative for a new focus.

Key department heads like Chief Couper and Pat Gadow, our Public Health Director, were passionate about improvements in city services achieved using Total Quality Management, but I knew that not all department heads were supportive. The conference with Deming ended worse than it started. I was even more suspicious of TQM.

The conference with Deming ended worse than it started.

~

The disastrous meeting with Dr. Deming behind me, I asked the comptroller to do an audit of the city's previous three years of TQM. I decided not to interfere with the ongoing TQM projects, but until the audit was completed, I suspended all new initiatives. I wanted independent verification.

Chief Couper, Pat Gadow, and Tom Mosgaller (former Mayor Sensenbrenner's TQM Director), and I continued working together despite our differences on TQM. Tom was relocated from the mayor's office to one between Public Health and Human Resources, adjacent to the city's animal control officer. There he remained, as he described it, "Living in the catacombs."

Things could only get better, and they did. While we waited for the report, Tom and I focused on the role of TQM in community life, not just city management. As we talked in our own space and time, we discovered a common set of shared values and attitudes. Saul Alinsky, the great community organizer had profoundly influenced both of us. My admiration for Tom grew.

Things could only get better, and they did.

Tom introduced me to the work of professor, author, and community organizer, John McKnight. McKnight, a close friend of Tom's, became a significant contributor to my views of organizational development particularly as to how city staff—from public heath to police and fire—could most effectively interface with the larger community. McKnight focused on analyzing the assets of a community, not the deficits—on building upon the strengths of the community, the people, the institutions, the businesses.

Instead of resenting me, Mosgaller built trust with me, which was only enhanced when the audit revealed that most TQM projects were successful. McKnight and Deming independently shaped how Tom and I approached community services.

Pat Gadow, a retired Navy Lieutenant nurse, and I quickly identified healthcare as a major focus for my administration. Pat, committed to the quality program, was a sound practitioner. I saw ample evidence in her staff meetings. Problems and mistakes were discussed without recrimination or blame but with the intent to correct mistakes.

We tackled the city's new and expanding challenges of race and poverty, with the staff recognizing its inadequacies—especially its own lack of diversity. Those who did not understand the challenge, particularly as it came to race and institutional racism, were not punished for past failures but were educated and coached.

Problems and mistakes were discussed without recrimination or blame but with the intent to correct mistakes.

There was no pushback but an excitement in facing a new purposeful challenge. The Department of Public Health was an organization guided by trust, not fear. This was to be our new initiative: delivering quality health services to Madison's Southside. The nurses, the infectious disease specialists, and epidemiologists were most enthusiastic, even though many of them did not fully understand the challenges of serving communities of color. The institutional challenges Pat Gadow and the staff faced were not unique among U.S. local healthcare providers in 1990. And it was not for lack of trying. UW Hospital, St. Mary's Hospital, and Meriter Hospital were all running programs designed to serve communities of color, but they were not working effectively.

Pat and I sat down and identified all the agencies, government and private, that should be involved in providing healthcare to the Southside. Besides the three major hospitals, we came up with the Dane County government, the Town of Madison, the University of Wisconsin-Madison

Schools of Medicine and Nursing, and a number of non-profits, many associated with the United Way of Dane County. No matter how one examined it, they were all failing to produce improved health outcomes for people of color.

The problem was that no matter what they did, they were white institutions, in fact, white male-led institutions. They did not have the trust of the community, nor did they provide residents with access. For example, an African-American or Asian young woman was not about to seek reproductive services from them. Pat, her staff, and I met with women of color and the South Madison alderman. After the initial meetings it was just Pat, her staff, and African American women, like community leader Betty Banks, who had been long involved in community healthcare. Betty recruited other women from the community, particularly from Mount Zion Baptist Church. They followed up with some joint meetings with me and my staff, but not with the contrary alderman who had earlier declared that we were designing a "welfare temple."

The problem was that no matter what they did, they were white institutions, in fact, white male-led institutions.

The recommendation from these discussions was to establish a community health facility on the Southside in the heart of Madison's lowest income areas, in the midst of the city's largest black population and the growing Southeast Asian and Latino communities. We listened to those doing the work, the patients. *We listened to the customer.*

We staffed the new facility with city public-health nurses, invited in Family Enhancement (a nonprofit that worked on early childhood development and parenting) and any other providers we could entice. We bought the old Knights of Columbus Hall, a fabricated metal building that reeked of beer, fish fries, and cigarettes. We cleaned it up and (despite the alderman's cheap shot, who called it a "welfare temple") we were in business. The official name was the "South Madison Health and Family Center," later renamed by the community "Harambee," a Kenyan word meaning "All pull together."

~

I had assumed the service area was for city residents who resided within a mile and half of the site, less than 10,000 people. Within a few months, however, Harambee was bursting at the seams, for the people we served were coming from beyond the city boundaries. Patients were coming from Green County, forty miles away. The largest non-city patient population was from the Township of Madison, a municipality distinct from the City of Madison. Pat's intake data showed that over 20% of our patients came from what was popularly referred to as "the Town of Madison."

I was not pleased. For years, the Town of Madison had underfunded their police and fire services, relying on the city of Madison to back them up. I met with the town chairman. When I asked him to take a lead and help in the management and cost of patients from his township, he was uninterested and suggested that the county government should handle things. "Dane County government provides our health services, especially those childhood immunizations you are doing. Refer them there."

I met regularly with Pat Gadow, who reminded me that our mission was to expand health services. She challenged me, "Let's see if I have this right? A mother comes in with her two-year old toddler who should have had the first childhood immunization eighteen months ago. I am to give them a referral to the county office which is seven miles away? If the immunizations are already more than a year overdue, what do you think are the chances that she will make it over there next week without a car?" Enough said, we continued serving everyone who came through the door.

The bad news was that by 1995 we were out of space. But the good news was that right across the street was a mostly vacant strip mall with an empty bowling alley, which already housed the South Madison Public Library branch. Armed with the statistical proof as to how many families we served and the kinds of services provided, the previously skeptical city council approved a multi-million renovation of the old bowling alley with local and federal Community Development Block Grant (CDBG) funds.

From the beginning we needed more operational support and funding as we were continually expanding our services. Pat Gadow went to work. The problem was that our initial foray into the Southside was not supported by all of the medical, health, and family-support institutions. Rather than isolate them or call for their defunding and more money for us, we doubled down in involving and convincing them to embrace our new design.

Pat's first stops were the University of Wisconsin-Madison's medical school and its world-class teaching hospital. They were still a "No." Undaunted, she went to her friends at the UW-Madison's School of Nursing. They were more receptive to the city proposal, which offered something previously marked by failure—the opportunity to provide meaningful healthcare services to the women of underserved communities.

Suddenly, the university was "in." Perhaps inspired by the nurses, other providers began committing to staffing Harambee–including UW-Madison's hospital and medical school, Meriter Hospital, and St. Mary's Hospital. Access Community Health Center, a nonprofit community-based healthcare provider, was also quick to join. Group Health Cooperative opened its own facility across the street. Dane County came in to help with non-city residents.

In these changing times, Pat and her leadership team instilled a new sense of purpose for our Public Health Department. The staff was let loose to design their new delivery systems, using continuous improvement tools. After the extensive and on-going discussions with community leaders and the patients—that is, our customers—there was continual review and data collected on patients' health. Sexually transmitted diseases, low birth weight, smoking cessation, and cancer screening were all part of the effort. This transition continued as the patients (customers) moved to become decision makers in our health care system. As Betty Banks wrote:

> This entity (The Harambee Collaboration) was committed to "leveling the playing field" of decision making, which ensured that residents had a say in the delivery services and governance. They were not "on the outside looking in" or told what was best for them. Service providers involved them in decision making, listened to what they had to say, and were guided by their wisdom.

In the private sector, there is today widespread recognition that your partners and suppliers must also adhere to the same principles of quality as you do. A lawn mower manufacturer will fail if the outsourced rubber wheels fail, for example. The same is true in the public sector.

The critical piece in the success of the Harambee Collaboration was the independent Harambee Board, a community-based guidance team. They met regularly and were part of the management group who consulted with the healthcare providers. We needed a supplier who could deliver the *trust* that we could not produce on our own. We needed a partner who better knew the needs of our patients.

The Harambee Board members went into the neighborhoods, the homes of the patients. They saw the young pregnant women on the neighborhood streets, in the churches, and community facilities. They served as a constant reminder, "Are you getting enough rest, eating right, limiting your drug and alcohol consumption, not smoking?" They did something that doctors and nurses, mostly white, could not do.

Now we could provide virtually every health service, including an early childhood initiative, short of surgery and behavioral health services. Harambee was multicultural and multilingual.

~

In 1998 something unusual occurred, eventually gaining national attention. A noticeable decline in Dane County's African American infant mortality rate was reported.

That decline was to continue through 2002 when it fell as low as white infant mortality compared to both local and national standards. It was the first known example of the black-white gap closing in any one state or county, according to the *Newsweek* article, "A good mystery: infant-mortality drop in Wisconsin." Medical journals featured articles about the phenomena: they found no scientific advancements, no identifiable medical treatments to account for the positive outcomes. I knew it was because of the Harambee Collaboration.

A noticeable decline in Dane County's African American infant mortality rate was reported.

I had been out of office twelve years by 2009, however, when Jennifer Lord, the Harambee staff director informed me that the current city administration was *defunding* Harambee. Her position had been eliminated. What the city had really defunded was the role of the women on the board. Betty Banks and I joined together, but our best efforts to save Harambee failed. In "The Long Game," an unpublished document she wrote about the Harambee Center, Betty said:

> The South Madison Health and Family Center-Harambee was defunded and disbanded in 2009, ironically, this was the year that the county's black-white infant mortality gap returned. Because of politics involved in the "death of the Harambee Center," politicians and decision makers refuse to acknowledge the groundbreaking work of Madison's Harambee Center and its contribution to the dramatic drop in Black infant deaths and the mysterious irony of the closing of the Center and the infant-mortality spike in 2009.

We had never set a mathematical goal of reducing African American infant mortality or reducing low baby birth weights, the major cause of infant death. We simply designed a quality healthcare system. The quality staff we assembled all made a commitment to respect and serve the customer, their patients, but there was one essential ingredient that only the community leaders could provide—and that was the *trust* needed to attract those fearful patients.

By 2011, demographic reports made it clear that in so many areas—health, education, income—the Dane County disparity between whites and Blacks was enormous. Almost all the gains in these areas made from the early 1990s until 2008 were wiped out, reversed by the Great Housing Recession. The old adage "Blacks are the last hired and first fired," was proven once again.

For years, people who found fault with the mission of a government agency or failed to understand its mission did not attempt to correct it; rather they cut its budget. Member of Congress did that with the Environmental Protection Agency (EPA). President Reagan did that with the Department of Housing and Urban Development (HUD). President Trump did that with the U.S. Postal Service.

Even people of goodwill can react negatively to government programs or agencies when they do not understand their mission. The nation's healthcare systems, both local and national, were designed without recognition of the need to build trust with low-income communities and communities of color.

The nation's healthcare systems were designed without recognition of the need to build trust with communities of color.

No more proof of that is needed than the challenge of Covid-19 and getting people immunized in 2021. The challenges of seeking continuous improvement to social programs, of course, are not limited to healthcare. They are matched in job training, employment, criminal justice, housing, and our school systems.

Deming was right in 1989: He and his colleagues had every reason to be concerned about failure when there is transition at the top of an organization. But in my opinion what they missed was that leadership transition—whether fueled by ignorance or neglect—has an even more debilitating impact on unempowered communities that are not in a position to determine their own future.

~

Postscript: Modeled after the original South Madison Health and Family Center-Harambee, the new Harambee Village opened in 2014. Its aim is to create a more equitable healthcare system through improving health outcomes for mothers and babies, one family at a time.

Paul Soglin is a former three-time Mayor of Madison, Wisconsin, having served a total of 22 years in that office between 1973 and 2019. He was a fellow at the Institute of Politics at the Kennedy School of Government, Harvard University (1979) and taught graduate course in Public Management, Finance, Personnel, and Advanced Public Management at the LaFollette School of Public Affairs, University of Wisconsin-Madison for a dozen years between 1997 and 2020.

Questions for Reflection and Discussion

1. Have you experienced a transition from one manager to another? If so, tell what happened. If not, go online to BendingGranite.com and read the story "Never Say Die."
2. How can economically disadvantaged communities develop enough political clout to get their needs met? Which continuous improvement techniques and practices might help? Be specific.
3. How has the racial reckoning that has been happening in this country affected your desire to help lead change in your organization or institution? Explain your answer. Do you think that an emphasis on continuous improvement could be helpful in dealing with this issue? Why? How?

Be Curious, Get Furious, Experiment

by Kent Lesandrini

We measure everything at work, except what counts.

Margaret Heffernan

In attending the 100th birthday anniversary for George Box in 2019, I was struck by the number of stories from colleagues, students, and associates who referred to Monday Night Beer and Statistics—an informal venue George hosted in his basement that was open to students or faculty from any department at the University of Wisconsin-Madison. In *An Accidental Statistician,* George explained that he didn't want the discussions to be overly theoretical. People sat on an old sofa and an assortment of odd chairs. Coats and jackets were piled up in heaps on the ping pong table. George wrote: "Often people who had brought a problem and received some help would let us know in subsequent sessions how their project was getting on, and a number of discoveries and more than one publication with multiple authors came about as a result...."

I did not move in those circles then, so I wasn't fortunate enough to attend any of these. I really like the informal and interactive feel of these basement sessions, however, and I'd like to share my reflections as if we were together in George's basement, with you sitting on that old sofa—perhaps with a beer or a root beer or one of George's home brews. I can't hear you respond, of course, but be sure that I'm only testing ideas with you as a point of departure for more discussion. All is provisional here in this space.

~

I came to the Quality Improvement (QI) movement via Russel Ackoff's Idealized Design—an architectural approach to planning. You begin with the premise that everything has been destroyed. If you were starting from scratch, what would you create? This means first you begin with design specifications: "What kind of house do you want to build?" This is the initial conversation you have with an architect to create a blueprint. For organizations or departments, this leads to questions of purpose. Specifications can take shape around feasibility, logistics, values, or aesthetics.

These are conversations we don't always have before trying to repair the deficiencies of the current system. But what is the future we are trying to create? Or ideally, how should the present system work? Each area redesigns itself in collaboration with internal users and (occasionally) external partners. For a mailroom or IT department, for example, there would be only internal users on the planning team. QI methodology becomes critical at this stage in redesign of work processes or systems.

"Teaching is an obstruction to learning."

How do people learn? Working with a hospital's x-ray department one time, we began by trying to define "quality" for the area. Staff were expounding on equipment, accuracy, and technical results when a female technician spoke up. "Have any of you had an x-ray here lately?" she asked. "I came in over the weekend for a possible tailbone fracture. The tech didn't want to hear my story—she just needed a work order. I had to strip below the waist and put on a gown (which, by the way, wouldn't tie). Then I had to climb onto a cold table. She did a good job on the X-ray. No complaints, but I felt like a slab of meat in the process. How does that fit into our quality of care?"

In the initial training, we had talked at length about customer perspective, but none of it registered until she described her patient experience. Which brings me to the real point here. It's very tempting to put people through 3-4 days of intensive training prior to implementation. The deepest learning, however, seems to occur experientially—first by trying to figure out what "quality" really means for your work and second by applying data analysis and using efficient tools to solve the real problems you face. Everything else is theater. Russell Ackoff, a pioneer in organizational and systems theory, went so far as to say, "Teaching is an obstruction to learning."

Most adults learn best by finding their way into the questions. How do we provide enough initial awareness and knowledge to let people start experimenting? Of course, I could be completely wrong about all of this. I'm often wrong. What's been your experience? Anyone want another beer?

~

The French proverb—attributed to Jean-Baptiste Alphonse Karr—is difficult to refute: "The more things change, the more they stay the same."

Why do people change? When I became Director of Personnel at Central Life, a health insurance company in Madison, my first assignment was to implement a non-smoking policy. We offered multiple cessation programs to assist smokers. I interviewed people afterward who tried to quit. There was one theme among people who were successful. This was not connected at all with programs or tools for cessation.

The people who quit were all *moving toward* instead of *giving up* something. One woman had a daughter who was pregnant. The grandchild could not stay with her if she was a smoker. A man had recently experienced severe shortness of breath. He was very clear about wanting to breathe without fear. Both were moving toward a desired future rather than just changing an undesirable behavior. Change is not rational—it operates through imagination and will. This is why stories are more useful than theories. But stories only go so far. What's in it for people to change?

~

In describing Appreciative Inquiry, Sue Annis Hammond poses the question "What's working around here?" as a prelude to "What problems are you having?" This is an important reframing. It goes deeper, however. I would suggest it is vital to enter the reference frame of the organization, its culture, and its individual people before trying to imagine any kind of real change. What has made them successful? What keeps them coming to work each day? If you truly appreciate the core, you can build from there.

It is vital to enter the reference frame of the organization before trying to imagine any kind of real change.

Without knowing the reference frame, you are simply the most recent in a series of imposed programs or enlightened, but short-lived, initiatives. People are smart—they know when they're being discounted, patronized, subtly coerced or artfully "handled." People can smell it. Speaking of which, is that popcorn ready yet?

~

This is ridiculous, but I've seen it so many times I need to mention it: With major change, it seems there are often one-third who embrace it immediately, one-third whom you will never engage no matter how hard you try, and a middle third who are trying to figure out what they think. You must expend energy on all three groups, of course, but it's a question of how to invest limited time and energy to get traction for moving forward. Early on, I spent lots of time and emotional energy on those most stridently opposed–trying to win them over. Gradually I learned there is more leverage in amplifying the energy of those truly excited about change and helping the middle third find a way in on their own terms. Many who are opposed "norm" to the center as things evolve. Some leave, and that's O.K. too. But I was definitely a slow learner on this point.

There is more leverage in amplifying the energy of those truly excited about the change.

Does this Rule of Thirds mirror your own experience? If so, shouldn't it be on the back of a cereal box or in a fortune cookie or something? Or maybe I'm just fixated on threes.

How do you make change stick? In a scene from the film The Big Lebowski, Cowboy (played by Sam Elliot) is sitting at a bar in a bowling alley in Los Angeles circa 1991 when he provides this enigmatic counsel: "A wiser fella than me once said – sometimes you eat the bear, and sometimes the bear, well, he eats you." Now, to get the full impact of this scene, "bear" has to be pronounced "b'ar." The Dude (played by Jeff Bridges) is drinking a white Russian and is at the end of his rope, depressed and forlorn. The Dude responds to Cowboy: "Is that some kind of Eastern thing?"

We've all been there. You do all the right things, it seems to be working, gaining momentum, and then something happens—a new leader, an external change, an internal implosion—and everything unravels before your eyes. In reply to The Dude's query ("Is that some kind of Eastern thing?"), Cowboy says, very seriously, "Far from it."

But I think it *is* an Eastern thing. Don't you? Discuss this amongst yourself while I find George's bathroom.

I'm back. Did you resolve the Big Lebowski question? Is it an Eastern thing? Do we have any Taoists in the group? Any Lao Tsu fans? Here's a passage from the *Tao te Ching* over 2000 years old:

> Do you think you can take over the universe and improve it?
>
> I do not believe it can be done.
>
> Sometimes things are ahead and sometimes they are behind.
>
> Sometimes breathing is hard, sometimes it comes easily.
>
> Sometimes there is strength and sometimes weakness.
>
> Sometimes one is up and sometimes down.

In thinking about how to make change stick, here are three questions to consider:.

1. *What's in it for them?* Begin from the reference frame of those who must change. Why would they be drawn to this? What's in it for them? Learn more from them; frame the change from their vantage point.
2. *Whose initiative is this?* It's tempting for leaders to champion initiatives–providing charismatic vision. Is the initiative identified primarily with one person (a change agent) for its energy? Or does it have a life of its own? A self-organizing energy at different levels?
3. *Can change keep changing (a shapeshifter) while maintaining its purpose?* When circumstances change, agents often lock into prior positions and tactics. Is there a deeper game that might be played in another way or on another level? As in our lives or relationships, change can often clarify and deepen purpose.

There are no easy answers to these three questions. Despite all our efforts, sometimes change doesn't stick. There are lots of things you can do to make it more likely to stick, but there are no silver bullets or absolute guarantees. Every one of us sitting in this basement has a story here in failed implementation. What do *you* do when the b'ar eats *you?*

But maybe this leads to a deeper question: What really matters over time? How do we evaluate efforts? Who can be sure of the impact we're having?

Fifteen years ago, I was going into University Bookstore in Madison when a friendly-enough-looking fellow stopped me. "Are you Kent Lesandrini?" It was too late to lie. "Were you a Teaching Assistant for an introductory English course at the University here in the late 1970s?"

Guilty as charged. *Was he still upset about a grade I gave him?* I wondered. "Well, I thought it was you," he laughed. We shook hands. "I wanted to tell you how much I enjoyed your discussion section. The course was just a requirement for me because I was on a science track, but those discussions really had an impact." I was stunned. Who knew? The truth is I had always felt like a complete failure as a teacher. Oddly, I did remember him. He was quiet, didn't say much, but wrote thoughtful essays. What a serendipitous meeting for me.

"Are you Kent Lesandrini?" It was too late to lie.

Who knows what impact we're having—for good or ill? Or what the ripple effects of an experience can have as they spread invisibly from the work we are doing? Are these effects any less real because they are intangible? Let's come back to the project above where you did all the right things but for whatever reason the project was short-circuited or later undercut. How do you measure what happened? Or what impact your effort had? Are the only true measures of a project the outcomes that have tangible (that is, quantifiable) metrics?

But before we dive down an epistemological rabbit hole here, do I smell coffee? I could use a cup of coffee before we tackle this next one.

~

I'm not quibbling with the importance of measures. I'm asking: Who can assess the ancillary impacts of even a "failed" project on the individuals involved? Or on the culture in some direct or indirect way? Did employees gain valuable leadership experience, preparing them for more responsibility? Were new partnerships forged with key stakeholders outside the organization? Did people get to know one another better and learn to work more effectively together? Perhaps the impact was latent—an experience that seasoned the organization for something more sustainable later.

Here are six wholly indefensible pronouncements to stimulate further thinking and discussion next week here in George's basement. Feel free to talk back to the page. You'll feel better.

1. The greatest barriers to implementation of quality improvement (or any methodology) arise from unnecessary dogmatism regarding its tenets.
2. Extensive training is ineffective in launching the enterprise. People learn within the context of identifying and solving the real problems they face.
3. Glowing after-the-fact project reports mask the messiness of life lived. More often, you feel like you're getting nowhere until you look back and realize you've actually done something.
4. Proverbs for Paranoids, 3: "If they can get you asking the wrong questions, they don't have to worry about answers." (see Pynchon, 1973, p. 251).
5. Despite the 85/15 rule (that 85% of problems are caused by the system itself), individuals *are* important…and often the key to successful implementation.
6. Most critical to success is a subversive and playful orientation to these challenges—an irrational optimism and persistence in the face of ongoing setbacks and discouragement.

The only one of these statements I will defend to the death next week is the last one. Without it, the work of leading improvement becomes lifeless. But that's just my opinion, and I have been known to be wrong.

~

George Box, Bill Hunter, and Stu Hunter epitomize this spirit in their book *Statistics for Experimenters.* Inside the front and the back covers of the second edition are 60 aphorisms—some their own and others ranging from Sophocles to Yogi Berra. Many of these are mischievous and playful. One of my favorites is from R.A. Fisher: "The best time to plan an experiment is after you've done it."

Statistics for Experimenters opens with lyrics from Cole Porter's song *Experiment (1933).* You can hear it sung on YouTube in a vintage recording by Gertrude Lawrence. Herein lies the title of my story tonight. The song ends:

- **Be Curious,** Though Interfering Friends May Frown.
- **Get Furious,** At Each Attempt to Hold You Down.
- **Experiment,** And You'll See.

Clearly these three were having some fun while making serious contributions to statistics and experimentation. I would suggest a spirit of play is critical for any enduring effort and often connected with discovery. George Box beautifully captures this spirit of playful mayhem and serious purpose in his oft quoted: "All models are wrong; some models are useful."

I have one of my favorite cartoons in my wallet. There's no caption, but I call it the "Metaphysical Box Score." The cartoon constitutes my concluding thoughts tonight. Pass this around.

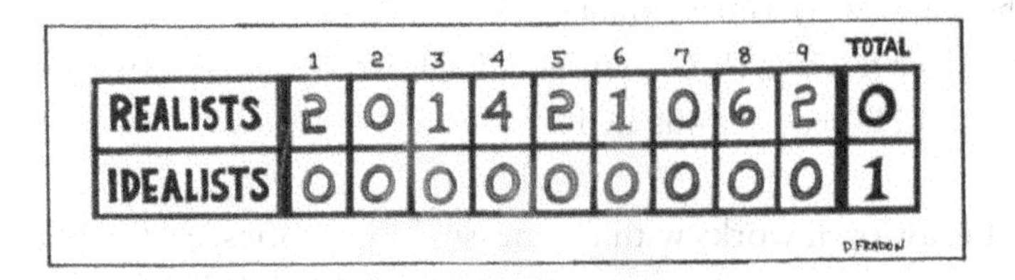

Dana Fradon, *The New Yorker*

Of course, I could be completely wrong about this. I'm often wrong. But I'm pretty sure about this one. If you disagree (and you might), then get some more coffee or another beer or whatever you're having and keep talking. I'm going home. But for me, until next week at least, the Metaphysical Box Score stands.

References

Box, G. E., Hunter, W. and Hunter, J.S. (2005). *Statistics for experimenters* (second edition.) Wiley-Interscience.

Box, G.E. (2013). *An accidental statistician: The life and memories of George E.P. Box*. Wiley.

Detrick, G. An interview with Russel L. Ackoff. (2002). *Academy of Management Learning and Education.* https://ackoffcenter.blogs.com/ackoff_center_weblog/2016/12/-an-interview-with-russell-l-ackoff.html.

Hammond, S.A. (2013). *The thin book of appreciative inquiry.* (third edition). Thin Book Publishing.

Heffernan, M. (2015). *Beyond measure: The big impact of small changes.* Simon and Schuster/TED.

Porter, C. (1933). *Experiment.* Warner Brothers, Inc.

Pynchon, T. (1973). *Gravity's rainbow.* Viking Press.

Tsu, Lao. *Tao te Ching* (F. Gia-Fu and J. English translators). (1972). Original work published circa 400 BCE.

Kent Lesandrini works with businesses, universities, and public sector organizations on strategic planning, organizational development, and change initiatives. He trained with Russel Ackoff and members of Interact from the Wharton School of Business. He occasionally gives presentations integrating scientific theory, the arts, and business to promote dialog within organizations and across disciplines or industry sectors. Kent lives in Madison, Wisconsin, and claims that at one time he knew how to play the accordion. We can neither confirm nor deny this claim at the time of publication.

Questions for Reflection or Discussion

1. What is the value of learning in informal settings (outside of classrooms or formal professional development)? Describe one such venue where you have learned some important things. Name one or two of the things you learned.
2. Are some things worth doing, even if they fail? If so, describe one that you were involved in or observed and tell why it was important.
3. Have you seen the author's "rule of thirds" in action when it comes to making change? We must expend energy on all three groups, of course, but which group do you aim your change efforts at: those enthusiastic, those decidedly opposed, or those who are skeptical but waiting to decide? Why, and is it working for you? Explain your answer.

It's in the Water

by Jim Bradley

Start where you are. Use what you have. Do what you can.

Arthur Ashe

Gatherings in Madison, Wisconsin, often begin with an acknowledgment that we are meeting on the ancestral lands of the Ho-Chunk, home to the indigenous *people of the sacred voice* for over 12,000 years. Appreciation is also expressed for the Ho-Chunk's stewardship of the fresh water and rich soils that sustain life in our community. The Ho-Chunk heritage, coupled with our unique and abundant natural resources, inspire what we call "seven-generational thinking," which means assuring that our actions today will benefit those seven generations hence.

Madison is an isthmus, a narrow strip of land nestled between two fresh-water lakes, Mendota and Monona. The majesty of lakes Mendota and Monona serve as a constant visual reminder of our individual and collective responsibility to preserve and protect the natural environment. Madison's legacy in environmental leadership and stewardship includes Aldo Leopold, noted naturalist, and Gaylord Nelson, former governor, U.S. senator, and founder of Earth Day. They, among many others, taught us that responsibility of stewardship is often best addressed by thoughtful study and informed action. Frameworks of guiding principles have been central to the Madison community's learning and aligned action for improvements today and well into the future.

Stewardship is often best addressed by thoughtful study and informed action.

W. Edwards Deming's system of Profound Knowledge was foundational in the quality improvement movement. Similarly, *The Natural Step* by Karl-Henrik Robért offered guiding principles for seventh-generation thinking in environmental sustainability and resiliency practices. Both frameworks are holistic, humanistic, and rooted in continuous improvement. They also require a discipline of root-cause analysis to understand complex systems and identify leverage points for lasting systemic change.

Two local not-for-profit organizations—comprised of committed individuals and organizations across a wide range of industries, educational institutions, and governmental entities—led the development in Madison of a culture that applied the frameworks and shared lessons learned in leading change to a wide variety of issues. Formally incorporated in 1987, the Madison Area Quality Improvement Network (MAQIN) focused on quality management. Sustain Dane, founded in 1999, led the charge on sustainability. Central to both efforts was the visionary leadership and hands-on involvement of Brian Joiner. Recognizing the leverage and indispensable influence of city government, Joiner and other volunteers led training sessions with City of Madison staff in both Profound Knowledge and The Natural Step. The city, with leadership support of successive mayors Joe Sensenbrenner and Paul Soglin, operationalized water-quality management and sustainable/resiliency practices with skilled staffing, departmental purpose statements, and aligned work plans.

The ripple effects of MAQIN's and Sustain Danes' foundational work with community-based organizations are wide-spread and lasting, aided by a constancy of purpose at the heart of all continuous improvement. If you look, you'll find teams working on systemic improvement virtually everywhere. Simply put, like the visual reminders of lakes Mendota and Monona, it's in the very water of Madison.

~

"Change happens when inspired people take action," the mantra of Sustain Dane, says it all. For over twenty years Sustain Dane has inspired, connected, and supported people to accelerate sustainable actions for community wellbeing. Initial efforts were directed to education through neighborhood and business learning circles, and the sale of residential rain barrels. (See "One Family at a Time" by Karen Crossley.) The organization expanded its reach and impact with focused training and projects based in city government and schools. An active network of businesses, non-profits, and governmental entities now gathers regularly learn and share best practices.

"Change happens when inspired people take action."

The Wisconsin organization Rooted (formerly the Center for Resilient Cities) used the guiding principles of resilience found in the natural world to develop and implement green infrastructure planning spanning education, food systems, urban/community gardening, and neighborhood center services. Its Badger Rock building is a LEED-award winning platinum multi-purpose building that serves as a place for neighbors to gather and connect. Badger Rock Middle School is a charter school focused on project-based learning. Recently acquired by the Madison Metropolitan School District, Badger Rock will be expanded to include a neighborhood elementary school.

The Clean Lakes Alliance is devoted to improving the water quality of the lakes, streams, and wetlands of the Yahara River Watershed. The Alliance is a unique partnership of diverse stakeholders who are building on and expanding upon decades of ongoing efforts to preserve and restore our waters. Central to the Alliance's mission is a commitment to the science of water stewardship and root-cause analysis to identify and remediate legacy practices that have degraded local waterways and Madison area lakes.

In the 1990s the United Way of Dane County and the Madison Community Foundation, two vital community non-profit funders, collaborated to learn about and employ the concept of "building community assets" espoused by professors John McKnight and Jody Kretzmann of Northwestern University that encourages organizations to conduct a strength-and-needs analysis to direct their charitable giving. With McKnight's guidance, they began to identify and map community assets, investing in a virtuous cycle of building on community strengths. These significant non-profits have distinct missions with some overlap. For years, rather than competing, they have collaborated and supported each other to the benefit of the community.

~

Finally, and a good place to end the remarkable collection of stories in this book, what are some of the human, geographic, social, political, organizational assets that exist in your community that would help support and nourish continuous, positive change efforts? What is happening now that is working well in your community, and what can be learned from it?

The geographical position of Madison, between two magnificent lakes, has surely shaped our city's distinctive culture of sustainability, conservation, and cooperation. The understanding that we humans also impact our beautiful and fragile blue boundaries continues to influence and energize local leaders and change agents to seek current solutions with an eye toward their benefits...even seven generations into the future.

Reference

Ashe, A. (2001). Arthur Ashe Quotes. BrainQuote.

Jim Bradley has been CEO of Home Savings Bank, Madison since 1985. Jim's board service with community-based nonprofits includes the Madison Area Quality Improvement Network (MAQIN), Madison Community Foundation, Sustain Dane, Downtown Madison, Inc., Destination Madison, and several others.

Questions for Reflection and Discussion

1. Do volunteers get paid? In what ways? Tell one story about yourself or someone you know who got "paid" to volunteer.
2. What are the seven-generational issues around water that the human race must consider? What other "big" issues face us? Which one do you care most about? Why?
3. Name three human, geographic, social, political, organizational assets that exist right now in your community that might help support and nourish continuous, positive change efforts. What might you do to help recruit them in your efforts to lead systemic change efforts on the issue you care most about?

Epilogue

Leading Change Now

The greatest predictor of leadership success
is the desire to grow as a leader.

Sugarman, Scullard, and Wilhelm

We hope these 30+ stories inspire you to act. As we stated at the beginning of *Bending Granite,* our world has complex, gnarly problems that good intentions alone can't address. And there are wonderous things we can create and build if we have the know-how.

Small or expansive—you may want to improve the effectiveness of your meetings, or redesign a critical service for your customers, or build an energy self-sufficient world. Throughout the stories in this book, current and past leaders spanning decades have shared their approaches, challenges, and successes in addressing a broad range of problems in every type of organization.

You will note that all of the authors paid attention to three essential elements for leading successful change: purpose, processes, and people. We have deliberately chosen these leaders and their stories to illustrate principles and practices that are fundamental and enduring, tested over time, and ready for you to adopt and adapt to in your world now.

~

Here, we offer a number of immediate actions you can take to improve your own changemaking skills, so you can help lead your organization, institution, or community to become "greater and more beautiful than it was."

Get really good at asking questions.

As a leader, you can believe you have to know everything. And in some ways, you'll think your team expects that of you too. What we have learned is that it's more important to know the right questions to ask than to know the right answer out of the box. A few fundamental questions to always keep in mind are:

- What are you trying to accomplish? What is your purpose?
- How will you know that a change is an improvement?
- What steps can you propose that will result in real, measurable improvement?

- Who will help you and how will you begin?
- How can the changes you make be continually improved?

Early on, you may fear that if you ask questions you might be seen as clueless and weak. We learned that our staffs knew so much more than we did about certain things and that most of them were willing—no, happy—to share what they knew. They appreciated being asked.

Some things you have to decide on your own, and some things you can delegate to the people doing the actual improvement work. That is where the art of leadership comes into play—knowing which one is which. In the end, however, you will always make better decisions after consultation with others.

The skill of asking the right questions extends to getting feedback from your customers, users, and other stakeholders and then using that information. It's critical to ask questions to understand their wants and needs, and to learn about their experiences with your products and services. To ignore this can be catastrophic.

Use the Plan-Do-Study-Act Cycle to guide change and improvement.

PDSA provides a simple but powerful model for leading change and making sure the actions you take are, in fact, improvements.

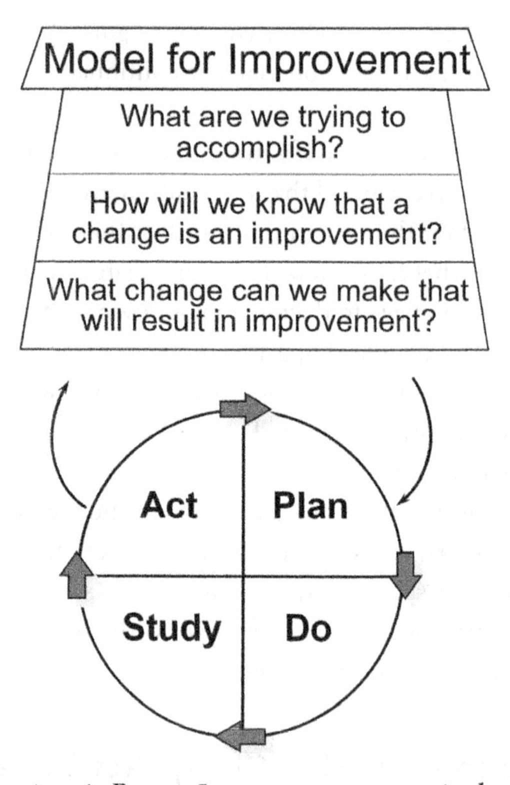

Associates in Process Improvement, www.apiweb.org.

The cycle of improvement begins with "Plan"—working to understand the situation as thoroughly as possible and then planning the strategies, both for immediate action and for continual improvement.

The "Do" step includes implementation and collecting data on results for the Study step. (When you plan any change, decide then and there who will be responsible and when for checking on progress and results.) PDSA assumes that adjustments will need to be made as you proceed with implementation, because systems behave in predictably unpredictable ways. Thus, the "Study" step provides the opportunity to really examine what is happening—are things proceeding as you had hoped? Finally, in the "Act" step you will typically *adapt, adopt, adjust, or abandon* the original plans for improvement. Any complex issue may go through multiple spins of the PDSA cycle, thus PDSA is, in essence, "continuous improvement."

Learn how to facilitate a productive meeting.

In most of the 20th century, leaders and managers interacted primarily one-on-one with individuals. Now they interact mostly with teams, and often, virtually. How can you help people use their time together productively?

Excellent design and facilitation are even more essential for virtual meetings. Some resources to help you do this are below. At least make sure one of your trusted team members can facilitate a good, interactive meeting, especially when a decision must be made. In today's complex and time-competitive environment, it's important to get a lot of options on the table quickly, and neutral group meeting facilitation can help make that happen.

Know how to flow-chart a process.

A *process* is a set of activities done to create a product or service. Of all the QI and Six Sigma and Lean tools, knowing how to create a flowchart of a process is the one you cannot do without. It is an essential part of all the stages of PDSA. Flow-charting is deceptively simple: Create a map or picture of the steps; use boxes and arrows to show the direction of the steps that need to be taken; and place a diamond to show each place a decision must be made and who needs to make it. All organizations, institutions, and communities include hundreds to thousands of processes that interact with and depend on one another. Continuous improvement is not just about changing the org chart or whose job it is to do something. It's about helping all of these processes (some of which are hard to see) function smoothly and together. A leader who really understands this is positioned to be successful.

What are the most important processes you are responsible for? Which is most critical? Sit down with your team and draw out how that process works now, step by step, using boxes or with self-stick notes. Arrange them in sequence. If you have never done this, it will be an eye-opener for you and everybody else. You will likely find that different people do different things, in different order, for different reasons. Generally, this is not a good thing, because you don't want a lot of variation in your most important activities. Variation can lead to errors and waste. If there are points where team members are empowered to make decisions to best serve customers, this should be clearly noted in the sequence.

Processes degrade naturally over time as people come and go and team members lose sight of the original purpose. Sometimes you can improve a process just by creating a visual flowchart because you can quickly identify where there might be delays or errors. As you make improvements to the process, create a flowchart illustrating the steps and sequence of the new process.

You and your team need to be able to understand what is really happening in your most important processes. A flowchart is a way to do this. And besides, they are kind of fun to do together.

Sustain efforts through leadership changes.

Leaders come and go. We have seen too many improvement and innovation efforts discontinued because they are seen as a priority owned by the previous leader. All new leaders have things they care about. It might be addressing a crisis that threatens the organization, or a vision they have for a new product or service. How can you help address a new leader's priorities? Watch for significant events or challenges and turn them into opportunities for improvement. Help the new leader see how these tools, techniques, and facilitation skills can further their own priorities.

Create or join a community of practice.

A community of practice (popular in healthcare and education, among other sectors) is a group of people with a shared interest who learn to do things better by interacting with each other regularly. The community of practice can be within your own organization, in your community or city, or even statewide, national, or international.

Find others who are leading change, and then learn and work together. This can be informal—as described in Denis Leonard's story in this book, "A Deeper Sense of People and Purpose"—or more formally through an organized network. And you can join us at BendingGranite.org to see and learn more. There you can gain much from learning from others, including how they approach similar problems or issues. Or you can identify common issues and work together to develop solutions that serve the greater good.

Every community of practice needs a convener to keep it alive. This role takes time and perseverance, but the payoff is learning, new connections, as well as recognition and appreciation from your peers. So, whether you are joining a group that already exists or creating a new one or joining us online, the idea is to find a way to share, learn together, and grow as a leader of change.

Value the People Closest to the Work

Most people—do their best work when they feel respected and appreciated. How do you give recognition to other people in your organizational settings? How could you make your appreciation known even more clearly? Everyone doing their jobs well makes it more likely that you will succeed too. Remember to thank them.

Be Truthful. This can be easier said than done. Sincerity and forthrightness on your part, however, will build trust and the respect of others. Share information. As systems thinking genius Donella Meadows advises, "Do not sequester information." Share as much about what you know as you can with your team and others who may need the information. It is a show of respect and can be an accelerator for improvement as team members see the bigger picture.

Define and share the personal principles and values that guide your journey to become a leader of change. Keep those values out front. Use them to shape your decisions and reactions and to inspire others.

Start small.

Even the biggest transformations can begin with small demonstrations. Pilot projects are marvelous organizational learning opportunities. An advantage of starting with pilot projects is that if the effort is truly innovative, a pilot won't be as threatening to the prevailing culture as a full-scale change could be. A pilot will also provide data that hopefully supports doing more of the same or at least points out the potential pitfalls. At the same time, you will develop champions in the organization who understand and are as passionate and willing as you are to advocate for innovation with their colleagues.

Again, it is better to start small and have a great success than to experience a big, visible failure. You can have a mountain of a goal in mind, but a couple of small changes can be the first shovelfuls toward that goal. Then you can go big.

Check out the Baldrige standards and self-assessment tools.

There are lots of assessment tools out there, but we recommend you start with Baldrige, considered the grand-daddy of the rest of them. The no-fee Baldrige PDF assessment "Are We Making Progress?" provides questions around Leadership, Strategy, Customers, Measurement, Workforce, Operations, and Results. Any of these questions would make great discussion topics for a meeting or retreat or simply to ask yourself and your colleagues. They can also become the basis of an all-out assessment of your organization, institution, or community. Baldridge is quite instructive, especially for noticing blind spots in your existing processes.

You may want to consider becoming what's called a "Baldrige examiner." This will allow you will see and rate how top-performing organizations are exemplifying high-quality standards. You will bring a lot of insight back to your organization and will enhance your own leadership capacities and reputation.

~

Our Next Steps

For our part, we have expanded this book into a virtual format—adding stories, podcasts, and reviews online to help us all continue to connect and learn from one another. Visit our website at BendingGranite.org. There you can find valuable interactive resources to support you and opportunities to share with others around emerging ideas and approaches to change and improvement. We hope to meet you all there, at least virtually.

~

Your Next Steps

Remember that wherever you are, you already have a circle of control and an even wider circle of influence. You don't have to wait for your boss or the CEO or anyone else.

- Complete the Personal Action Plan that is free at BendingGranite.org.
- Visit BendingGranite.org for inspiration and new stories and information or to tell others of your own experience at leading change.
- Download the Bending Granite process improvement charter from the website and get started!

~

Thank you for being willing to consider becoming a leader of change. Give it a try. Let us know how it goes.

Reference

Sugarman, J., Scullard, M., and Wilhelm, E. (2011). The 8 dimensions of leadership: DiSC strategies for becoming a better leader, Berrett-Koehler Publishers.

Appendix

Resources and Connections

Classic Books

The number of book choices on leading change today can be overwhelming. These classic books below offer solid advice and can help you focus on purpose, processes, and people.

Bringing Your Strategic Plan to Life: A Guide for Nonprofits and Public Agencies by Kathleen A. Paris, 2011.

The Essential Deming: Leadership Principles from the Father of Quality by Joyce Orsini (audio version available), 2012.

The Fifth Discipline: The Art and Practice of the Learning Organization by Peter Senge, (audio version available), 2006.

Fourth Generation Management by Brian L. Joiner, 1994.

The Improvement Guide: A Practical Approach to Enhancing Organizational Performance by Gerald L. Langley, Ronald D. Moen, Kevin M. Noland, Thomas W. Nolan, Clifford L Norman, and Lloyd P. Provost, 1996.

The Leader's Handbook: A Guide to Inspiring Your People and Managing the Daily Workflow by Peter R. Scholtes, 1998.

Real People, Real Work by Maury Cotter and Lee Cheaney, 1990.

The Tipping Point: How Little Things Can Make a Big Difference by Malcolm Gladwell (audio version available), 2002.

Current Resources

Alignment, Process, Relationships: A Simple Guide to Team Management by Steve King, 2019.

Baldrige Excellence Framework by NIST, National Institute of Standards and Technology (customized books for Business/Nonprofits, Health Care and Education), 2021-2022.

Community: The Structure of Belonging (2nd edition) by Peter Block, 2018.

Excellence in Higher Education Guide: A Framework for the Design, Assessment and Continuous Improvement of Institutions (8th Edition) by Brent Ruben (workbook also available), 2016.

NIATx Easy and Powerful Process Improvement for Behavioral Health. https://www.niatx.net/.

Reveille for a New Generation: Organizers and Leaders Reflect on Power compiled and edited by Gregory F. Augustine Pierce, 2021.

The Surprising Power of Liberating Structures: Simple Rules to Unleash a Culture of Innovation by Henri Lipmanowicz and Keith McCandless, 2014.

Switch: How to Change Things When Change is Hard by Chip Heath and Dan Heath (audio version available), 2020.

The Team Handbook (3rd Edition) by Peter R. Scholtes, Brian L. Joiner, and Barbara J. Streibel, 2018.

Upstream: The Quest to Solve Problems Before They Happen by Dan Heath (audio version available), 2020.

Professional Development Providers

These are providers we have worked with. There are many other excellent organizations providing learning events today as well. Look for those who provide follow-up coaching, training, and continuing learning resources, rather than just a one-time event.

American Society for Quality (ASQ), https://asq.org/.

Focus on Facilitation: A Community of Practice (monthly no-fee learning events from University of Wisconsin and Madison College), https://focusonfacilitationcop.com/.

Industrial Areas Foundation (IAF): A Network of Institutionally Based Community Organizations, https://www.industrialareasfoundation.org.

International Association of Facilitators (IAF): Promoting the Power of Facilitation Worldwide, https://www.iaf-world.org/site/.

Journey of Collaboration: Unleashing Group Power, Darin Harris and Steve Davis, https://www.journeyofcollaboration.com/.

Leadership Strategies: Michael Wilkinson, founder, https://www.leadstrat.com/.

Network for Change and Continuous Innovation (NCCI): Higher Education Focus, https://www.ncci-cu.org/.

Wisconsin Center for Performance Excellence, https://www.wisquality.org/.

Zing Collaborative: Sarah Young, founder, https://www.zingcollaborative.com/.

Our Website

https://www.BendingGranite.org